MISTER, ARE YOU A PRIEST?

Mister, Are You a Priest?

Jottings by Bishop Edward Daly

EDWARD DALY

FOUR COURTS PRESS

Published by
FOUR COURTS PRESS
Fumbally Lane, Dublin 8, Ireland
email: info@four-courts-press.ie
http://www.four-courts-press.ie
and in North America by
FOUR COURTS PRESS
c/o ISBS, 5804 N.E. Hassalo Street, Portland, OR 97213.

ISBN 1-85182-591-6

A catalogue record for this title
is available from the British Library.

Printed in Ireland
by Betaprint, Dublin.

Contents

Illustrations

Illustrations occur between p. 128 and p. 129.

1   Tom & Susan Daly 1933.
2   1939.
3   As first year seminarian 1951/2.
4   First Year Class, Irish College, Rome, 1951/2. *Standing* (l. to r.) Christy McLaughlin, Tom Egan, Seamus Casey, Martin O'Grady, Niall Molloy. *Sitting* (l. to r.) Michael Walsh, John Hanly, Tommy O'Reilly, Seamus Creighton, author.
5   Ordination to Diaconate, Basilica of St John Lateran, Rome, 1956, Father Dominic Conway, Spiritual Director, Irish College, centre.
6   Ordination to Diaconate, Basilica of St John Lateran, Rome, 1956.
7   Ordination to Priesthood, St Patrick's Church, Belleek, 16 March 1957, with mother and family (l. to r.) Marion, Anne, Dympna and Tom.
8   Ordination to Priesthood, 16 March 1957, with Bishop Neil Farren, clergy and altar servers.
9   Father Michael McMenamin, parish priest in Castlederg.
10 Father McMenamin and Bishop Neil Farren.
11 A wedding in St Eugene's Cathedral, Derry. Owen Dawson and Patricia MacCafferty, October 1970. Courtesy of Patricia Dawson.
12 Speaking at the final performance of a pantomime in St Columb's Hall, Derry, 1966. Courtesy of Eamon Gallagher.

Preface

On 29 January 1998, Mr Tony Blair, the British Prime Minister, announced to the House of Commons the establishment of a new Inquiry into the events in Derry on Bloody Sunday 1972. Lord Saville would chair a tribunal of three.

Subsequently during September and October 1998, Eversheds, the solicitors for the Saville Inquiry, were in correspondence with me seeking a statement on the events of 30 January 1972. The solicitors forwarded me copies of various contemporaneous statements that I had made at that time.

I began work on the preparation of a statement for the Saville Inquiry and all kinds of memories, happy and unhappy, came flooding back. This sparked the beginning of the jottings contained in this book and it just built up from there. I describe these as jottings, because that is what they are. This was never meant to be a comprehensive story, merely a rag-bag of memories.

I had just reached the point in the story where I was about to be ordained as Bishop of Derry. Then early in the year 2000, illness and major surgery intervened. As the illness seemed likely to be with me for some time and I did not feel like continuing the work, I decided to submit the story for publication at this stage.

Few Irish diocesan priests have attempted to publish an autobiography in recent years. Perhaps fools rush in! These jottings may serve to put on record one priest's story of his childhood, his studies for the priesthood, his life and work and his joys and tribulations as a priest in parish ministry in the North in the late 1950s, 60s and early 70s. The latter part of the story covers an important period in

Derry's political and social history and in the history of the North.

I hope that these jottings may offer some insight into the life and ministry of a Catholic priest in a troubled area during that period. I was not unique. There were many other Catholic priests engaged in similar work at that time in Derry. Only a few of them are mentioned in the book. They were caring, dedicated, generous and courageous colleagues. None of us was perfect; we shared many of the human imperfections, but I think that all of us tried to serve the great people entrusted to our pastoral care to the best of our ability. Some, like Bishop Neil Farren, Tony Mulvey, Joe Carolan, Martin Rooney, Tom O'Gara and James Clerkin have gone to their rest. Some have resigned from the active priesthood to take up secular life. Some are still serving as priests in various parishes. I considered it a great privilege to have served with all of them as brothers in the priesthood.

I gladly dedicate this book to them.

May 2000

CHAPTER 1

Childhood in Belleek

Birth and the border – trains and fairs – Major and Madame -
primary school and Master Egan – arrival of the GIs –
an aeroplane crashes – a country shop – wakes and funerals –
Father Ó Ciaráin and his castle – sport and drama -Belleek Pottery

Most of my life has been spent living and working within three or
four miles of the border between Northern Ireland and the
Republic of Ireland. I grew up in Belleek in County Fermanagh in
Northern Ireland but I was born in the West Rock Nursing Home
just across the Irish border in Ballyshannon in County Donegal. I
was never quite sure whether the decision that I would be born on
the Donegal side of the Irish border was a deliberate political decision or merely a matter of convenience! I have spent the rest of my
life, apart from six years studying in Rome and a brief period in
Dublin, living and working just within the border on the Northern
Ireland side. I dislike giving the six separated counties their formal
title of Northern Ireland, although I will feel obliged to do so, from
time to time, in these jottings, in the interests of accuracy. I prefer
to call that area 'The North' or 'The Six Counties'. The border sep-
arating those Six Counties from the rest of the island of Ireland was
imposed twelve years before I was born. The consequences of that
imposition dominated and shaped my adult life in many ways.
However, it did not greatly impinge on my childhood because, at
that time, I was never really aware of the significance of the border.
It was just there, a dry-stone wall along the field behind our home.
It was a line, but invisible and largely irrelevant.

The most interesting stories of childhood always seem to be

11

those of a troubled childhood. I had a blissfully happy childhood. I was the eldest of a family of five. I have three sisters, Marion, Dympna and Anne and one brother, Tom. My parents were very happy and loving and caring. They worked hard and provided well for us. We were not poor but we were not rich either. Little was wasted. We lived just outside the village of Belleek about four hundred yards from the border. My father, Tom Daly, had been actively involved as an officer in the IRA in the War of Irish Independence. I only became aware of this in my late teens. He never talked to us about his involvement in this struggle. Perhaps he did not wish to expose his children to the harsh realities of those cruel times. He left Ireland, for a time, after the conflict. In the late 1920s, he inherited a small grocery shop from his uncle and returned home to Belleek. He developed the grocery business and he was also the local undertaker. My mother, Susan Flood, originally came from Pettigo, a village about twelve miles from Belleek. The War of Independence impacted on her also. As a young girl, she was evacuated from her home for some months in 1922. Her first cousin, Patrick Flood, an IRA volunteer, was shot and killed in Pettigo in April 1922. The conflict with the British continued in the Belleek/Pettigo area long after the Anglo-Irish Treaty was signed in December 1921.* There was considerable dispute and conflict about the precise delineation of the border in that area. Despite their background, my parents were not politically active after they got married. I remember them as moderate Nationalists. They were married in January 1933. I was born in December 1933.

Belleek in the 1930s and 40s had a population of less than three hundred. The River Erne tumbled and cascaded its way past the village towards the sea. Just above the village, a set of huge sluice gates painted deep crimson signalled the point where Lough Erne ended and the River Erne began. Below the sluice gates, there was an ancient, narrow stone bridge overlooked by an eighteenth century fort that was known locally as 'The Battery'. There were beautiful waterfalls over which the water, liberated from the sluice gates,

* See the article 'The Struggle for the Belleek-Pettigo Salient 1922' by John B. Cunningham in *Donegal Annual*, 1982 (Donegal Historical Society, Ballyshannon).

gushed and raced and poured and the dominant sound and background music of my childhood was that of the nearby river. The River Erne, at that time, was rich with trout and salmon, and anglers came from far and wide to fish there. There were spectacular fishing spots, waterfalls and deep dark pools in the shadow of trees. There were eel weirs, too, for the harvesting of eels at certain times of the year.

Another sound of my childhood was that of steam locomotives and trains. The Bundoran branch line of the Great Northern Railway ran alongside our house and the trains majestically thundered or trundled past, hissing white steam, and rattled over a metal bridge across the Erne on their way to or from Ballyshannon. The trains were a constant source of curiosity and fascination to eye and ear. The nearby village railway station was one of my favourite childhood haunts. I spent hours in the signal cabin or on the platform, as passenger trains came and went. I watched as goods trains shunted cattle wagons and freight wagons into sidings. Everything was transported to Belleek by rail, from hampers of fresh bread to bales of bacon, to the clay and coal for the pottery. I had no doubt what I wanted to be when I grew up, an engine driver on a steam train. That, I felt, would be true bliss. Indeed, if truth were told, I still hanker after that particular calling.

One of the many excitements of early childhood was the monthly fair day, on the seventeenth of every month, except when that date fell on a Sunday. The farmers from the surrounding area drove their cattle and brought cartloads of pigs and bonhams into the village. The carts with bonhams were covered with sacking to keep them from escaping. Horses and donkeys, too, were offered for sale. I do not remember many sheep at the fair. Each farmer drove his cattle into the village. It could be one beast or ten or twenty head of cattle. Sometimes they travelled many miles. They arrived early in the morning to get a prominent position on the street. After acquiring such a location, they were fully occupied keeping the little flock together until the beasts were sold. There was much shouting and swearing and wielding of sticks. On occasions, the cattle were not sold or a satisfactory price could not be obtained and then the long return journey had to begin, driving the cattle back along the road, home to the farm. The cattle dealers, who bought livestock, came mainly from Enniskillen and Irvinestown, Dromore and Omagh. Everywhere there was the buying and selling, the bargaining and the slapping of hands when deals were done. Then there were second-hand clothes dealers, called cantmen, and tinkers selling tin cans and porringers and saucepans; there were musicians and ballad singers singing and selling their song sheets. The cantmen set up their stalls, and the fitting of second-hand garments went on all day, even in the pouring rain. Jackets and coats were tried on and either selected or rejected. All this business was transacted on the main street, which was the only street. It was a very wide street. The animals that were sold were usually driven to the railway station to be transported to their unknown destiny. The pubs were packed all day and late in the evening, a few people would be 'the worse for wear'. The men drank at the bar and the women discreetly had a little tipple in the snug. As well as a business occasion, the monthly fair day was a social occasion. It was exciting for a youngster, ever changing, noisy, full of vitality and interesting, colourful characters and smells. Our route home from school took us through the village. On a fair day, it took longer than usual to get home. We stood and gazed at everything that was going on. At the end of the fair day, the street was in a terrible mess, but nobody minded too much.

In addition to the shop, my father had a small farm and fattened a few cattle. The days when the cattle were brought to the fair to be sold were particularly exciting. Would they be sold? Would the price be good? We kept a few cows and a flock of hens, a vegetable garden and a potato patch. It was good to be able to live mainly on food that was produced around the house at home. It was exciting, too, to go out and search for eggs that the hens had laid in all sorts of hidden places in the garden at the back of the house and then see them being boiled for the tea and eating them. It was a little more emotional when we had roast chicken! Drinking water was obtained from a spring well down beside the railway line, which for some reason unknown to me was called 'The Gullet'. Haymaking in midsummer and threshing corn in late summer and early autumn were particularly satisfying and enjoyable times. There isn't a more beautiful smell than that of freshly cut grass, and there are few more enjoyable experiences than having a mug of hot tea in the field in the midst of haymaking. Expeditions to the bog with a neighbour to cut and save turf were other treasured experiences.

The home of the McGonigle family, who farmed nearby, was possibly my favourite calling-house as a child. Although it was on the outskirts of the village, it was a country house, with a half door, a huge blazing hearth fire with pots and a steaming jet-black kettle always on the crook. Mrs McGonigle was a kind and welcoming woman, as was Packie, her husband, her son Seán, and all her family. The population of Belleek was more than ninety per cent Catholic, but our immediate neighbours across the road, the Mackeys, were Protestant. They and their housekeeper, Nellie Warke, were dear and kind friends of mine in my childhood and for as long as they lived. They had a lovely old guesthouse, called Heronshaw, in a magnificent setting overlooking the river, and I spent many happy hours and days there. Commercial travellers stayed there, and so did anglers, and many of the same people returned year after year. I was never conscious of any difference between the Mackeys and ourselves, apart from the fact that we went to different churches on Sundays.

Just off Cliff Road, between the village and our house and on the other side of the railway line, was the imposing black-and-white structure of the RUC (Royal Ulster Constabulary) barracks. As a child I was not aware of the political significance of the RUC barracks in that location, literally right on the border. The senior police officer, Head Constable Briggs, and his family lived in married quarters attached to the barracks for a few years. His son, Ronnie, who was the same age as me, played with us at that time. We played occasionally in the spacious grounds surrounding the barracks. Our favourite game was cowboys and indians. Ronnie's father, on one occasion, showed us the barracks cell or 'the black hole', as it was known. It was a somewhat unnerving experience. I remember being extremely curious when I saw wanted notices, with mug shots, being posted on the barracks notice board. The notices were an appeal for information about IRA prisoners who had escaped from Crumlin Road Prison in Belfast. Twenty years later, I came to know the family of Hugh McAteer, who was one of those escapees, a leading IRA figure, whose picture was posted outside the barracks. I am sure that, because of his background, my father had reservations about my recreational activities around the barracks. Perhaps Head Constable Briggs had similar reservations. However, I was never aware of such uneasiness from either side.

A little further down Cliff Road, there was the Egg Store, where the farmers and their wives brought their eggs and sold them. The eggs were then sorted, boxed and dispatched. There were several fascinating machines there to sort the eggs into various groups according to size. Each egg was held up to a light bulb by one of the workers and illuminated to test its freshness or otherwise. I am sure that a more efficient method of testing and sorting eggs has been invented since then. With other children, we roamed around and we had free and unimpeded access everywhere to pursue our child-ish curiosity. The neighbours were wonderful though there were some neighbours' dogs that we were afraid of.

Talking of dogs – about a mile further down Cliff Road, the road we lived on, and across the border in County Donegal, was Cliff House. Major Moore lived there. He was an impressive and imposing figure, an elderly retired major from past and distant wars. Cliff House was the 'Big House' in the area. It stood on a superb site set in the woodland at a dramatic bend in the river. It was a majestic stone building surrounded by conservatories and it had beautiful gardens. Though my friends and I were fascinated by it, we were afraid to go near the house and always kept a respectable distance. There was a hint of mystery and danger about it and we were afraid to go too close. We were certain that if we went closer, wild dogs would come rushing out to attack us, or some other mis-fortune would befall us. The Major came walking into the village, striding erect with a walking stick, up Cliff Road and past our house, to post letters from time to time. His wife, whom we knew as Madame 'Beedo', possibly Bidault, was a particularly striking figure. She dressed elegantly in long skirts down to her toes, always wore a very large and decorous hat with a dark veil hanging down from it over her face. She was usually accompanied by a fearsome bull ter-rier, which frightened us out of our wits as she made her way past our house every Tuesday afternoon to purchase some magazine or other in Belleek and to bring letters to the post office. For some strange reason, and without any evidence whatsoever, we came to the conclusion that she was Hungarian! She and the Major were like figures from a Brontë novel and were a source of enjoyable curiosity. I never remember them walking into Belleek together. They were always alone. Many years later, I was discussing the Moores with an elderly person from Belleek. I described Madame Bidault as Major Moore's wife. The old woman smiled at me in a strange kind of way!

I started school in the autumn of 1938. The Commons Primary School was a small national school consisting of two classrooms with about fifty pupils on rolls. The facilities were primitive. Little had changed since the school was built in the latter part of the nineteenth century. The toilets in the schoolyard were crude and basic, little more than a hole in the ground. There was a tiny porch, where we hung our coats. The classrooms were furnished with ancient, long, heavy wooden desks that stretched the full width of the room. Inkwells were set into the desks at various points. The ink was prepared in the classroom from powder and water. In the colder weather, a roaring turf fire was lit in each of the classrooms and on wet mornings we were allowed to hang our coats to dry on the fireguard. On some very cold days, the teacher would gather the entire class around the fire to give a lesson. Dog-eared schoolbooks were passed from one generation of pupils to another.

My first teacher was Miss Rogan. She taught me for my first three years in school. She was from Ballyshannon, a member of a family that is internationally famous for its creative skills in tying and designing fishing flies. Miss Rogan expressed that inherent family creativity in her wonderful teaching skills. She taught us reading and writing; she taught us, in a particularly memorable way, about the surrounding wild life and nature; she instructed us in our faith and prepared us for First Confession and First Communion. The prayers that Miss Rogan taught me have remained with me all my life and are still among my daily prayers. I keep referring to her as 'Miss' Rogan. It occurs to me that I never got to know her Christian name! I suppose it is a measure of the respect in which I have always held her.

After completing the first three years, we graduated to second class and moved into the Master's room. Master P.J. Egan was a plump, bald man from the west of Ireland. The school was his whole life. He was a superb teacher. The available facilities, by today's standards, were primitive; his main resources were text-books, the blackboard, pencil and paper, and his own ingenuity and flair for teaching. He shared with his pupils his love of reading and introduced us to that great pleasure which I have enjoyed through-out my life. He loved poetry, especially Yeats and Wordsworth. I can still clearly remember him reading Wordsworth to us in the spring when the 'hosts of golden daffodils' were all around us. He intro-duced us to *The Wind in the Willows* and *Treasure Island*. Patricia Lynch, the Irish writer of wonderful children's books, was another of his favourite authors. Along with Robert Louis Stevenson, she became one of my childhood favourites. I read all of her books sev-eral times. I could identify with the characters and the activities she wrote about. Master Egan even introduced us to Shakespeare. He despaired of my dreadful handwriting, as many others have done in the years since then. There are some things that even the best teachers are unable to rectify! At the Commons School, I learned mental arithmetic in a way that I never forgot. I use the same tech-niques to this day. As was the case in all schools at that time, Master Egan delivered corporal punishment when he deemed it necessary. The instrument of punishment was the leather strap and it was painful. But he was fair. I always consider myself as having been par-ticularly blessed by my two inspirational primary teachers. We brought a bottle of milk and a few slices of bread and butter to school with us and we ate this during the lunch-break. During the war years, I seem to recall, bottles of orange juice and cod liver oil were distributed in the school. Every pupil walked to and from school. Parents did not come to the school to collect us – we made our way to and from school with other pupils. The bigger children accompanied smaller children. Some walked several miles, morning and evening, in all kinds of weather. A few pupils came in their bare feet, except in the depths of winter.

On our way to and from school, there were lots of adventures. One route to school took us up a narrow lane past the black zinc shed in which Bill Thornhill lived. Bill was somewhat eccentric. He had long grey hair, shaved about once a month, and smoked Wild Woodbine cigarettes incessantly. He lived alone. There were always rats to be seen around his shed, which he befriended and fed. He gave names to many of his rats and called them his 'wee dearies'. He always seemed to be in good form, had a few drinks when he got his pension and offended nobody. Nor did anyone offend him. It was considered daring to walk along that lane past Bill's shed.

My normal daily route to school took me through the village and past St Patrick's church. It was customary for me and the other pupils who passed that way to call in for a short prayer on the way home from school. Prayer and churchgoing were very much part of the life of the community and were taken for granted. When I was about eight or nine, I volunteered to be an altar server, and Master Egan taught myself and some other boys the responses, '*Ad Deum qui laetificat juventutem meam*', and all the other beautiful sounding and mysterious words of the Latin Mass. Eventually, we began serving Mass. I greatly enjoyed that experience. There was something magical and mystical about it that appealed to me. The Latin words and the incense and the candles and holy water enhanced the attraction. There was something of the theatre about it.

The Second World War was raging in Europe and in Asia during much of my time in primary school in the early 1940s. Despite the fact that we lived in a tiny little backwater on the very periphery of Western Europe, the war impinged on our lives in many ways. Possibly the single most drastic impact on a primary school child was the rationing of sweets and chocolate. Even with a father who had a shop, sweets and chocolate became scarce commodities, which could only be obtained and enjoyed on rare occasions. Food was rationed. Clothing was rationed. Petrol was rationed. An air raid siren was tested from time to time, and we were all issued with gas masks. Thankfully, the siren never heralded a real air raid and there was never any cause to use the gas masks. The dramatic announcement on the wireless of the Japanese bombing of Pearl Harbour is the earliest event in the war that I can remember with any clarity. We heard it in our kitchen from the huge brown Marconi wireless set, with its wet and dry batteries. We had just come in from morning Mass on Monday, 8 December 1941. It was a holy day. That was a dramatic moment, which I can still recall very clearly. Some time before then, refugee children started to arrive from Belfast and Glasgow and various parts of England. Children were evacuated from the big cities to live with families in safer areas. Most of the refugee children who came to Belleek were relatives or friends of the host families. Some were not. We knew them as 'the evacuees', and they were welcomed into our community. Then, within view of our house and a few miles away to the southwest, two huge metal radio masts were erected at Dernacross, several hundred feet high. They could be seen on the skyline for miles around. Even before December 1941, the RAF flying boats of Coastal Command had established a base on Lough Erne nearby, and for the duration of the war the magnificent and beautiful white Sunderland flying boats and less beautiful grey Catalinas were a constant daily feature overhead. They were *en route* to anti-submarine and convoy escort patrol over the Atlantic. Years later, I became aware that they were making use of the Donegal Corridor negotiated between de Valera and Churchill. Otherwise those aircraft would have had to make a lengthy detour over Counties Tyrone and Derry to reach their patrol areas over the Atlantic Ocean. Several RAF personnel were based at the radio station around the aforementioned radio masts at Dernacross. There were many hundreds of British and Canadian RAF men at the bases between Belleek and Enniskillen. Then, sometime in 1942, the Yanks arrived.

The introduction of the American GIs to a sleepy little closed community like ours was dramatic, to say the least. The Americans set up a radio base with huge masts and antennae at Magheramena, a few miles outside Belleek. This was presumably a radio beacon to guide aircraft flying in over the Atlantic from the United States to some of the air bases in the North and in Britain. An American GI was the first coloured person I ever saw in the flesh. The GIs were very kind to the children of the area. They had lots of sweets and Hershey chocolate bars and chewing gum and all kinds of goodies, which they distributed generously. They called at the school in their jeeps to deliver candy. They held parties for us school kids at regular intervals, but especially at Halloween and Christmas. They gave us rides on their jeeps and trucks. They played baseball on the Main Street and got very drunk from time to time. Late in the evening on one fair day, a group of GIs spotted a forlorn man with an unsold donkey and they bought it from him. Then they went into a pub, purchased a basin full of Guinness and offered it to the donkey to drink. It was the only time I ever saw a drunken donkey! The GIs entered into the local folklore and several of them married local girls. They were a source of constant fascination. During 1943 and the early months of 1944, there were huge build-ups of Allied troops in County Fermanagh, particularly around Enniskillen, as they prepared for the invasion of North Africa and continental Europe. They were around in their thousands. It was all very exciting for a ten-year-old. More and more planes were flying overhead, including fighter aircraft, like Spitfires and Hurricanes, occasionally towing target drogues behind them. There was also an increasingly constant stream of large bomber aircraft, especially Flying Fortresses and Liberators, coming in from North America, being ferried over to take part in the European bombing campaign. Cycling trips along the lovely shore road between Belleek and Enniskillen afforded a spectacular view of flying boats at anchor on Lough Erne. On a few occasions, we were lucky enough to see a flying boat land or take off. There were tanks and armoured personnel carriers and Bren gun carriers on the roads, with thousands of troops in full camouflage battledress engaged in military manoeuvres.

The single most dramatic and memorable event of the war occurred for me in the early afternoon of Saturday, 12 August 1944. It was a beautiful bright sunny day and we were engaged in haymaking on a hillside in the high field behind our house. It was in the early afternoon. We heard an aircraft approaching and there was a sound like backfiring and bangs from its engines. When it came into view, it was a Sunderland flying boat. It was flying very low and circled several times; thick black smoke was streaming from one of its engines. We were told subsequently that, as it was circling, it was jettisoning depth charges and fuel into the bog lands below. Suddenly, about two or three miles from where we were, it seemed to attempt to land, and crashed in a bog between the townlands of

Cashelard and Corlea across the border in County Donegal. There was a thunderous rumbling noise when it hit the ground, a sound that echoed around the surrounding hills. I cannot remember seeing a fire. We immediately left the hayfield, ran home, grabbed our bicycles and pedalled to the scene as fast as we could. But the Garda Síochána were there before us and members of the Irish Army were also soon on the scene. Many other local people gathered. We watched from a road about two hundred yards away from the crash site and saw some wounded survivors being taken away on stretchers. The aircraft had crashed across a narrow bog road. It had broken into pieces, the tail section being clearly recognisable. There was a crew of twelve, three of whom lost their lives in the crash. They were all members of the Royal Canadian Air Force.* The Irish soldiers threw a cordon around the area and eventually chased us and other civilians away. On following days, the whole area was shaken with huge explosions when the Irish Army detonated some of the jettisoned depth charges. The crash was the talk of the area for a long time afterwards. When the security was taken away, people searched the remaining debris. Aeroplane glass, the thick glass from aircraft cockpits and windows, was a much-prized item at that time. People made rings and other ornaments from it.

As I got older, I became fascinated by the war, especially after D-Day when I became aware that many of the soldiers who had been based in Fermanagh in 1943 and the early part of 1944 were by then fighting in various campaigns in mainland Europe. Master Egan taught us geography using the war maps that appeared in the newspapers at that time, with great dark arrows pointing out the various attacks and counter-attacks across Europe and Asia. I can still remember the precise location of unlikely places such as Coblenz and Essen, Bastogne and Arnhem, Iwo Jima and Nagasaki.

When I was about nine, my father allowed me to help in the shop. I had played around there for many years, but now it was serious – I was on the staff! The country shop, even during wartime,

---

*   There is mention of this crash in an interesting article 'World War II Plane Crashes in Co. Donegal' by Gerard A. Hannigan in *Donegal Annual*, 1991 (Donegal Historical Society, Ballyshannon).

was a wonderland for a nine-year-old. Whilst the rationing and shortages limited the stock to very modest proportions, there was still a great variety of goods on sale. All kinds of groceries were available, as well as meal and flour; hardware implements like spades and shovels, veterinary pharmaceutical products for warble-fly, hoose and all kinds of other ailments, as mysterious as they were unpronounceable. Dry batteries were stocked for wireless sets, and people left their wet batteries to be charged from time to time. My father repaired wireless sets, as a hobby, and people brought them to him when there were problems. The shop offered a great opportunity to meet people and to be at ease with people. A man called Eddie McGonagle assisted my father in the shop. Eddie was a great character and a source of much wisdom. I loved being with him. By the time I came to know him, he was already advanced in years and had worked in the shop for most of his life. I spent hours with him in the store, filling and weighing quarter- and half-pound bags of tea from tea chests, bags of sugar from hundred- weight jute bags and half-stone bags of flour. Nothing was pre-packed at that time. People came into the shop at the same time on the same day each week. Eddie and my father knew what they wanted before they asked. The farmers and their wives came in their horse-carts and pony-traps. Coupons were required for virtually all staple goods. The coupons from the ration books had to be cut out, carefully put away and counted at the end of the week or month and returns made to the local Food Office in Irvinestown. My father often involved my sister, Marion and myself in cutting out, sorting and counting the ration coupons. It became a family event. Like us, most people in the locality were self-sufficient. They or their neighbours had hens and a few cows. Nearly every family churned its own butter and baked its own bread. But supplies of tea and sugar were a particularly acute problem. There were variations in availability and supply on both sides of the border, with the result that smuggling in both directions was a major industry. Everything from cattle to tea and sugar was smuggled. There was a contest between the ingenuity of the smuggler and the vigilance of the customs on both sides of the border. People along the border were able to have the best of both worlds.

My father, as already mentioned, was also the local undertaker. At that time, the country undertaker's responsibility was merely to prepare and supply the coffin. The family, or a neighbour of the deceased, washed and prepared the corpse a few hours after death. The body was then laid out on a bed in the room, or, in some cases, the kitchen, for the duration of the wake. The undertaker also provided other needs, such as tea and sugar, and clay pipes and tobacco and cigarettes. A discreet bottle of whiskey, if it could be acquired during wartime, would not go amiss either! I carefully watched in fascination as my father and Eddie prepared many coffins, lined them and inscribed and fixed the breastplate and other outer fittings. They fitted out the coffins in the back store amidst the meal and flour bags. I remember being particularly distressed on one occasion as they prepared a child's white coffin for someone younger than myself. When the coffin was prepared, they went to the house of the deceased to deliver it, usually on the night before the funeral. The coffin was usually left in an outhouse until the morning of the burial, when members of the family would place the corpse in it. A little grey trailer, which my father towed behind the car, was the means of transporting the coffin from the shop to the house of the deceased. My father didn't have a hearse and, anyhow, in most cases, on the day of the funeral, the coffin was carried from the home to the church on the shoulders of male members of the family, however distant that may have been. I was always impressed by the care and respect and sensitivity with which Eddie and my father carried out these tasks. My father always attended on the morning of the funeral and assisted and supervised in the burial. During school holidays, I often accompanied him to funerals.

My father's work as undertaker took him to two parishes and four different churches. As a result, I was in frequent contact with many priests whom I came to know and respect. As an altar server, I was in regular contact with the priest based in Belleek, but as a result of attending funerals with my father I frequently met priests attached to other churches and parishes. They were all very kind to me. Some of these priests would have called in the shop also. One priest who particularly fascinated me was Father Lorcan Ó Ciaráin. He lived in a castle at Magheramena, about two or three miles outside Belleek. It had formerly been the dwelling of local gentry. I don't quite know the story of how it came to be parish property or how a priest came to be living in such an edifice. It was strange that such a building should be the parochial house. It was an impressive, if somewhat dilapidated building with large draughty rooms. It was the biggest house that I was ever in as a child. In the autumn every year, coming up to Halloween, Father Ó Ciaráin invited people out to the castle where, in a large room, the floor was covered with apples which had been picked from the adjoining apple orchard and he encouraged them to help themselves which they did. He was given to telling tall and fascinating stories. He specialised in ghost stories. During our Halloween visit for apples, he always had a new ghost story. He was very elderly when I first came to know him. Not surprisingly, Magheramena Castle was disposed of after Father Ó Ciaráin died in 1945. The other priests were less colourful but they were all very caring to families at times of sickness and death and carried out their duties with great dedication and generosity. Virtually all of the priests whom I knew in my childhood came from County Monaghan. I thought that that was the place from which all priests came!

There were plenty of recreational activities in Belleek during my childhood years. From early on, I enjoyed watching anglers fishing in the river. My parents must have taken a hint because when I was about eight years old, they gave me a fishing rod as a Christmas present. From then on, I did a little fishing myself. However, I had more enthusiasm than skill where angling was concerned. With other boys from school, I enjoyed cycling and roaming around through the fields and along the river.

But the main recreational activity was watching and playing Gaelic football. There was a very active GAA club in Belleek. Although Belleek was in County Fermanagh, the local club at that time played in County Donegal. The pitch, across the border in Corlea, was rented from a farmer and was very basic, just a reasonably flat field with goal posts which struggled to remain perpendicular. There were no dressing rooms; the players changed into their playing gear behind a hedge. Some of the players were our local heroes. There was room for people of all ages – even for children in juvenile teams and competitions. It is to their great credit that the GAA was, at that time, the only organisation that provided healthy recreation for young people in almost every parish in Ireland. The wonderful commentaries on big games by Michael O'Hehir on Radio Éireann on Sunday afternoons were a significant factor in the popularity of the GAA and the lives of people throughout the country. Those commentaries thrilled everyone, young and old. My father, a keen footballer in his younger days, was also a devoted football fan. I travelled with him by train to many big matches in Dublin and Cavan and elsewhere on Sundays. The Great Northern Railway laid on special trains for every major sporting occasion. I remember being particularly thrilled on one occasion in Breffni Park in Cavan when my father pointed out Michael O'Hehir to me as he sat in his shirtsleeves in the radio commentary box. He was more famous then than many of the players. The first time I was ever in Dublin was to see an All Ireland semi-final in 1942 or 1943. Many of the finest footballers in the country were in the Irish Army during World War Two. Some of them were based at Finner Camp, an Irish Army base situated between Ballyshannon and Bundoran. They played regularly in local games and it was a bonus to see some of the great national stars of the sport, household names, in action locally.

There were cultural activities too. Anew McMaster and the Carrickford companies paid visits from time to time. These were repertory companies that toured small Irish towns and performed a different play every night. They were a feature of Irish rural life at that time and I gained my first taste for the theatre from them. They achieved remarkable performances with very basic facilities. Lighting was often sourced from hurricane lamps. The companies were made up of colourful characters on and off the stage and they brought a frisson of excitement into our lives. They stayed in a local boarding house and performed in McCabe's Hall, a hall owned by the village blacksmith. The Irish playwright, Lennox Robinson, wrote a lovely play based on these companies, called *Drama at Inish*. There was a local amateur dramatic group at that time called the Border Players who staged some splendid productions. No wonder. The producer was an Irish Customs officer based in Ballyshannon.

His name was McCann. He later became Director of the Abbey Theatre, Tomás Mac Anna. On Sunday afternoons, especially in winter, when there weren't any football matches, I cycled, with other local children, to the Rock Cinema in Ballyshannon, four miles away, to attend the matinee. My favourite films were Westerns and the serials that were shown each week. The local area was also a centre for Irish traditional music. There were many excellent musicians, particularly fiddlers and accordion players.

At home, too, there were lots of social activities. There were always people calling in house for a chat. At Christmas time there were visits from the Mummers. There were card games and board games and the family Rosary at night. But listening to the wireless set, the radio, was my favourite pastime and my window on the outside world. It was a simple, uncomplicated lifestyle.

The Pottery horn or hooter punctuated the day, dictating the start or the end of the working day or lunch-break. Belleek Pottery was and still is the focus of the whole village. It has provided good employment for local people for more than a hundred years. The workers were and still are the backbone of the local economy and of the local community. The Pottery also generated and supplied electricity to the village at that time. In many ways, the presence of a craft industry of such quality and prestige protected Belleek from the searing poverty and subsequent emigration that bedevilled many other rural areas of Ireland at that time. For the duration of the war, the Pottery was deprived of its primary market in the United States. So the workers confined themselves to the production of plain earthenware rather than the more exotic fine china. The skills involved in some of the Belleek products are quite amazing. The older craftsmen, like Michael Dolan, were rightly held in almost reverential awe in the locality when I was child. I remember being extremely proud when I saw 'Belleek' listed as a noun in the *Collins English Dictionary*: 'a kind of thin fragile porcelain with a lustrous glaze, named after Belleek, a town in Northern Ireland where such porcelain is made'.* An indigenous craft industry producing a

---

*   *The Collins English Dictionary* (London, 1986).

high-quality product is a wonderful blessing for any small community.

My holidays during childhood were spent with relatives. I had lots of cousins around the same age as myself. I particularly enjoyed going to Dungloe in West Donegal where my aunt lived. It is a lovely area. I also greatly enjoyed holidays with aunts and uncles and their families in Donegal and Pettigo. In Pettigo, my uncle had a public house. This provided another set of experiences. At that time, brown wooden casks of Guinness were sent out by rail from Dublin to every town and village in Ireland. In my uncle's pub, a lot of time each morning was spent in the bottling shed transferring the Guinness from the casks to bottles. The bottles had to be washed, then filled and then corked. All this was done by hand, apart from a primitive contraption, coated in white enamel with six protruding copper pipes, into which the contents of the wooden cask were decanted and transferred to the bottles. The bottles were stored for a few days before serving. Whilst it was not, by modern standards, the most hygienic operation, I enjoyed participating in it. During one or two summers, my parents rented a bungalow in Rossnow-lagh, a seaside resort in County Donegal about eight miles from home. Although Rossnowlagh has a wonderful beach, the seaside, for some reason or another, held few attractions for me as a child. On most days, whilst the family were in Rossnowlagh, I was glad to travel with my father to help him in the shop in Belleek.

I was lucky to be blessed with such a happy childhood. I had good and loving parents, excellent teachers, and a wonderful, enjoyable, interesting and healthy environment in which to experience my childhood years. It was a carefree time. But things were going to change.

CHAPTER 2

Not the Happiest Years

*Boarding in St Columb's College – homesickness -
severe regime – the sweet smell of chips –
enjoyable holidays – isolation from outside world -
deciding on a career – chemistry or priesthood?*

I could have stayed at the Commons School until I was fifteen years old. However, my parents wanted me to have a secondary education and go to a secondary school. This created a problem. There was no Catholic secondary school for boys in County Fermanagh at that time. Anything other than a Catholic school was unthinkable. To be enrolled at our own diocesan college, St Macartan's College, Monaghan would have involved spending the first year exclusively learning Irish before the studies proper would begin. The same difficulty would occur if I chose to attend the secondary school in nearby Ballyshannon. So it was decided that I should sit an entrance examination for St Columb's College in Derry. Derry was the nearest large city. It seemed very far away from home but there was no other option. Master Egan prepared me for the examination.

The entrance examination took place in the Loreto Convent in Omagh in April 1946, and about six weeks later, I was informed that I had been accepted by St Columb's College and had been awarded a scholarship. I didn't quite know whether to be pleased or disappointed. I wasn't very enthused with the thought of leaving home and going so far away. Boarding school didn't exactly appeal to me.

My parents brought me to Derry to start my new life on Tuesday, 3 September 1946. It was my first time in that city. As we entered the grounds of St Columb's, I quickly realised that it was a far cry from the Commons School to which I had been accustomed. It seemed so big. Many other parents were there with their sons, none of whom I knew, and none of whom my parents knew. Someone, I think it was a senior pupil, showed us to the dormitory and the cubicle where I would sleep for the next year and then brought us on a quick guided tour of the college; the refectory, the chapel, the study hall, the football pitches; and the museum! Then came the dreaded, tearful moment when my parents departed and I was on my very own for the first time in a strange and not very friendly environment. I had come out of a community in which I knew everybody and into a community in which I knew nobody.

My only knowledge of boarding school prior to my arrival in Derry was gleaned from comics and books. Tales of Billy Bunter in the *Dandy* or *Beano* comics was not the best of preparation for life and survival as a boarder in St Columb's in the 1940s, nor indeed was *Tom Brown's Schooldays*.

There are two things that I still remember clearly from my first week as a pupil in St Columb's College. The first memory is of the Dean reading the College Rules in the chapel. I remember having the distinct impression that it would be much easier to get expelled from the college than to stay there. This puzzled me and, in subsequent years, I confess, often tempted me. I also remember going through the ritual of being 'ducked'. This involved first year students being chased and caught by older boys, dragged to the nearest tap and drenched to the skin. It was part of the initiation ceremony.

We were told, at some stage, that we were in St Columb's to be educated for life in the great wide world in the second half of the twentieth century. There were some very gifted teachers. It was fascinating to be introduced to new subjects like chemistry and foreign languages like French. After my experience as an altar server, it was good to learn more about Latin. It was interesting to have a variety of teachers, a teacher for each subject rather than one teacher for all subjects.

However, I found the adjustment very difficult, for several reasons. The primary problem was that I greatly missed my parents and family. I was dreadfully homesick for weeks and weeks. At twelve years of age, it is traumatic to be completely cut off from your parents and family for three months at a time in such an alien environment. At home, I had shared a bedroom with my younger brother. Suddenly I was in a tiny wooden cubicle in a large dormitory, with about forty or fifty other boys of my own age. Sleep was never a problem, although getting up after a rising bell early in the morning in a cold dormitory and washing in cold water did prove to be a challenge. Food was scarce in those post-war years. Perhaps, it was not the best time in history to be in boarding school. Hunger was ever-present, and this was aggravated by the fact that close to the college, and well within smelling distance, there was a bakery and a fish-and-chip shop. Both, of course, were strictly out of bounds and, in any case, would have been beyond our financial means. In the morning, the scent of freshly baked bread and pastry wafted over the college wall. After an inadequate meal, on dark winter evenings, the seductive smell of chips frying in the Southend Fish Saloon made the pangs of hunger more acute. Although the Abercorn Bakery has long gone, there is still a fish-and-chip shop on the site of the Southend Fish Saloon in Bishop Street. Every time I pass by, I recall hungry nights in St Columb's. Parcels from home and the generosity of friendly and co-operative day pupils, who shared their lunches with us, allowed us to survive.

There was another smell that permeated this area of Derry. The Gas Yard, dominated by huge gasometers, was down in the Bogside, a few hundred yards behind the College. The smell of coal gas is a smell I always associate with those years spent in St Columb's. The Gas Yard is now gone.

Because of the fact that we were all in the same position, there was ample scope to form good friendships with fellow boarders. Boarders provided a good support for one another. We shared food parcels from home. There were lots of opportunities to engage in sporting activities, which was good. I was introduced to the game of soccer, which I had never seen before. We were able to watch Derry City play in Brandywell Stadium on Saturday afternoons from a vantage point in the college grounds, albeit against college rules. I had taken piano lessons all during my childhood and had made reasonable progress. My mother, at one time, taught the piano to chil-

dren. However, in St Columb's, there was a choice between continuing piano lessons or sport. I chose sport. I greatly enjoyed the
sporting activities but I have always regretted not continuing with
my piano studies. I envy those who can play the piano or any musical instrument.

Priests made up more than half of the teaching staff. Whilst I
had been aware that there would be priests on the teaching staff,
meeting priests in this new context initially perplexed me. I was further bewildered when the strap was produced. Whilst I was prepared to accept punishment, I had not been prepared for the shock
of receiving physical punishment from priests. I had had a very
happy relationship with priests in my parish at home. But this was
different. The strap appeared often and a great number of teachers,
cleric and lay, used it. The punishment, often arbitrary, frequently
verged on the brutal. It was painful and humiliating. The use of the
strap was not confined to the classroom. Boarders often experienced
severe penalties for minor infringements of rules, long after class
was over. On occasions, punishment was meted out without the
recipient fully understanding why he was being punished. Reasons
for the punishment were not given. You did not ask questions. But
in the 1940s, that, apparently, was the accepted norm. Few complained and one could expect little sympathy, even from the most
caring of parents. 'You were not punished unless you deserved it',
would have been the likely response. So you just stuck out your
hand and took 'your medicine'. The bullying was not confined to
the staff. Some prefects seemed to perceive their position as a
licence to beat up younger pupils. This was known as 'bashing'. It
was a severe, harsh and often cruel regime.

We attended class each day from Monday to Friday and for a
half day on Saturday. Boarders spent hours every evening in supervised study, and this was particularly painful at weekends. Sunday
always seemed to be a particularly long and dismal day. Those who
had relatives in Derry or a visit from parents on Saturday could go
out into the city with them. I did not have any relatives in Derry and
my parents were unable to come to visit me because of petrol
rationing. It was virtually impossible to make a return journey in
one day from Belleek to Derry by public transport at that time. So

from that early September day in 1946 until the day I went on my Christmas holidays, I was not outside the college gates. And it was the same for most of my first three years in St Columb's. I seldom had the opportunity to leave the College grounds from the start of term to the holidays at the end of each term. After spending my childhood years wandering freely wherever I wished over a wide area, either on foot or on bicycle, I was now confined to a small area within the college grounds. I wrote to my parents each week. They wrote to me keeping me in touch with everything that was happening at home.

One of the happiest journeys of my life was the journey home by train on that morning two or three days before Christmas 1946. I can still remember it clearly and recall the growing excitement as I approached Belleek, counting down the stations – Irvinestown, Kesh, Pettigo, Castlecaldwell, all the familiar landmarks and then home. My mother and brother and sisters were waiting on the platform to greet me. We hurried from the station to the shop, where my father and Eddie were busy with the Christmas rush and on to our home and the first good meal for three months. It was a wonderful Christmas spent rediscovering friends and places that I had sorely missed.

However, all good things come to an end. I remember pleading with my parents at one stage during the holiday to let me stay at home. I did not want to go back to St Columb's. Returning to boarding school, after the first holiday at home, was particularly difficult. My parents endeavoured to explain to me that it was for my own good. So some time in the second week of January, I embarked on the return train journey, on my own. I had expected that I would meet some other returning pupils along the way. Yet, despite checking at every station platform, there was nobody I recognised on that particular train. They must have travelled on an earlier train. The train got into Derry about 7.30 p.m. It was a very dark, cold night. I had a big case loaded down, mostly with food. I suddenly realised that I didn't know how to get from the station to the college. I had never undertaken that journey before on my own. I headed out of the GNR station hauling my case and finished up on Foyle Road under Craigavon Bridge, not knowing where I was going. At that stage, I felt very sorry for myself, sat on the case and burst into tears. Within a few minutes, a kindly man came along. He asked me what was the matter. I explained my problem to him. He said, 'Don't worry. I'm going that way. I'll take you there.' He picked up my case and walked me the whole way to the college gates in Bishop Street. I never found out who he was. It was my first personal experience of the great kindness of Derry people.

I spent five years in St Columb's College. There were some good times, some brilliant teachers and interesting things to learn. There was a fine academic education. Sporting activities were most enjoyable. I met and made some very good friends. However, on the whole, I did not find it a good experience. It was not the happiest time in my life.

One of the more unpleasant experiences took place during the month of January in my second year in St Columb's. One member of our class committed a relatively trivial offence. This gradually was exaggerated out of all proportion by the Dean and transformed into a major breach of rules. The offender had already been in trouble with the authorities, so we all decided to protect him. He refused to admit the offence. Everyone in the class, about twenty of us, was individually questioned about the matter. We all refused to co-operate with the investigation. So we were all punished. All privileges were cancelled for the remainder of that school year. We were not permitted outside the College, even if parents came to visit; we were not permitted to receive parcels from home, parcels on which we depended so much and there were some other less painful penalties. The punishment was vastly disproportionate to the offence. I told my parents of this, when informing them that the weekly parcels could not be sent. Four months later, on a weekend in May, my parents had managed to accumulate sufficient petrol to come to visit me. I warned them that I would be refused permission to go out with them. But they said, as it was their first visit in two years, the Dean would surely acquiesce. The incident had occurred months before and they presumed that it would be forgotten. They came to Derry and the Dean did not acquiesce. He refused permission for me to go out for a meal with them. I was angry and hurt by the humiliation of my parents. It was the first time that they had managed to visit me in the two years I had been in the College. Thirty years later, the Dean was a colleague of mine in the Irish Episcopal Conference. We became good friends and colleagues. I often wondered if he remembered that day in May 1948. We never got round to talking about it. In any case, my anger and hurt had long gone. He was acting, perhaps, in the tradition of the time. It was a bad, cruel and unchristian tradition.

There was a profound feeling of isolation from the world outside for which we were allegedly being prepared. Although there were some very accomplished athletes and footballers among the pupils, we did not compete with other schools in any sporting competition. Newspapers were forbidden, and we were not allowed to listen to the radio. Some pupils tried, with varying degrees of success, to build crystal radios. Despite some ingenious efforts in radio engineering, reception from these radio sets, even when audible, was indistinct. They were also invariably hunted down and seized by the Dean. They were easy to detect, because apparently they caused scratchy interference to reception on the Dean's own wireless set! From the college, the turrets of Derry Prison were clearly visible. The years in the college were something that had to be undergone, like a prison sentence. Ultimately, I kept my head down and 'did my time'. I enjoyed what I could in St Columb's College and endured the remainder. I suppose that there were many similar boys' boarding schools at that time.

A place in St Columb's where I did find some comfort was the College Chapel. The beautiful stained glass windows behind the main altar captured my attention. Various panels portrayed Jesus working with Joseph in the carpenter's workshop, Jesus speaking and teaching the doctors in the Temple and Jesus challenging the young man, the story from chapter 18 of St Luke's Gospel. As a young person, I always found those windows inspirational and comforting. They taught visually and very powerfully the sacred nature of work, knowledge and service. Subsequently, as a bishop, in my homilies to pupils in that same chapel, I often used those windows to illustrate what I was saying.

My parents realised that I was very unhappy in St Columb's, and as there was no alternative college, endeavoured to make my holidays as enjoyable as possible. I spent most of the days working in the shop and on the farm and thereby earned pocket money. I played a lot of football and went with my father to many big club and county Gaelic football games. I listened to music on the radio and gramophone and went to the cinema in Ballyshannon and to the summer shows in Bundoran. I loved to visit Quigley's Music Shop in Ballyshannon and to purchase gramophone records (78s) and sheet music of popular songs. Quigley's was a wonderful treasure trove of musical paraphernalia. Bundoran and Rossnowlagh were easy to reach by bicycle and we did a lot of bathing in the breakers there.

During the latter years of the 1940s, Belleek and Ballyshannon were at the centre of one of the biggest civil engineering projects in Ireland at the time – the Erne Hydroelectric Scheme. This involved building two huge dams across the River Erne at Cliff, beside the aforementioned Cliff House and at Cathleen's Falls outside Ballyshannon, and harnessing the waters of the river to generate electrical power. Hundreds of workers were brought in to do this work. On Sunday mornings, with other local people, we walked to Cliff to view the work on the construction of the huge dam being built there. It was a massive and spectacular building project. Sadly it necessitated the demolition of Cliff House. The huge river was diverted into a specially built channel or bypass, whilst the dam was being constructed. Ballyshannon and Belleek became boomtowns. Two splendid new cinemas were built in Ballyshannon. New shops were opened. After the war, Belleek Pottery returned to making its characteristic Parian china. It was a very exciting time in the area. Everything was wonderful for me until each holiday approached its end.

In my last year in St Columb's, I had to give some thought to my future career. At that time, there were no careers teachers or guidance counsellors. I gave consideration to several careers. I was interested in teaching or going to Queen's University in Belfast to study analytical chemistry or medicine. Then one day, early in 1951, I first heard of what was called the Bishop's Examination, or to use the colloquial term 'the Bishops'. This was an examination for those who expressed an interest in joining the priesthood of the Derry diocese. I applied for this examination. I have often since wondered why I chose to become a priest. I have often been asked the reason why I opted for priesthood. To this day, I am unable to find a simple answer to that question. There was no tradition of priests in the family background. I was certainly greatly impressed by almost all the priests I met in my early childhood. I was very impressed by some, though not all, of the priests on the staff of St Columb's. Four priests on the College staff particularly impressed me for their kindness and care, in an atmosphere where kindness and care were not in plentiful supply. (I am now aware that the priests on the teaching staff of St Columb's, at that time, received only a tiny percentage of their salary. The remainder went towards the maintenance of the building and to subsidise the fees of the pupils. It was a difficult assignment for many of them. I am sure that some of them were unhappy to be working as teachers. They, too, like their pupils, led fairly Spartan lives.) Apart from the fact that my religious faith was always important to me and I was attracted by the idea of service to people, I cannot specify to this day why I chose priesthood. There certainly was no 'Damascus' moment! I suppose that it could be said that I drifted into it. In any case, I sat the Bishop's Examination and was accepted as a seminarian to study for the priesthood of the diocese of Derry. With several of my classmates, I was nominated to study in St Patrick's College, Maynooth. Initially, I must confess that I perceived it merely as another career option that might be changed at a later date. I sat the Senior Certificate examination with my classmates in June 1951. I applied for entry to Queen's University in Belfast to study analytical chemistry as well, just in case.

I told my parents about my interest in the priesthood during my Easter holidays. They had been asking me during that final year about what I intended to do with my life, what career I planned to follow. They did not pressure me in any direction. When I told them of my interest in priesthood, they expressed surprise but said that if that was what I wanted they would support me in my wish.

I did not know how to tell my friends in Belleek that I had decided to be a priest. My initial plan was to tell nobody except my parents. I was not quite sure how they would react. I decided to tell just one close friend. Her reaction was less than encouraging. She thought that I was mad! I swore her to secrecy and she never said a word. I asked my parents to do the same. I did not want local people around Belleek to know of my decision until I was ready to go to the seminary. I still wanted to keep my options open. I still wanted to be free to change my mind. I was having an enjoyable time during my last summer holiday before going to the seminary when, to my horror, a local newspaper reported that I was going to study for the priesthood. I feared that a certain distancing would take place amongst my friends after this announcement. To my relief, that did not happen. Nobody changed his or her attitude to me. They carried on in the same carefree manner as before. Everyone was very relaxed about it. Whilst the fellows said nothing, some female acquaintances gently teased me about my decision. The premature announcement did not spoil that summer. I had a good time. A good time in Belleek in the early 1950s was relatively innocuous!

I was to begin studies in Maynooth in early September 1951. Then there was a bolt from the blue. On 5 September, I received a letter from Bishop Neil Farren, my bishop in Derry, telling me that he was nominating me for a scholarship and giving me an opportunity to go to the Irish College in Rome to study for the priesthood. Another student, who was to study there, had withdrawn. I was shattered and so were my parents. It was a short and succinct letter. Whilst it appeared that the bishop seemed to have left my options open, our local priest in Belleek advised me that such a letter from a bishop constituted an offer that 'could not be refused'! It was my first taste of how difficult and surprising ecclesiastical obedience could be.

I had never been out of Ireland in my life. The thought of going to a foreign country was something that I had never contemplated when considering priesthood. I began to think that I had made a terrible mistake and wondered what alternative career options were still open at such a late stage. Analytical chemistry seemed to be immensely attractive once again. A second letter from Bishop

Farren arrived some days later, accompanied by a letter from the Rector of the Irish College. He suggested that I contact a Michael Toal who lived outside Omagh. He was a fourth year student in the College, who was home on holiday. My parents drove me to Omagh that very day and we spent the evening talking to Michael. Whilst I was appalled to learn that students in Rome were only allowed home once every two years, Michael spoke in glowing terms of the Irish College and of life in Rome. This conversation gave me considerable reassurance. I had gone to Omagh wondering how I could get out of this dilemma but I returned home in a more positive frame of mind. I would give it a try. Besides I had three or four more weeks at home than I had expected. We were not to depart for Rome until the beginning of October.

I spent some time purchasing various items that were required for Rome. A passport had to be acquired and travel tickets had to be purchased. The nearest travel agent at that time was in Dublin! As the eldest member of the family, I was very conscious of the fact that all of these expenses placed a considerable financial burden on my parents. Four members of the family were younger than I was and one of my sisters was in boarding school at that time. The youngest, Anne, born whilst I was in St Columb's, was just a few years old. My parents never once complained. I was increasingly sad and lonely at the thought of leaving my parents, brother, sisters, friends and Belleek for two long years. Three-month stretches in St Columb's College were bad enough. But two years in a foreign country! It seemed like an eternity.

CHAPTER 3

Irish College, Rome

To Rome by sea and rail – what is pasta? – first sight of a Pope –
seminary life – Villa Irlanda and Formia – a trip home –
theology studies – Parente and Piolanti – a month in Perugia –
subdiaconate – big decisions – father's illness

The first week of October 1951 brought a mixture of emotions.

Taking leave of Belleek and my family and friends was painful. My father and mother drove Michael Toal, myself and another Derry student, Brendan McGinn, to the other end of Ireland to begin our journey to Rome. The journey from Belleek to Cobh in County Cork took a whole day.

We stayed overnight in the Commodore Hotel in Cobh. Before going to bed that night, I spent a long time with my parents in their room. It was the first time that I ever had a real and open heart-to-heart talk with both of them together. I expressed concern about the financial burden that I had brought on them by my decision to study for the priesthood. They reassured me about this. They told me that they were very happy about my decision to study for the priesthood but that they also would respect any subsequent decision if I decided that I could not embrace such a calling. I thanked them for all that they had done for me. Before going to my own room and to bed, we prayed the Rosary together as we had often done as a family in the evenings in the kitchen at home.

The morning came and it was time to say farewell to my parents. The farewell at Cobh was different than the first farewell in Derry five years earlier. I was older and somewhat more emotional. My anxiety was exacerbated by the fact that I wasn't sure that my

40

decision to study for the priesthood was a correct one. I felt quite insecure. In fact, that morning I was convinced that I had made a disastrously wrong decision. Two years seemed like such a long time to be away from home.

I do not know who planned the route for that journey from Ireland to Rome but more than a dozen of us set off together from Cobh. For decades, Cobh had been Ireland's great transatlantic emigration port for people travelling to America to find new opportunities and a new life. We were going east rather than west. It was a dramatic manner in which to leave Ireland for the first time. We left the quay at Cobh on a tender with a large number of people. The views of the cathedral and the town of Cobh from the sea were spectacular. Then as we steamed seaward around a headland the huge bulk of the SS *Washington*, an American passenger liner, suddenly came into view. It was anchored in the mouth of a bay. It seemed massive. We boarded it from the tender through a small door in the side of the liner and were allocated our cabins. Excitement and expectation gradually began to overcome the loneliness and sadness.

The SS *Washington* had been a troopship during the World War Two. The crew were American. The quality and the quantities of food were incredible. The menus took our breath away. I had never before heard of many of the items listed in them. We berthed in Southampton on the morning after we left Cobh. In Southampton harbour at adjoining berths we saw the *Queen Mary* and the *Mauritania*, legendary Cunard liners that I had often read about. Someone had given me a gift of a Brownie Kodak box camera and I began to put it to good use. We sailed from Southampton that evening and when we woke up the following morning, we were berthed in Le Havre in France.

We disembarked in Le Havre after two very enjoyable days and nights on the ship and took the train to the Gare St Lazare in Paris. We had booked into a small hotel in the Latin Quarter. There followed a couple of very interesting and enjoyable days in Paris, climbed the Eiffel Tower, walked the Champs Élysées, viewed the Arc de Triomphe, visited Notre Dame, La Madeleine, Montmartre and other places that had free admission. Paris was exciting and exhilarating. It was my first experience of being in a situation where few spoke English. I had an opportunity to try out the French that I learned in St Columb's. During all of these excursions, I got to know my fellow students who were travelling in the party. They came from all over Ireland. We all got along very well and greatly enjoyed our time together. I felt that I was going to be happy among them. This experience was certainly going to be different than St Columb's.

The last part of the journey was completed by rail, travelling from the Gare de Lyon, through Switzerland to Italy. It was a wonderful and fascinating trip, completed in just over twenty four hours. The Great Northern branch line to Bundoran was a child's train set compared with this. The train had to slow down here and there to pass over temporary bridges, which replaced bridges destroyed or damaged during the war. Even then, six years after the war ended, the debris of war could still be seen here and there in the towns and cities. I sat glued to the window, spellbound by the countryside, stunned by the beauty of the mountains and the lakes of Switzerland, fascinated by the long tunnels, mystified by some of the unfamiliar crops in the fields and hillsides.

The first part of the journey through Italy was through the darkness of the night and early morning. We were due to arrive in Rome around 9 a.m. From first light, we gazed through the windows at this country that was to be our home for the next six years. It was different than anything we had ever seen before. There were few green fields. Everything was brown. Quaint little towns clung to hilltops. People, men and women, were working in the fields and vineyards from first light. As we neared Rome, our anticipation grew. The one building with whose outline we were all familiar was St Peter's Basilica. We were sure that, once we could see it, we would have arrived in at our destination. But we didn't see St Peter's. Instead we saw endless streets of very dowdy tenement houses with washing strung from balcony to balcony across the street. We seemed to travel for ages through densely packed housing before eventually arriving at the station. Stazione Termini, completed just a year earlier for the 1950 Holy Year, was hugely impressive. We engaged a number of taxis to transport our luggage and ourselves. The scene outside the station was chaotic – animated, noisy, hot and crowded. In a few minutes, we arrived at the Irish College on Via Santi Quattro. The rector, Monsignor Donal Herlihy, warmly welcomed us. Each of us was shown to the room allocated to us. The ceiling was very high and the floor was tiled with terrazzo tiles. The room was dominated by a huge window fitted with a wooden shutter to shade against the sun or to keep out the light during siesta. There was a chair, table and bed, wardrobe and small chest of drawers. It was simple but it was adequate.

The Irish College in Rome was founded in 1628 and has been located in various parts of the city since. It was founded at a time when it was increasingly impossible to educate priests in Ireland. Irish Colleges were established in various parts of Europe during the seventeenth century to ensure that the training and formation of Irish priests for Irish dioceses would continue. The present building, which houses the Irish College in Rome, was opened in 1926.

Much of the first week in Rome was spent on a silent six-day retreat! It was a strange introduction to seminary life. The retreat director was interesting and encouraging. The food was mystifying. There was pasta each day – spaghetti, penne, risotto and so on. I had never seen pasta before in my life. I didn't know whether it was vegetable, animal or mineral. There was also red wine available at lunch each day. I was rather shocked by this because I was a teetotaller and a member of the Pioneer Total Abstinence Association; and not just a Pioneer, but I had strong views about young people drinking alcohol. We were on retreat with complete silence, so I was afraid to ask anyone about these matters. I noticed that several of the other newcomers like myself were a little reluctant to touch these strange dishes, and pushed the food around the plate rather tentatively. However, after a few days, hunger overcame such reservations. The most serious problem for me during that week was that I ran out of cigarettes during the second day of the retreat and I was too terrified to break the silence to ask someone else for a cigarette! The heat was also quite intense. I listened with fascination to the bewildering cacophony of sound from the surrounding streets. The whine of Vespa scooters and the incessant blowing of horns were a feature. The tolling of countless church and monastery bells marked out the hours. On the second day of the retreat, I found my way to the roof of the College and looked at the view. The Irish College is situated on the Coelian hill. The view from the College roof is breathtaking. The instantly recognisable dome of St Peter's Basilica could be seen to the north and a multitude of towers and spires and domes and buildings of all shapes peppered the skyline. A huge hospital dominated the foreground to the east; this explained the constant whine of ambulance sirens, which persisted through most days and nights. To the southeast were distant hills with clearly discernible clusters of houses and villages, which I later came to know as the Alban Hills. All of this heightened the expectation. The sun was warmly shining out of a clear blue sky. This was going to be a really exciting city to live in.

The retreat ended. There was much to talk about, much to discover. I was assured that wine was a necessary accompaniment to pasta. I was introduced to Italian cigarettes, a brand called Nazionale, which were foul. Then I had my first experience of the city of Rome. My first trip through the city was to a beatification ceremony in St Peter's Basilica. I was filled with excitement and anticipation on the way there, as we walked through the streets in the early Sunday morning. We passed the Colosseum and the Forum as we made our way to St Peter's across the Tiber River. I was surprised by the brown colour of the Tiber. Then along the splendid Via della Conciliazione and into Piazza San Pietro and the first sight of the awesome Bernini colonnades reaching out to embrace everyone and the magnificent façade of one of the most famous churches in the world. My first sight of a Pope was deeply moving experience. Pope Pius XII was carried into crowded St Peter's on the Sedia Gestatoria* with pomp and splendour to the sound of blaring trumpets. His face was so familiar. The scene was wonderful. It was sheer theatre. I felt quite overcome by it. From our vantage point, we could not see much of the actual ceremony after the Pope was carried past us and we could not understand

---

* This was the ceremonial chair on which, at that time, the Pope was borne aloft into St Peter's. The chair was carried on the shoulders of members of the papal household. It has not been used since the time of Pope Paul VI.

much of what was said, apart from the familiar parts of the Mass. The music and singing were magnificent. Looking around the crowds, including all colours of skin and all kinds of dress, I became conscious of the universality of the Church, embracing all races, cultures and classes. I came back to the College filled with enthusiasm. I was already happy in Rome and much more at ease with my decision to study for the priesthood. I was even learning to enjoy the amazing variety and goodness of pasta!

There were nine other young Irish men in my year in the Irish College; each of us aged around seventeen or eighteen. There was one from Galway, two from Meath, one from Mayo, one from Kerry, one from Offaly and three from Roscommon. We attended lectures in the Pontifical Lateran University. It was quite near the Irish College, just a few minutes' walk across Piazza San Giovanni, the great square of the Basilica of St John Lateran. The lectures in the various subjects were delivered in Latin or Italian. It was somewhat daunting. We had a crash course in Italian and the benefit of notes in English taken by generations of students before us. Most of us had taken Latin as a subject in secondary school, but secondary school Latin and spoken Latin are quite different. The ability of some of the professors and lecturers to speak fluent Latin at machine-gun speed did not assist our understanding. The student body was made up of students from Czechoslovakia, which at that time was behind the Iron Curtain, and students from various parts of Italy and ourselves. Many of the Czech students had made enormous sacrifices to study for the priesthood. They had escaped from their homeland and were out of communication with their parents and families. We studied logic, ethics, metaphysics, philosophy and psychology and various other subjects. We endeavoured to grapple with Hebrew, taught through the medium of Italian that we didn't understand! But the Lateran University was a pleasant place and we made a lot of friends there. Lectures began at 8 a.m. and ended at 12 noon. There were afternoon and evening lectures from time to time.

Our daily routine was to get up at 5.25 a.m. then have morning prayer and quiet meditation in the chapel from 5.45 until 6.15. Mass was celebrated at 6.15 and at 7.00 we had breakfast. We were at the

university for 8.00 and returned from there at 12 noon. There was
a short period of prayer before lunch at 1.00. After lunch, there was
a siesta until 3.30, when we had a period of recreation or an opportunity to go out sightseeing in the city. In the evening there was
study, prayer and recreation. It was a good and healthy routine. The
rector, Monsignor Donal Herlihy, the Vice Rector, Monsignor
Kevin McCabe and the Spiritual Director, Father Dominic
Conway, treated us as adults. These three men guided us and cared
for us, physically and spiritually, in an exemplary manner. They
were firm and demanded high standards but they were fair and most
caring. I had great respect for all three of them and that respect
grew as the years went by. The Irish College was also blessed by the
presence of the St John of God Sisters. They had a convent in the
College grounds and they supervised the cooking and looked after
our physical welfare when we were ill. They were wonderful and
dedicated women who brought a feminine and maternal dimension
to our life in the Irish College. Their presence had a considerable
and positive influence on our formation.

At that time, all priests and seminarians in Rome had to wear a
soutane or cassock. This was worn at all times when out in the city
and at most times when in the College. When walking in the city,
we were required to wear the traditional round hat with a broad
brim and seminarians at the various colleges had to wear a garment
called a *soprano*, a black outer cape with distinguishing marks that
identified the particular College attended. The Irish College students wore a black *soprano* with a narrow red stripe. It certainly
caused one to stand out. But we were not as prominent as those
from the German College. They were required to wear a bright red
cape and a red cassock and they could be seen coming from a long
distance away. The conventional wisdom at the time suggested that
they were required to wear this distinctive garb because, sometime
in the nineteenth century, German College students had over-
indulged and misbehaved in a Roman tavern. As a result there was
a colourful Roman solution for a German problem. After getting
over the initial inhibitions, the Roman clerical dress was not a problem. When in Rome ...

I was utterly captivated by the city of Rome. Almost fifty years later, I am still captivated by it and greatly enjoy my visits there. There is so much to see. There is so much vitality, variety and excitement in the place. Within a one-mile radius of the Irish College, there is the Colosseum, the wonderful eleventh century basilica of San Clemente with its amazing excavations, the Roman Forum, the basilica of St John Lateran, the Scala Sancta (Holy Stairs), the basilica of St Mary Major, the basilica of Santa Croce with its relics of Christ's Passion, the old city walls and aqueducts, to mention just a few of the major sights.

There are several Romes. There is imperial Rome, given expression in the Roman Forum; early Christian Rome, as experienced in the catacombs; Renaissance Rome with all its architectural and artistic splendour; and modern Rome. Each is full of interest. A few times each week, at the insistence of Monsignor Herlihy, we walked out in a group of five or six, called a *camerata*. A senior student was in charge and we systematically visited the city – churches, museums, art galleries and other sites of historical, cultural, religious or architectural importance. On other occasions, we went sightseeing in smaller groups. I have always felt a deep sense of gratitude to Monsignor Herlihy for offering us this encouragement and affording me that opportunity. He even whetted our interest by scheduling the reading of *Ave Roma Immortali*s during meals in the refectory during our early months in Rome. This classic book on Rome by Francis Marion Crawford gives dramatic insights into the city's colourful, ageless and varied history.

Walks in Rome, at that time, were always full of pleasant surprises. One could visit the church of Santa Maria del Popolo, and gaze in admiration at the light and shade of Caravaggio's wonderful paintings; and then a short distance down the Via del Babuino, Gregory Peck and Audrey Hepburn were filming *Roman Holiday* on the Spanish Steps and around the Piazza de Spagna in the presence of excited crowds. Nearby is the house where John Keats, the poet, lived and died in 1821. Every day brought its quota of delightful and pleasant surprises – a beautiful church, an interesting painting or fresco or just merely soaking up the atmosphere of the city and watching the passing parade from a sidewalk café whilst enjoying a cappuccino.

Most ordinary Italians, in the 1950s, did not know where Ireland was! When one spoke of 'Irlanda' or described oneself as 'irlandese', they immediately interpreted it as 'Olanda' or 'olandese'. They thought that we were Dutch! It took quite an amount of explanation to correct this misapprehension. Ireland and things Irish did not then impinge much on the life of the average Italian in the streets or shops. Things are different now.

I exchanged letters with my parents almost every week and with other members of my family and relations from time to time. It wasn't difficult to think of things to write about because so many new and interesting things were happening almost every day. I was living in a new environment, in a new country among new friends. I was being treated as an adult rather than as a child. I had not been happier since I left primary school. However, the first Christmas was lonely. It was my first Christmas away from my family. Christmas, at that time, was not celebrated in Italy as it was in Ireland. The sixth of January, the feast of the Epiphany was the day on which the Italians exchanged gifts. But they had wonderful Christmas cribs in the churches and outdoors in some of the piazzas, most notably the living crib in the Piazza Navona, the beautiful piazza with the superb fountains. In the Irish College, we always had an enjoyable celebration at Christmas. The religious celebrations were beautiful and meaningful. We entertained ourselves with a dramatic production and concert. Over the Christmas holiday period, each year, we also exchanged visits or played football matches with other national Colleges in Rome, like the English, Scots and North American Colleges.

The big annual celebration, however, was on 17 March, St Patrick's Day. The Irish in Rome, with many others who had the most tenuous of links to Ireland, celebrated the national festival with unbounded enthusiasm. The morning was given over to religious celebrations, whilst the afternoon and evening were usually dedicated to celebrations of a somewhat less religious nature. The Irish Ambassador to the Holy See and the Irish Consul to Italy both joined us for lunch in the Irish College, accompanied by various

Cardinals and other VIPs. I always appreciated the fact that, no matter how distinguished the guest, Monsignor Herlihy always insisted that all of the students would participate in any meal or celebration. The junior students served the lunch, as they did on all major occasions. The Irish tricolour flew from the front of the College alongside the papal flag. The Irish Ambassador to the Holy See during my early years in Rome was Joseph Walsh, a somewhat inscrutable and ascetic figure. At that time, there was no Irish Ambassador to Italy, just a Consul.

Whilst we had exams in mid-year, the first major university examinations came in June at the end of our first year. The weather during the preceding month was exceedingly warm, making study difficult. The studies involved frantic efforts to achieve some fluency in Italian and an adequate knowledge of the courses studied. Such knowledge was acquired from the notes of former students and documents called *dispensae* issued by the various professors and lecturers, as well as reading and studying books and other material relevant to the courses. The examinations at the end of first year were all oral examinations. The results were based on performance during the year and in the examination itself. The examiners were lenient on first years from abroad. They were tolerant of our inadequacy in Italian. Despite that leniency, I failed in three subjects in the examinations at the end of first year! Justice was done! I was more fascinated by the city of Rome and my new surroundings than by the study of academic subjects. However, on my second attempt and after more application to study and improved ability in Italian, I managed to pass the exams when I took them again at the beginning of the autumn semester. The Italian word for 'failed' is '*bocciato*', possibly the origin of the English word 'botched'.

My improved ability in Italian could be attributed to the fact that we spent every other summer in Italy. In the early days of July 1952, after the examinations were completed and the university closed down, and the students due to return to Ireland had departed for home, the remainder of the college community, Rector, Vice-Rector, Sisters and students, decamped from the intolerable heat of Rome for the villa. The Villa Irlanda, as it was called, was located about one hundred miles south of Rome between the coastal towns of Formia and Gaeta. The complex consisted of three buildings. One of these buildings was a convent in which the Sisters lived. Another building housed the Rector and Vice-Rector and guests, as well as the library and other communal facilities. The main building accommodated the students and there we had our refectory and chapel. The whole complex was set among tomato gardens and vineyards. It was located right on the beach on the Gulf of Gaeta. It was a superb location. There were mountains behind and the sparkling Mediterranean in front. The island of Ischia could be seen through the haze to the south. The complex was purchased by the Irish College in the 1930s and used throughout the forties, fifties and sixties as a summer villa. It was sold in the 1970s and is now a fine hotel.

During my first summer in the villa, I learned to swim. Before learning to swim properly, however, I had a narrow escape from drowning. A wooden diving platform, which students in former years had constructed, was anchored some way from the shore and, one day when I overestimated my swimming ability, I panicked and found myself in serious difficulties when trying to swim to the platform. I was fortunate to be rescued by another student, Brian O'Rourke from Carlingford. (Brian has since gone to his rest.) Apart from that slight mishap, the stay in Formia was blissful. We had a very relaxed timetable. For most of the day, apart from periods designated for prayer or worship, meals and some light study, we were free to swim and dive, sunbathe, learn Italian from conversation with local people, engage in walking trips and cycling trips and read books. 1952 was the summer of the Helsinki Olympic Games and I learned a great deal of Italian from reading the reports of the Games in Italian sports newspapers, like the *Corriere dello Sport*. Emil Zatopek, the Czech athlete and a fellow-countryman of some of the students at the Lateran University, was one of the great heroes of those games. Our families sent us copies of the Irish newspapers, particularly the Monday editions, with all the sports reports. We explored the area around Formia and Gaeta by foot and on bicycle. We climbed the mountains that lay just behind us to the east. Among the places we visited was the celebrated Benedictine monastery and burial place of St Benedict, Monte Cassino. The monastery, with its commanding and dominating position on a mountaintop, was the scene of a fierce and prolonged bombardment and battle in World War II. When I first visited Monte Cassino, about eight years after the battle, the abbey was still in ruins because of the Allied bombardment. In September, a group of us went to Naples and visited Pompeii and Capri. During our visit, we witnessed the liquefaction of the martyr's blood on 19 September, the feast of St Januarius, a bizarre and remarkable Neapolitan spectacle. One has to experience a celebration in Naples to understand the full meaning of celebration. Those months in Formia bound us together as a unit in friendship and fellowship. However, we still keenly looked forward to going home the following summer.

After the summer holiday, it was back to Rome. There were new students to greet and old friends who returned to continue their studies. Among the new first-year students was one of my closest friends from childhood, Seamus McManus from Belleek. Seamus had opted to study for the priesthood of the Armagh archdiocese. During subsequent years in Rome, it was wonderful to have someone from Belleek with whom to share many things. During my second year in the Irish College, in 1953, Pope Pius XII named Archbishop John D'Alton of Armagh as a Cardinal. John D'Alton was a past student of the Irish College and many members of the student body were involved in the various ceremonies associated with his elevation as a Cardinal. Almost all the members of the College of Cardinals were in Rome for the occasion and most of them visited the new Cardinal in the Irish College. It was a great opportunity to see and meet, albeit briefly, people like Cardinal Spellman of New York and Cardinal Gilroy of Sydney and many other prominent figures in the world Church. Among the visitors to the College was Monsignor Montini, later to be Pope Paul VI.

The years in Rome were interspersed with various big occasions. There were visits from Irish Presidents, Taoisaigh, Government Ministers, Bishops and other prominent figures in Church and State. Monsignor Herlihy ensured that we were involved in all these occasions. But, as students, we most enjoyed visitors or pilgrims from our own locality or diocese. There were many of these, both clergy and laity. Tourism was just beginning to open up after the war. The package tourist had not yet arrived. But there were many hardy individuals who did make their way, by train or car, and even a few who cycled the whole way from Ireland to Rome. I enjoyed showing visitors around the city. It is a most pleasurable experience to share your love of a place with a visitor.

I experienced my first Roman ordination ceremony in 1953, when a number of the students from the Irish College were ordained to the priesthood. Ordination ceremonies in Rome at that time were marathon affairs. The ceremonies usually began at 7 a.m. and were not completed on some occasions until mid-afternoon, and all this whilst the participants were fasting! At each ordination ceremony, there were dozens of candidates for Tonsure, for First and Second Minor Orders (Porter, Reader, Exorcist. Acolyte), Sub-Deacon, Deacon and Priest. It was difficult enough for the candidates but it must have made even greater demands on the officiating prelate. Cardinal Micara officiated at many of these ceremonies in my time in Rome. It was a good experience to see friends and fellow students, with whom one studied, prayed, shared meals and played football, being ordained to the priesthood. Almost every week I spent in Rome affirmed my decision to be a priest.

I gave considerable thought to the issue of celibacy. The Spiritual Director, Rector and various Directors of Retreats regularly encouraged us to think carefully about this matter. I had thought about it before making my decision to enter studies for the priesthood. I had a few girlfriends during my holidays from St Columb's College, but none of the relationships were very serious or prolonged. They were just young people of my own age whom I enjoyed being with. Young Italian women are particularly attractive. Spending much of the summer on the beach in Formia certainly concentrated the mind! As I got older and about to enter my twenties, I had to confront this issue. I had to face up to the reality and consequences of the decisions I would be required to make. The consequence of celibacy that I found most challenging was that it obliged me to sacrifice the opportunity of ever being a parent. However, no firm decision was made at this stage. I didn't have to make a final decision for a few more years. But the issue was frequently in my mind.

From Easter 1953 onwards, I looked forward eagerly to my first holiday at home for two years. I longed to hear the voices of my parents again and to see them and my brother and sisters. We couldn't telephone home at that time and our only contact was by letter. I looked forward to being in Belleek again and meeting all my old friends. With a couple of other students, we planned an interesting route home. We went overland by rail. We first visited Florence, then Venice, on to Vienna, through Germany, up the Rhine to Amsterdam and on to London. We had a fascinating trip. We enjoyed the museums and buildings and art treasures of Florence, the unique beauty of Venice, the experience of Vienna, which was still recovering from the war with the Red Army still in prominence. We went to see La Bohème at the Staatsoper. We arrived in London a few weeks after the coronation of Queen Elizabeth II and London looked magnificent. It was a first visit to all these cities and it was exciting to visit places that one had only seen in photographs in geography books and newspapers. We stayed in a lodging house in London belonging to an Irish woman, Mrs McCoy, in Victoria. Irish College students had stayed with her for years and years on their way to and from Rome. There were similar stopping-off points, established over the years, in cities all over Europe. Mrs McCoy was like a mother to us and we experienced our first taste of bacon and eggs for two years on our first morning in London. I also recall that the first time I saw an English-language programme on television was in Mrs McCoy's in late June 1953. It was a cricket Test Match. We ran out of money in London and had to leave a day earlier than planned for the last leg of our trip!

If the departure from Ireland through Cobh was emotional, the first return to Ireland was equally emotional. We travelled by train from London to Holyhead and by steamer to Dun Laoghaire. I still remember being overcome at seeing the spires of Dun Laoghaire through the light mist on that beautiful summer morning. Air travel has taken much of the pain and excitement out of leaving or returning to one's homeland. There is something very emotional and romantic about leaving or arriving by sea. It is a more gradual and tempered form of arrival or departure. We said our goodbyes to one another and I made my way to Amiens Street Station in Dublin to catch a train for the last leg of my journey. It was the Bundoran Express, which primarily carried passengers who were making the pilgrimage to Lough Derg. It didn't stop at stations in the North. It was the fastest train home, making the journey in less than four hours. It was lovely to experience the familiar surroundings and smells of the Great Northern Railway and the excitement equalled that of my first return home from St Columb's College at Christmas 1946, almost seven years earlier. I had just a few pence left in my pocket and I couldn't care less. I counted down the stations again like I did on my first trip home from St Columb's. It was wonderful to see the unchanged familiar landmarks – Irvinestown, Kesh, Pettigo, Castlecaldwell, and through Belleek and over the metal bridge across the Erne, and my first sight of our house. I was quite overcome. My father and mother and my brother and sisters were all waiting on the platform in Ballyshannon. It was a wonderful moment. Tears flowed. It was great to be with the family once again.

The first week home was sheer bliss. Being with my parents again was a source of great warmth. It was exciting to see how other members of the family had grown up in the meantime. There was so much to talk about, so much catching up to do. I had missed my parents and family greatly during the two years in Rome – the only negative aspect of my years there. It was lovely to meet old friends and visit familiar places again. It was the custom then for clerical students to wear a black suit all the time whilst on holiday. However, I reverted to my ordinary casual clothes after a few days. I was conscious of the fact that, in a small community, I was expected to live up to the calling I had received. People were somewhat over-respectful and that made me uncomfortable. But after a week or so, people thawed out and treated me as they did in years gone by. I soon became more relaxed and less self-conscious. I began to work in the shop again and help with the hay and other activities, which I enjoyed. I went fishing and played football and cycled to the cinema in Ballyshannon a few times every week.

The Rector of the Irish College had advised me to have a swelling on my right cheek attended to whilst I was at home on holiday. It was badly swollen since my final year in St Columb's College. I went to my local doctor and he referred me to a specialist in Belfast. I was admitted to hospital there in the first week of August for minor surgery. However, the 'minor surgery' was a disaster and, to my dismay, I ended up spending four weeks in hospital in Belfast! I had to leave hospital with my jaw and cheek more swollen than it was before. Four precious weeks were lost from the holiday to which I had looked forward so much. I persisted with the swollen right cheek for twenty more years. It didn't cause me any pain. It generated questions like 'Do you have a toothache?' and less charitable remarks from time to time, but that didn't worry me. The experience of surgery during that precious summer prompted me to leave well enough alone. The remainder of that summer holiday passed very quickly. I attended the All-Ireland Football Final in Dublin in late September. The All-Ireland Football Final was the occasion for a reunion of all the Roman students who were home for the summer and an opportunity to purchase books and other odds and ends for the year ahead. It was also an opportunity to plan travel arrangements for the return journey.

We travelled back to Rome in early October, stopping here and there along the way. Monsignor Herlihy was utterly horrified that a group of Irish College students spent three days in Florence on their way back to Rome without ever visiting a museum or viewing any of the wonderful sights of that city. Instead they opted to spend the three days in Florence in a bar playing snooker! The Rector was aghast. After the mandatory stop at Mrs McCoy's in London, with a few others, I opted to travel via Paris and Lourdes and then along the south coast of France, the French and Italian Rivieras, stopping here and there on the way, and so on to Rome along the west coast of Italy. It was a good trip. I remember being very impressed and moved by Lourdes on my first visit there. It was to be the first of many visits. I have to confess that on our way to Rome, we looked in on the casino in Monte Carlo and observed the gamblers at play. Fortunately Monsignor Herlihy did not hear that! It was a wonderful way to see the Continent. We had to travel to Rome in any case and the rail fares were relatively cheap, and the variations from a direct route did not cost that much extra. I thoroughly enjoyed those student journeys to and from Rome.

When Monsignor Herlihy heard that I had spent four weeks of

my holiday in hospital, he immediately suggested that I go home the following summer instead of spending the holiday in Formia at the villa. It was typical of the man. He was the essence of kindness. He taught me a great deal about the importance of caring.

In my third year in Rome, I began to study theology. In the course of these studies, we met for the first time two professors who had notorious reputations, Pietro Parente and Antonio Piolanti. They were both brilliant men, dynamic lecturers who spoke fluent classical Latin, lengthy sentences with the verb at the very end. Parente taught dogmatic theology and Piolanti taught sacramental theology. They considered the Irish somewhat uncivilised compared with their own cultured countrymen. They suggested that the Romans never reached Ireland and it showed! They were highly suspicious of 20th-century French writers and theologians and both were fervent disciples of St Thomas Aquinas. They were deeply conservative and very fearful of Communism. They got more worked up and excited about theology than most of their Irish listeners about football! Piolanti was an impassioned speaker and sweated profusely, dabbing his forehead with a large handkerchief. They were truly characters. I hate to think of how they must have felt when the Second Vatican Council overtook them. As noted already, most of the examinations at the Lateran University at that time were oral examinations and marking was based on performance, attendance, attention and written work submitted throughout the year, as well as performance at examination. Parente eventually became an Archbishop and Cardinal. Piolanti did not reach those dizzy heights. Another of our professors, Ermenegildo Florit, who lectured in New Testament Scripture, also became a Cardinal and Archbishop of Florence. Pietro Palazzini, who was our professor of moral theology, also became a Cardinal and Prefect of the Congregation of Causes of Saints. We were in formidable company.

In our third year, we received tonsure. This was formal admission as a candidate for the priesthood. It was the first ministry conferred at every ordination ceremony in Rome. It also entailed having a little patch of hair about the size of an Irish pound coin shaved on the back of the head. It was a mini version of the large tonsure that some orders of monks receive. I was captivated by the fact that every barber in Rome knew how to do it. During the remaining years in Rome, we had the tonsure shaved on during each visit to the barber, except in the month or two before holidays in Ireland when vanity got the better of custom. Many of those with receding hairlines feared that the 'holy patch' might be misunderstood as a bald patch or some nascent dread disease of some kind or another. I was already rapidly losing my wavy locks at that stage, which made it difficult for the barber to find a hairy area in which to insert a bald patch! Many of our Italian fellow students had a more radical form of tonsure. They were required to have their heads completely shaved. This was certainly penitential, particularly for young Italian males, many of whom found it difficult to pass a mirror without taking out a comb and touching up the coiffure!

During our third year, we were becoming more and more fluent in Italian and more and more at home in Rome. There was the usual round of sightseeing, having the odd meal out in a trattoria at holiday times and taking trips to various parts of Italy during breaks from university. Around this time, with a few other students, I managed to indulge my interest in Italian Serie A Football by attending games from time to time. Roma and Lazio were the home teams in Rome and I had the opportunity to see some memorable games with Fiorentina (the most successful team in Italy at that time), Juventus, Milan and Inter. There were some wonderful players. Italian football has been an abiding interest throughout my life since then.

We went to the cinema occasionally. I saw *The Quiet Man* dubbed in Italian. In Italy, it was entitled *L'Uomo Tranquillo*. It was hilarious to see and listen to Maureen O'Hara, John Wayne and Barry Fitzgerald speaking Italian in a rural dialect surrounded by the magnificent West of Ireland scenery. It added greatly to my enjoyment of the movie. The Italians have great skill in dubbing films.

But, as well as play, there was a lot of study to be done and there was an excellent structure of community worship and prayer and meditation within the Irish College community. The Rector and Spiritual Director took a personal interest in each of us and in our progress, both spiritual and academic. The entire student body at that time numbered around forty. It was a relatively small community and we had an opportunity to get to know one another, warts and all, extremely well.

One of the features of the Irish College was the number of aircraft flying low overhead. The College appeared to be on the approach flight-path for Ciampino Airport, which was the primary airport for Rome before the new international airport at Fiumicino, was opened. Among the spectacular aircraft flying over at this time were the Comets. These were the first commercial jet aircraft. They were flown by BOAC on routes to Africa and Asia and Rome was a stopover point en route. The Comets were beautiful aircraft. Their distinctive sound caused everyone to look upwards when they passed overhead.

In our third year, an Australian, John Satterthwaite, joined our class. He was somewhat older and more mature than the rest of us. There were several Australians and New Zealanders among the students and they brought a new dimension and a whole new vocabulary to our student life. The surname 'Satterthwaite' caused great problems of pronunciation to the Italian lecturers and professors. It contained too many consonants and not enough vowels for an Italian to cope with!

I came home to Ireland at the end of my third year in Rome in the summer of 1954, the bonus holiday that Monsignor Herlihy made possible because of my misfortune during the previous summer. I had one of the best holidays I ever experienced. There were no stays in hospital. It was completely carefree. I was very happy and content in my choice of career. My parents were both well and healthy. Rationing had finally ended. Business in the shop was good. My sisters and brother were fine and everything in the world was just wonderful. I spent a lot of time that summer with my family. I grew particularly close to my father and spent a lot of time with him, talking and discussing things. He had been in Rome for a brief visit during a pilgrimage for the Holy Year 1950. He was intensely interested in all my experiences there and, with my mother, was keenly looking forward to attending my ordination in Rome. Seamus McManus was also home that summer and we were able to do a lot of things together. As in other summers, I made the pil-

grimage to Lough Derg. I went there with my brother. I was familiar with Lough Derg since childhood, because relatives on my
mother's side had a house on the island at that time to accommodate
some of the pilgrims and they also managed the boats out to the
island. So during summer holidays when I was much younger, I had
the opportunity to visit the pilgrim island occasionally. I remember
that when the time came to return to Rome at the end of that holiday, I found it more difficult and painful than it had been the previous year. I knew that I would not be back for two years and I realised
just how long that was from my previous experience.

During our fourth and fifth years of preparation for the priesthood, we continued our theology studies. I enjoyed study. Some
aspects of theology interested me and other aspects bored me. I
have always felt that our education in Sacred Scripture in the
Lateran University was hugely deficient, particularly our study and
understanding of the Old Testament. Scripture is a keen interest
and love of mine and I have always struggled to make up for the lack
of initial education in this basic resource for faith, preaching and
prayer. The holiday at the villa in Formia in the summer of 1955
was very enjoyable, though I missed home a lot.

I arranged to take a course in Italian literature, architecture, art
and music at L'Università per Stranieri (The University for
Foreigners) in Perugia in Umbria for the month of September.
With the encouragement of Monsignor Herlihy, I managed to get a
scholarship or grant for this course from the Italian Embassy in
Dublin. The course was memorable. Perugia is located right in the
heart of the area where the Renaissance occurred in the Middle
Ages, where Giotto and Raphael and Fra Angelico and Cimabue
and Filippo Lippi did their work, which revolutionised art. We visited Assisi, Arezzo, Siena, Spoleto and lots of other fascinating
places with university professors who were authorities on all these
artists and places. They acted as guides and gave us remarkable
insights. We viewed the work of all the masters of Italian art and
sculpture. There was also a superb music festival in Perugia during
that month and among the highlights was a memorable performance of Verdi's *Requiem* in the city's cathedral. The weeks in
Perugia provided a veritable feast of riches for eye and ear.

September 1955 was a month during which I felt enriched beyond measure.

I dutifully wrote a letter home every week during my years in Rome. I have always enjoyed writing letters. My father or my mother also wrote to me every week. They kept me abreast of news of the family and news about what was happening in Belleek and in Ireland. They also enclosed newspaper clippings and sometimes sent whole newspapers. I looked forward to their letters every week, though the vagaries of the Italian postal system meant that, from time to time, there would be some weeks without letters and on other weeks there would be a multiplicity of letters. In the late spring of 1956, I detected concern in my mother's letters about my father's health. My father never mentioned anything about this in his letters. I was worried for a time and looked forward a little apprehensively to the summer holiday when I could see things for myself. During that summer holiday, I hoped to make plans with my family for their attendance at my ordination to the priesthood in Rome the following spring. It was an occasion to which both my parents and myself greatly looked forward.

I was ordained to the subdiaconate in 1956. During that ordination ceremony, I took my vow of celibacy. I had had five years to prepare for that decision and consider it most carefully. During those five years, I had every opportunity to leave my studies for the priesthood, had I wished to do so. I knew that my parents might have been disappointed but I also knew that they would have supported and respected any decision I might have made. The authorities in the College would have adopted exactly the same attitude. Many of my contemporaries in lay life and schoolmates were already married and I often reflected on the likelihood that they had much less preparation for making an equally major lifelong decision than I had. I was fully aware that, by taking this vow, I would be forgoing many wonderful human experiences, especially marriage and parenthood. However, I was convinced that priesthood offered me a way of life that would be most fulfilling and challenging. I was very happy as a student for the priesthood. I was confident that I would be equally happy as a priest. So I took my vow of celibacy after due and lengthy consideration.

I also committed myself to pray the Divine Office every day. The Breviary, the three volumes from which priests read the prayers of the Divine Office, has been my constant companion ever since. The recitation of the Office brings structure and discipline into daily prayer. Ordination to the subdiaconate also committed me to wearing the clerical collar for the first time in Ireland, which was a rather strange experience, to say the least! I felt most inhibited wearing the clerical collar at first, particularly at home around Belleek. Once again my neighbours and friends made it easy for me.

However, inhibitions about wearing clerical dress was the least of my worries during that summer holiday at home in 1956. The sight of my father alarmed me when I returned. He had aged greatly and lost a lot of weight since I had last seen him two years earlier. He was still only fifty six or fifty seven years old. My mother and other members of the family were also deeply concerned about his health. Some weeks after I arrived home, he was persuaded to take a rest. So I accompanied him to the Causeway Coast in Antrim for a few days. He was far from well. We talked a lot. He told me how much he was looking forward to my ordination to the priesthood. I told him of my appreciation for all his kindness and encouragement to me. We talked about many things. Apart from a visit from my sister, Marion, who joined us for a day, it was the first time that we were alone together for a few days. When we were in North Antrim, we called on a family friend who was a doctor, Tom Wilson, in Ballycastle. He examined my father and had him admitted immediately for surgery to the Royal Victoria Hospital in Belfast. He was diagnosed as having cancer and was referred for radiation treatment to Montgomery House in Belfast. It was the first time in my life that I was confronted with cancer. The day that I heard his diagnosis, although I suspected bad news, was one of the worst days of my life. However, there was some comfort in the cautious hope of the doctors that radiation treatment might help. When he came home after the first bout of radiation treatment, he was in good spirits but clearly unwell. I never plucked up the courage to talk with him about his illness and the possibility of his imminent death. I didn't want to contemplate that and I don't think he wished to either. We both shared a love of cars and sport, especially Gaelic football, and we spent a lot of the time discussing those safe topics. But he hadn't his usual sparkle or interest. He was daily growing more tired and exhausted. I began to fear that he was going to die sooner rather than later.

I was broken-hearted.

CHAPTER 4

Great Sadness – Great Happiness

Meetings with Padre Pio –
20 February 1957 – retreat at the Graan –
an encounter with the B Specials – ordination and First Mass –
Arrivederci Roma

I returned to Rome with a heavy heart in early October 1956 for my final year of study and ordination to the priesthood. I flew to Rome for the first time. I wasn't in the mood for a protracted trip across the Continent after the experiences of the summer. During the early part of this final academic year, as well as our continuing theological studies, we had intensive preparation and training in the celebration of Mass and the ministry of the other sacraments. We learned and practised preaching skills. Whilst serious, this was hugely enjoyable. We criticised one another's preaching for content and delivery.

I greatly looked forward to my ordination but my enthusiasm was somewhat diluted by the growing realisation of the fact that it was most unlikely that my father could travel to Rome to attend the ceremony. Letters from my father became less frequent and, whilst he endeavoured to keep the bright side out for my sake, the deterioration in the quality of his handwriting betrayed his best efforts. In a letter written on 12 November, he revealed that he had suffered severe weight loss. At the same time, Seamus McManus' father, Patrick, was dying, so it was a sad period for both of us.

I discussed my concern and worry with Monsignor Herlihy, the Rector, and Father Dominic Conway, my Spiritual Director. Unknown to me, Monsignor Herlihy went to the Vatican and put a case for earlier ordination to the appropriate Congregation. He had hoped that it might have been possible to permit me to be ordained to the priesthood before Christmas. However, the Congregation declined, because I was too young, about to be twenty three in December; and had not completed the first semester of my final year of studies. A candidate for ordination, at that time, was required to be twenty-four years old and to have completed the first semester of his final year of theology study. The Congregation would have been prepared to dispense of either one of these conditions but not both. So my ordination remained scheduled on the same date as the rest of my class, 16 March 1957, in the Basilica of St John Lateran.

In mid-November 1956, when speaking with an Italian student in the university, I first heard about a remarkable Capuchin monk in a monastery in the small town of San Giovanni Rotondo, near the city of Foggia in the heel of Italy. His name was Padre Pio. I had never heard of him before. I asked Monsignor Herlihy if I could go to visit him and he willingly agreed. So on a wintry weekend in late November I travelled the long journey to the southeast by train and bus and eventually arrived at the isolated village and monastery of San Giovanni Rotondo. Early in the morning, around 5.30 a.m., I attended Padre Pio's Mass. There was a large congregation in the small church and the Mass went on for a couple of hours. Later in the day, I met Padre Pio. As I spoke Italian, I joined the lengthy queue and went to confession with him and spoke to him of my concern for my father and my approaching ordination. He was most comforting and spoke tenderly to me and prayed with me for some time. I returned to San Giovanni again during my Christmas holiday in early January. Michael Collins, another Derry seminarian, accompanied me on this occasion. As soon as I spoke, to my amazement, Padre Pio recognised me, despite the fact that he had hundreds of people coming to him every day and that the discussions took place in a darkened confessional box. Without my reminding him, he remembered what I had told him about my father and my pending ordination. He enquired about my father. Again he spent time with me and was most comforting. However, he did not say that my father would recover or survive until March. He inspired me. He had a presence, an aura about him, a dimension, which is very difficult to explain. He was one of the most remarkable persons whom I have ever met. I have never returned to San Giovanni Rotondo since that icy cold January day in 1957. I wish the memory of his intriguing physical presence there to live on.

I anxiously awaited every letter from home. My father and mother wrote regularly and tried their best to put a brave face on things. However, the continued deterioration in the quality of my father's handwriting communicated the real situation more effectively than any words. At Christmas my father had purchased our first television set. He was full of excitement, amazement and wonder at how a picture could be transmitted on the airwaves all the way from London to Belleek. Christmas 1956 was a particularly lonely time for me. I had always enjoyed Christmas in Rome. There was a certain degree of loneliness about being away from home but the efforts made by the College and all the social activities with other Colleges compensated in many ways. This time, however, I knew in my heart that Christmas 1956 would be the last Christmas when both my parents would be alive and I was the only member of the family away from home.

Early in the New Year, 1957, two of my uncles, unknown to me, went to visit Bishop Farren in Derry. My father's doctor had told them that there was no possibility of my father being able to make the journey to Rome in March. They enquired of Bishop Farren if there was any possibility of the ordination taking place in Ireland. Bishop Farren was aware of my father's illness, as I had informed him of it before I returned to Rome. He was full of sympathy and understanding. When my uncles approached him with their request, he immediately agreed to investigate the possibilities. He sought the permission of the Roman authorities and of the Bishop of Clogher and he contacted my uncles within a few days to say that he had obtained the requisite permissions and was prepared to ordain me in my local church in Belleek on 16 March, the same date as the class ordination was scheduled in Rome. Bishop Farren contacted Monsignor Herlihy, who informed me of the new arrangement. I was pleased that now there was a possibility of both my parents being present at my ordination. However, I was also disappointed that I would not be ordained in Rome with the other members of my class with whom I had shared so much over the previous six years. I had also looked forward greatly to showing my parents and brother and sisters and relatives around Rome. That was not going to happen now. I planned to go back to Ireland a few days before the ordination ceremony after making my ordination retreat with my classmates in Rome.

On the morning of Friday, 15 February, Monsignor Herlihy asked me to come to his room after Mass. He told me that he had received a telephone message from my uncle that my father's condition had seriously deteriorated and he thought that I should go home at once. He invited me to telephone my uncle there and then from his room. It was the first time that I had ever made a telephone call from Rome to Ireland. I had a short conversation with my uncle and he advised me of the gravity of the situation. He said that my father could die at any time. Monsignor Herlihy made all the arrangements and that night I was aboard a BOAC flight from Rome to London. The plane flew into an electrical storm somewhere over the Alps! There was a huge flash and a very loud and frightening noise. We had to make an emergency landing at Nice in the South of France! It was just my second journey on a plane. However, all was well. After a short delay to ensure there was no damage to the aircraft, we resumed our journey and got to London and flew from there to Dublin. I arrived home on the Saturday afternoon. Everyone was gathered in my father's bedroom and he was very weak. He recognised me immediately and greeted me with a smile. His voice was very faint and he was emaciated. The next few days and nights were spent at his bedside, with my mother and other members of the family. We talked and we watched and we prayed as my father's life on this earth ebbed away. The local priests and Doctor McCollum, the family GP, were very kind and supportive and so were our neighbours. My father died quietly and peacefully with all of us around his bedside on Wednesday, 20 February 1957. There followed the wake. For two days, friends and neighbours came to our home to offer their sympathy and their prayers. People were most supportive and this helped us to cope with our profound grief.

I cannot recall any of the details about the funeral except for one. As my father's remains were about to be removed from our home to the church on the evening before the funeral, two men, unknown to any of us, appeared. They wished to place an Irish tricolour on my father's coffin for the removal to the church. They said that they were fellow Republicans and wished to honour a colleague. My mother and the other adult members of my family circle refused to agree to this. I agreed with them. The men were courteous and did not persist and left our home forthwith. It was not the last time in my life that I was to be confronted with issues related to flags on coffins!

After the funeral, there was an unbearable silence and exhaustion in the home. We found comfort in prayer and visiting my father's grave. My brother, Tom, was hoping to go to university in the following September. My older sister, Marion, was teaching in Derry. Arrangements had to be made about the running of the family shop. It was decided that Tom, my sister Dympna and my mother would handle things until the summer and then long-term decisions could be made. I began to appreciate even more the sacrifice that all the members of a family are asked to make when one member of the family decides to enter the priesthood.

In the short term, I had to make arrangements for my ordination. I was not sure if the offer to ordain me at home still stood after my father's death. I contacted Bishop Farren and, once again, he was very considerate and supportive. He said that it was unthinkable for my mother and other members of the family to travel to Rome in the circumstances. He said that the ordination would go ahead in Belleek on 16 March as planned. I contacted Monsignor Herlihy by telephone and he was also happy with this arrangement. We decided, as a family, that there would be a very simple celebration.

I made arrangements to have my ordination retreat in the Passionist monastery at The Graan in Enniskillen, about twenty-five miles from home. It was good to get away to the peace and quiet of the monastery. I was physically and emotionally drained and I was also somewhat angry with God. However, I experienced and found great peace in The Graan. The priest who was directing my retreat suggested that I read and reflect on a selection of Psalms to assuage my anger and hurt and grief. The Psalms can give wonderful comfort at times when we are angry or confused or perplexed by the things happening around us. It was the first time that I felt some real consolation and comfort after my father's death and I prepared to face the future. During those six days of reflection and rest and prayer, I began again to look forward to my ordination and priesthood. Among other things, I renewed practising my Celebration of Mass to prepare for the real thing in a few days' time. We had been taught the Celebration of Mass in Rome. I completed the retreat and planned to return to Belleek to spend the night before the ordination with my mother and other members of my family.

At that time in early 1957, the IRA was conducting a campaign of bombing in the North. On the night before my ordination, I had an insight into some of the complexities of the Northern situation. A priest friend, who had very strong Republican views, was driving me home from The Graan to Belleek. It was a wet, murky, dark and dismal night. Suddenly a red light was waved on the road ahead of us. We stopped the car. Out of the shadows, men in black uniforms carrying rifles appeared from the hedges. They were B Specials! Although I had heard many horror stories about them, it was the first time that I had ever encountered them in real life. 'What's your name?' my priest friend demanded in a loud voice as soon as one of them approached the car. The B Special responded, in a surprised tone 'That's just what I was going to ask you.' My priest friend said that he would give our names only if they would first give their names. There was a stalemate, which went on for some time. Eventually we were ordered out of the car and made to stand at the side of the road whilst the car was searched. Scarcely a car passed whilst we were standing there. It was a lonely road. I was terrified and was certain that someone would be arranging my funeral rather than my ordination on the following morning. Eventually, soaked through, we were allowed to go on to Belleek. We did not tell them our names and they did not tell us their names! My priest friend was cock-a-hoop. He lustily and loudly sang 'Kevin Barry', an Irish rebel song, for the remainder of the journey home. 'In Mountjoy Jail one Monday morning ...'.

St Patrick's Church, Belleek, was the scene of all the great sacramental moments in my life. I was baptised, made my First Confession and received my First Communion there. I called in to say a prayer there going to and from the Commons School. I served there as an altar boy. By a strange coincidence, Bishop Farren administered the sacrament of Confirmation to me there in 1942, because, at that time, the Bishop of Clogher had died and the new bishop had not been appointed. He came to Belleek again on Saturday, 16 March 1957, to officiate at my ordination to the priesthood.

It was a simple but beautiful ceremony. It had none of the splendour and magnificence of the Roman ordination ceremonies, but, on the positive side, it lasted under two hours rather than six or seven hours. It was the first ever ordination ceremony in the parish. There was a packed congregation. I found it a very moving and uplifting experience. I was conscious of the fact that my classmates were being ordained in Rome at the same time. I was conscious, too, of the spiritual presence of my father, to whom I owed so much. With my mother, he had conveyed to me by word and example the importance of my faith, my religious beliefs and so many other values. The congregation present in the small church was made up of relations, friends and neighbours – people among whom I had spent my childhood: people whom I had served for many years in my father's shop, school friends, people with whom I had played football. They were all there. Master Egan was there and Miss Rogan, my primary teachers, to whom I was so deeply indebted. The ordination ceremony is a beautiful liturgy. To understand the Catholic priesthood, it is necessary to read the ordination liturgy. The translation of the liturgy into the vernacular has, in latter years, made its significance and inherent teaching more accessible to those who would not be familiar with the Latin.

After the ceremony, I joined Bishop Farren and the other clergy for a simple lunch in the Central Hotel in Bundoran. After the lunch, I returned to the family home in Belleek and joined my mother and family and relatives who had gathered there. It was a pleasant day and it made a small contribution to assuaging the pain of loss and the grief after my father's death.

On the following day, St Patrick's Day, I celebrated Mass for the first time. Again the celebration took place in St Patrick's Church. This was an awesome experience. At that time, Mass was celebrated in Latin, with the celebrant's back to the people. Reciting the familiar Latin prayers and invocations to which I had responded as an altar boy in that same church twelve years earlier seemed strange. Preaching to one's own family, relatives and neighbours can be a daunting prospect. The coincidence of the first Mass and St Patrick's Day made this somewhat easier. After the Mass I administered an individual blessing to the people. They were very kind and supportive and encouraging. It was a most humbling experience.

There wasn't much time to celebrate or stay around home after the ordination. I had been home since mid-February. There were studies to be completed, papers to be submitted, essays to be written, final examinations to be taken, loose ends to be tied up. So a few days after the ordination, I returned to Rome. My classmates, the staff and fellow students in the College were very welcoming and comforting. We exchanged our mutual experiences of the last momentous month.

But the final months of work had to be undertaken. We refined further our Celebration of Mass and preaching and celebrated parish Mass here and there in churches around Rome. We had some useful talks on the celebration of the sacrament of Penance and ministry to the Sick. We completed our programme of lectures at the university and prepared for our final examinations in June. There was extremely warm weather in June 1957, up in the nineties. It was difficult weather for study and, as was often the case at that time of year, we studied during the night and slept during the day.

Another event, which happened during those last months in Rome, was a visit of the Northern Ireland International Soccer team who played Italy in a qualifying round of the World Cup in the Olympic Stadium in Rome. Things were a lot different than they are today. The Italian sports newspapers had very little information on the Northern Ireland players. We were able to supply some information and photographs from programmes for international matches in Belfast. We visited the Northern Ireland team in training and met the players, people like the great Danny Blanchflower, a wonderful player, whose skills the Italian fans admired, A few of us attended the game. Italy won 1-0, a goal scored from a free kick bent round the goalkeeper. Northern Ireland acquitted themselves very well. They eventually qualified for the World Cup in Sweden after two eventful and tempestuous matches with Italy in Windsor Park in Belfast in the autumn of 1957, both of which I also attended.

The final examinations came in June. All the members of our class got through with varying degrees of success. The small group of us had become a family in the six years we spent together. We forged very good and close friendships. I can truthfully say that, although we had spent six years with one another, there was never a serious word or difference between us. This was another painful parting. We were leaving Rome and the Irish College too. We all were agreed that it would be *arrivederci* rather than *addio*. I loved my years in Rome, despite the sadness that came with my father's death. Rome is a remarkable city and Italy is a wonderful country. It is so rich in culture and vitality of all kinds. I admire the Italian people and love their attitude to life. I am happy exploring ancient churches and buildings in the cities or discovering treasures of art and sculpture in the little towns and villages that have clung to hilltops for centuries. I enjoy Italian food and wine. I like their football and music. The sunshine also helps.

From a Church point of view, perhaps, things were dull during our years in Rome. Pope Pius XII was in his declining years and nothing very exciting was happening. The group of students who replaced us and began their studies in October 1957 were to experience the death of two Popes, two Conclaves and Papal Elections, the wondrous pontificate of Pope John XXIII and an Ecumenical Council of the Church, the Second Vatican Council. They really had a powerful and rich experience.

I considered myself very fortunate and blessed to have studied in Rome and particularly at a time when Monsignor Donal Herlihy was Rector of the Irish College. He was an astute Kerryman, a scriptural scholar who gave marvellous talks on the Pauline epistles. He was witty and urbane. Above all, he was caring for his students. He was one of the individuals who had a major influence on my formation as a priest. Just seventeen years later, he was a colleague in the Irish Episcopal Conference.

It was good to get out of Ireland, too, and particularly the North, for a number of years at that stage of life. Living on an island can lead to more than geographical insularity. In Rome, the exposure to different cultures and the mixing with students from all over the world in that great cosmopolitan city was a broadening experience for which I will always be grateful. It was very affirming at that early age to experience the universality of the Church in such a powerful manner and to meet young men like myself from all kinds of backgrounds and cultures and from all over the world who were studying for the priesthood. Besides, it introduced me to a country that it has been such a pleasure for me to visit ever since. For that, I will be forever grateful to Bishop Farren who decided to send me to the Irish College in Rome to study for the priesthood.

CHAPTER 5

Curacy in a Border Town

Castlederg – living in 'digs' – a mixed community –
Black Men – teachers and children – the pastoral round –
dances and whist drives – a belt of the crosier – Father Peadar
MacLoinsigh – Ruby Murray visits – 'Robert Emmet' found not guilty –
the bishop's meal and a nervous parish priest

The first parish to which a priest is called to serve always retains a special place in his affections. The first parish to which I was called was the parish of Urney. This was a parish that straddled the border. One of the parish churches was located in Castlederg in County Tyrone and the other church was located in Doneyloop in County Donegal. I was appointed as curate in Castlederg. The majority of the parish population resided in the Castlederg area. All of the cross-border roads in the area had been blown up because of the prevailing security situation. A direct route between the two parish churches was only a matter of four or five miles. However, with the cratered roads, a car journey from Castlederg to Doneyloop meant driving almost thirty miles.

Bishop Farren again showed kindness to me. He knew that my family and I were still grieving after my father's death and Castlederg was the nearest point in the Derry diocese to Belleek, about thirty miles away. He also advised me to live in 'digs'. The parish priest, Father Michael McMenamin, was very elderly and his housekeeper, Sarah, was even more elderly and frail, so it would not be convenient to live in the parochial house. I was the first curate or young priest to be appointed to serve in Castlederg for many years.

Before taking up the appointment, I spent a few weeks at home with my mother and family. We were still picking up the pieces after my father's death. I cannot now remember the details or the reason for the decision but my younger brother, Tom, who had just completed his second-level studies, unselfishly decided to forgo university studies to manage the family business on my mother's behalf. I cannot recall whether he or my mother made the decision or whether it was a family decision. He had always been anxious to go to university and pursue a career in one of the professions. Whilst it may not have been clear at the time, it was not a good decision and did not serve his best interests in the long term. It demonstrated once again the sacrifices that families are asked to make when one of their number opts for priesthood.

I took up duty in Castlederg in mid-July 1957. In my first week there, an elderly lady told me that I took up my appointment at a most inopportune time, just after a parish mission given by the Redemptorist Fathers who had preached their traditional diet of 'fire and brimstone'. She commented, 'There isn't a mortal sin or a half crown left in the parish.' Father McMenamin was a kindly man. He invited me to lunch during my first week there. He pointed out to me that a large new secondary intermediate school had to be provided and this would involve massive fund-raising, as the parish funds were very low. He was relieved that I had arrived and said that he would now be able to take a back seat. He told me to do whatever I thought was needed in the parish. I would have his full authority. It was heady stuff for a twenty-three-year-old! I was brought to earth when he told me that my income would be around six pounds a week, a forecast that proved to be considerably exaggerated!

I managed to get 'digs' in a boarding house owned by the McGoldrick family on the main street about two or three hundred yards from the church. It was a small and very busy house and formed another significant element in my learning experience. The rent and 'keep' cost three pounds a week, which was very reasonable. That left three pounds spending money. I had lived in Spartan conditions as a boarder in St Columb's College; somewhat less Spartan but basic conditions in the Irish College in Rome. Now I was destined to live in 'digs'. In the house that was my 'digs', there lived a man and his wife and daughter, Sheila, and a huge but docile

Alsatian dog called Silver. From time to time, other men would take lodgings there. In the small premises, there was a confectionery shop, an eating-house, a ladies' hairdressing saloon and out in the back yard a photographic studio and a printing works. As a result, it was a very busy place and there was a constant stream of people coming about one thing or another at all hours of the day and night. There wasn't much privacy but I was as happy as a sandboy. I soon became aware that few people in Castlederg seemed to go to bed before one or two o'clock in the morning. For the first few months I did not have a car so I got around the parish on a bicycle.

It was a community consisting almost equally of Protestants and Catholics. It was my first experience of such a community. There had been a few outbreaks of community tension in the aftermath of an election some months before I arrived. Within a short time after arriving in the parish, I had my first experience of the July/August Saturday night marching syndrome, when large numbers of Orange bands paraded in the town. I had never witnessed Orange marches or heard Orange bands before. On the last Saturday of August, I had my first experience of Black Saturday when the Black Men (Royal Black Preceptory) held their County Demonstration in Castlederg. It was a sight to behold. I have a lingering memory of coming back to my lodgings after hearing morning Confessions to find crowds of 'Black Men' having their lunch in my 'digs' and my room strewn with sashes and other paraphernalia, deposited there while they ate. I couldn't resist the temptation to rig myself out in a bowler hat and sash. I looked good in the mirror! I even had a black suit to complement the outfit. I was a true Black Man! I don't think the owners of the sashes were aware of the profession of the tenant of the said room.

I carried out a systematic and extensive programme of visits to the homes of parishioners. They were delightful and most welcoming people. There was an extensive rural as well as urban area. Most of the people lived in relatively comfortable homes. However, there were a few houses that were somewhat primitive. There was large-scale poverty and emigration. The Catholic people in Castlederg, at that time, were relatively poor compared with their Protestant neighbours. A high percentage was unemployed. Protestant farmers with extensive farms in the fertile Derg valley and Protestant merchants in the town dominated the local economy. The small Catholic farmers were to be found further up the hills and nearer the bogs. There were a number of Catholic publicans in the town. In that part of the North, the liquor trade seemed to be the only area of business in which Catholics had a strong foothold. The puritanical views of some Protestants on alcohol probably inhibited them from being involved in anything to do with 'the devil's buttermilk'. There were also a few shops owned by Catholics. I found that the Catholic people in Castlederg in 1957 had accepted their lot as second-class citizens. Despite the fact that they formed a little under half of the total population, they just didn't want any trouble or hassle and had settled for their lot. They were patiently tolerant in the face of Orange arrogance, especially during the annual summer marching season that had to be endured on a weekly basis for the best part of three months. It was a marathon endurance test in the face of provocative sectarian triumphalism.

In those first months of parish ministry, I greatly enjoyed the new experience of celebrating public Mass each day, but I was nervous about my preaching. The Mass at that time was celebrated in Latin, with the celebrant's back to the people. I felt comfortable with Latin, as I had become quite fluent in it during my years in Rome. I loved and still love the rhythm and the sound of the Latin language and the mystique it brought to the celebration of liturgy. The sermon had to be preached in English and that was a different matter. I spent many hours preparing sermons and I was often less than satisfied with the result of my labours. Fasting from the previous midnight was then the norm. Celebrating two or three Masses on a Sunday morning in different churches, travelling and preaching whilst fasting was daunting, even for a young person like me. It must have been even more daunting for elderly clergy. I greatly enjoyed going to Doneyloop on occasions for the second Mass on Sunday and having breakfast in Canning's house beside the church afterwards. Seldom did tea and toast, toasted on a fork before an open fire, seem so tasty and good.

Many hours were spent hearing Confessions. Castlederg was packed with shoppers from outlying areas and outlying parishes on

Saturday nights. It was the main shopping town for a very large hin-
terland. So I spent many hours each Saturday evening absolving the
sins of three parishes! I found hearing confession to be a very humbling experience. I never failed to be amazed that someone was prepared to confess and share their most intimate secrets and failings
with another person one-half or sometimes one-third their age.

Then there were the children. The schools opened in
September. This presented me with my first experience of standing
before a class of children. I realised very early on that it was fortunate that I did not choose a career as a teacher. I was not cut out for
that vocation! I have great admiration for good teachers and the
manner in which they can maintain the interest and attention of
their pupils as they gradually introduce them to the wonders of
reading and arithmetic and writing, and nature and religion. One of
the first teachers I met in Castlederg was a teacher of infants, a
woman called Lucy Hegarty. I could have stayed in her class for
hours watching her teach five- and six-year-olds. She fascinated me
as much as she fascinated them, with her stories and lessons and
songs and humour. She taught me a great deal about the skills of
teaching and unfolding the wonders of knowledge and faith to children.

There is a story told of Lucy Hegarty speaking to six-year-olds
about Mary being the mother of Jesus and explaining that she was a
virgin. One little girl, a member of a large family, put up her hand
and asked, 'Miss, is my Mammy a virgin?' Lucy rather forcefully
replied, 'Indeed she is not!' The little girl went home for lunch and
commented to her mother, 'Mammy, Miss Hegarty says that you
are no virgin.' A none-too-pleased Mammy smartly accompanied
her daughter back to school and demanded that Miss Hegarty
explain herself.

In my first month I began regularly visiting the sick, the elderly and the dying around the parish. I embarked on this ministry with
a certain amount of trepidation. But I quickly came to realise that it
was one of the most wonderful and fulfilling experiences of priesthood. My father's lengthy illness and death were still fresh in my
mind. I saw my father in many of those to whom I ministered in that
first year of priesthood and since. The faith of the elderly and dying

was an inspiration to me. Some of the elderly had lived through very hard times. A surprising number of the elderly women in the Derg valley, I discovered, had roots in West Donegal. They had been 'hired' as children or young teenagers to large farmers in West Tyrone, primarily through the hiring fairs in Strabane in the late 1800s and early 1900s. Some of them had painful experiences. There were exploited and abused. They had worked and laboured long hours for a pittance. But they had come through it all with wonderful dignity. There were men, too, who had been hired. Some of the hired men had married hired women. I also came across women who had worked for a Protestant farmer and fallen in love with a Protestant farm labourer. The Protestant farmer had introduced her to his minister and arranged for them to get married in the Protestant church and the resultant family were brought up as Protestants. Now fifty or sixty years later, this woman would contact me and ask to be received back into the Catholic Church. I had two such experiences during my five years in Castlederg. On one of these occasions, the woman's son, an Orangeman, came to see me late at night. His mother was dying. He asked me if I could come with him as she wished to see a priest. I had to enter the house via a back lane so that nobody would see me. Some of these people had come originally from Irish-speaking areas in County Donegal and, now, fifty or sixty years later, still prayed in Irish the prayers they learned on their mother's knees. They would say that prayer was a great comfort and strength to them during difficult times. I learned more about spirituality and prayer from visiting the sick and elderly than from any professor or spiritual director. Priests receive far more than they give as a result of their visitation of the sick and elderly. I quickly came to realise that I was only beginning to learn about priestly ministry.

There was a small hospital in Castlederg. Most of the patients there were elderly geriatric patients. There were the regular monthly rounds and the urgent calls to people who suddenly became ill or to accident victims. These created unforeseen challenges, among them breaking news of death to unsuspecting family members or relatives. I found myself, at times, attempting to console and needing consolation at the same time.

In this entire hectic round of activity, time had to be found for personal prayer. I tried to find this time early in the morning, before things started to happen, but it was difficult. The change from a structured seminary life to life in 'digs' in a busy parish is a huge challenge. The Divine Office is a great discipline and affords an opportunity to pray and turn to God at various times of the day. It offers a framework of prayer into which the day can be fitted. I have endeavoured to pray the Rosary most days since I was ordained to the priesthood. I have also tried to stimulate my mind and prayer by reading. I have to admit that there were times when I could not pray, periods when I neglected to pray, occasions when I felt too tired or lazy to pray. But I have always tried to get back to my daily routine of prayer.

My own youthfulness and inexperience and the respect in which the parishioners held me caused me considerable concern and made me feel inhibited and quite inadequate. There was a huge and almost inordinate respect for the office I held. I realised that this respect for priesthood had been won by generations of priests who had gone before me. I felt myself continually being placed on a pedestal. There are few more uncomfortable places than pedestals. During those early months, I spent a lot of my time jumping off pedestals whilst at the same time acknowledging due respect for the office of priesthood.

I was taught a useful lesson during my first months as curate. I had occasion to write to Bishop Farren about something or other. He returned my letter with a curt note appended to it stating, 'Your handwriting is illegible. Suggest you take typing lessons.' I took him at his word and took typing lessons, thus acquiring a skill that I have always valued. I was particularly grateful for his advice when computers arrived about a quarter of a century later.

I called with Father McMenamin every Saturday morning and told him about the events of the week that was ending and discussed my plans and suggestions for the week that was about to begin. We decided on the announcements for the Masses on Sunday morning. He was always terrified of the bishop! Every new initiative was immediately countered with 'What would the bishop think?' After I had been in the parish about six weeks, he reminded me once again of the necessity of raising funds for the proposed secondary school. He pointed me in the direction of St Patrick's Hall, the parish hall, across the road from the church, a strangely designed building with crenellations along the top. It was a relatively small hall, with a seating capacity of about 300, heated by open coal fires. There was a small stage and elementary catering facilities.

I had no experience of organising fund-raising functions, but fortunately there was a curate in the neighbouring parish who was very successful in this field. About eight or nine miles away, Father Leo Deery had been successfully organising functions in Drumquin for some time before I arrived in Castlederg. Like myself, he had been sent to act as 'nursemaid' to an elderly parish priest, and his parish, too, had to raise substantial funds for the urgent school-building programme that was taking place throughout the North in the late 1950s.

I took advice from Leo and initiated my own activities in Castlederg. It introduced me to a whole new world. A wonderful and energetic committee of women and men from the parish organised dances, concerts and whist drives. I was inveigled into establishing an amateur drama group and a musical society and producing various plays and pantomimes, despite having very limited prior experience in these fields. In the summer there were road races, cycle races, stock-car races, donkey derbies, duck races, football matches and various other events. For the next five years, there was a frenetic succession of all kinds of activities, most of which were very successful both from a social and financial perspective. Very large crowds came to St Patrick's Hall from far and wide. Up to seven or eight hundred young people, double its capacity, jammed into the hall for the weekly dances. It was the era of the Irish show-band, a remarkable phenomenon in Irish entertainment and social life. Extra accommodation had to be found to cater for the crowds attending whist drives. All of these were useful social activities, and an interesting side effect was the considerable boost that the success gave to the morale and self-esteem of the Catholic community. They took great pride in the success of St Patrick's Hall. The entertainment quality of functions there attracted quite a number of

Protestant people as well and this served to improve community relations, which was an important added bonus.

In the late autumn of 1957, with substantial financial help from my mother and the sympathy of a bank manager, I purchased a small car, an A35 Austin. Up until then I had got around on a bicycle or by hitching lifts. I had never driven a car before. The garage owner gave me two or three brief driving lessons and I was on the road driving on my own. There were no L-plates, driving test or R-plates at that time. The car enabled me to visit my mother and the rest of the family in Belleek more frequently. It was also of great help in getting around the parish, especially in responding to urgent calls.

There were few free moments but I enjoyed it enormously. The sheer variety of the work involved in parish ministry was exhilarating, exciting and challenging. Each day was different and often full of surprises. I had found precisely what I was looking for. Priesthood was all that I hoped it would be.

There were pitfalls, too. I had been a total abstainer from alcohol when I went as a student to Rome. During my time in Rome, where there was wine for lunch each day, I took wine and enjoyed it. However, I had scarcely ever taken alcohol in Ireland. One evening in late 1957, I was visiting a family in Castlederg. The woman of the house asked me if I would like to share a drink with her husband and herself. I agreed out of courtesy and had one small glass of whisky with them. A few days later, there were stories around the parish that the new young curate was 'a boozer'! At that stage, I decided immediately to become a total abstainer once again. I remained a teetotaller for the following fourteen or fifteen years. That small experience taught me to be circumspect. I learned that being a priest in Ireland at that time meant that one was constantly under observation and the slightest transgression was noted and commented upon, and often exaggerated out of all proportion.

The parishioners were not the only people whom one had to be careful about. Some time in November 1957, a number of parishioners asked me if it would be possible to have a Midnight Mass at Christmas. I asked Father McMenamin about it. As usual, he left the decision to myself. The people told me that they did not have a Christmas Midnight Mass for many years because of the fragile state of Father McMenamin's health. I went ahead and announced plans for the Midnight Mass. It was a decision greatly welcomed by the parishioners. Little did I know that it would be the antecedent to my first 'belt of a crosier'. Shortly after the announcement, I got a call to Bishop's House and asked why I had ignored diocesan regulations. I did not know what regulation I had breached! Then I was informed that Christmas Midnight Masses were strictly forbidden in the Derry diocese. Apparently, many years before, there was a fracas in some church or other as revellers emerged from a pub and found their way into the church whilst Midnight Mass was in progress. The result was that Christmas Midnight Masses were forbidden throughout the diocese. I pleaded ignorance. I was instructed to announce on the following Sunday that there would not be a Midnight Mass in Castlederg at Christmas. I was also wrapped over the knuckles for advertising parish dances in a local newspaper on one occasion. That was also forbidden. I came back to Castlederg licking my wounds and went to see Father McMenamin. He commented with a chuckle, 'Well, it just shows you that they don't teach everything in Rome.'

I was more fortunate than another curate in a small rural parish in County Tyrone about the same time who also advertised a parish dance in the local newspaper. Unknown to the curate, newspaper advertising of parish dances was forbidden! Another diocesan regulation. Bishop Farren sent a sharp letter to his parish priest severely reprimanding him and the curate for this transgression. The parish priest, who had a healthy disrespect for authority, promptly threw the letter into the fire. The curate, flushed by the success of his first venture into advertising, put an even bigger advertisement in the paper in the following week. Bishop Farren sent an even more irate letter to his parish priest, who promptly consigned it to his fire once again. The curate placed yet another advertisement the following week, but before the dance could take place the bishop arrived in the parish in person and 'interviewed' both the parish priest and the rather bemused curate, threatening them with all kinds of unspeakable sanctions. It didn't worry the old parish priest in the slightest but the curate was shocked. The local newspaper's advertising income dropped as a result. It didn't pay to advertise in the Derry diocese in the 1950s!

There were other matters that 'were not taught in Rome'. Castlederg was near to the boundary with the diocese of Clogher. The Bishop of Clogher at that time, Bishop Eugene O'Callaghan, had even greater problems about dancing than Bishop Farren. Dancing, for some strange reason, appeared to be a big issue with some Irish bishops in the 1950s! Bishop O'Callaghan had a regulation prohibiting his diocesans from going to dances in his diocese if the dancing continued beyond midnight. He further declared such activity to be a reserved sin,* as far as I can remember. I mentioned earlier about the big crowds at the dances in Castlederg that usually went on until two in the morning or later. In fact, most of the dancers did not arrive at the hall before eleven o'clock. I also mentioned the crowds who came to Confessions in Castlederg on Saturday nights. One could be excused for being tempted to suspect that there was a connection between these two phenomena! It is a poor sanction that does not benefit somebody.

I came to have great respect for the wisdom of older priests. I enjoyed visiting them. Whilst the younger clergy may have been 'streetwise', the older men were worldly-wise. In the two neighbouring parishes, the parish priests were in their seventies. Father John Lagan was parish priest in Ardstraw West. Although he was from Maghera in County Derry, he spoke with a slightly American accent. He had spent the first twenty-four years of his priesthood on loan to the diocese of Salt Lake City in Utah in the United States. He was quiet, shy and withdrawn, a very spiritual man. I always found his advice sound and encouraging. I chose him as my confessor. Father Peadar MacLoinsigh was parish priest in Aghyaran, a vast rural parish in West Tyrone. He was a well-known scholar and gregarious character, an incessant talker, but always interesting. Peadar was a wonderful host and loved hosting lunches for clergy and other guests. As his name suggests, he was a keen Irish scholar

---

*   A sin which, in normal circumstance, could only be absolved by the Bishop or a priest given special faculties by him.

and a native speaker from Cloghan in Donegal. He had a great love for books and a wonderful library and welcomed writers and historians to his parochial house. He had spent some years, 1912-19, on loan to a diocese in South Africa and was shocked and angered by what he had witnessed there. He had also served in Castlederg for fourteen years from the mid 1920s to the late 1930s. Peadar hosted his celebrated lunches about once a month; they began around one in the afternoon. Guests were seldom free to leave before eight in the evening. All of the time was spent sitting around the dining-room table. There were usually six to eight guests present. He invited me to lunch every few months and some of the occasions were really memorable. The food was good but the conversation was the most memorable element of Peadar's lunches. It is such a pity that he died without writing down his memoirs and experiences. He was the first contemporary of the War of Independence and Civil War whom I heard talking openly about those days in Ireland. I remember sitting, fascinated, listening to him and others engaged in conversation for hours on end. Peadar did most of the talking. He was a delightful soul and the source of much profound wisdom. He gave me much good advice on pastoral ministry.

After almost a year in Castlederg, I decided to change my 'digs'. The house I stayed in was too public both by nature and by its prominent location on the main street. Whilst I was happy to live there and the McGoldrick family were very kind to me, several parishioners suggested that I ought to move to somewhere more discreet. Castlederg was a small community and when an individual wished to discuss a private or personal matter with the local priest, he or she did not want the whole community to know about it. So I moved to another house, Cherry Cottage. I stayed there with Joe and Peggy Gallagher, a delightful couple.

In the meantime, I was finding my feet in priesthood. At that time, the local priest had to act as social worker, marriage counsellor, bereavement counsellor and youth counsellor, as well as attempting to deliver a dozen other services, which were not strictly related to priesthood. There were few social services provided by any other agency. I came to have great respect for the work of the St Vincent de Paul Society and its members, who discreetly helped and supported people who were in need. They did it in a way that respected the dignity of the individual. I was edified by the simple and uncomplicated faith of the people. It was a quiet time politically and community relations improved notably during my years in Castlederg, although I can only recollect meeting the local Church of Ireland or Presbyterian clergy on a few occasions. However, I met with many Protestant lay people and became quite friendly with a number of them.

I greatly enjoyed my activities in St Patrick's Hall. Some time in the late 1950s, a complete refurbishment of the hall was undertaken, including the laying of a new maple dance floor. I discussed with parishioners whom we could get to perform the opening ceremony. They decided that we should engage some big showbiz celebrity. The only 'big name' in showbiz whom I knew was the singer Ruby Murray. At that time, she had several records in the 'hit parade' and was one of the biggest names in the business in Britain or Ireland. I had known her many years before when, as a student, I regularly attended summer shows in Bundoran. At that time, Ruby was just starting out on her career. She played in shows in Bundoran for several seasons. Although I never imagined that she would agree to come to Castlederg, I managed to contact her through a mutual friend in show business. She remembered me from her Bundoran days. I invited her to perform at the opening of the hall. To my astonishment, she agreed to come. She came especially from England for that one engagement, arrived in Castlederg in a huge black limousine and gave a wonderful performance. Ruby was a humble and gentle person. There was lots of media interest in her visit and there were as many people outside the hall as inside. St Patrick's Hall was really on the map.

I gradually developed my interest in theatre, particularly in the production of plays. It is a most pleasurable experience and became my favourite hobby. It was also a wonderful way to get to know people. To take a play script and cast it and bring it to life on the stage is incredibly fulfilling. I assembled and auditioned a group of people, some of whom had brief theatrical experience and others were complete newcomers. Initially, we performed our productions locally. We were subsequently invited to perform in other parish halls in the area. Some of these were very small with the most basic stage facilities. A few of them did not have electricity even in the late 1950s. The stage and hall lighting was provided by Tilley lamps fuelled by paraffin oil. Two or three parochial halls in West Tyrone, at that time, were in converted lofts over disused stables. Despite the lack of facilities, there were always capacity audiences for the plays. In one parochial hall, the parish priest insisted on sitting in the front row. The audience applauded only when he applauded and laughed only when he laughed. It was somewhat bewildering and perplexing for the performers, but there was worse to come. After our performance there, he addressed the audience and thundered against the play and against us. At the end of his speech, we were unsure as to whether we or the play we had performed were the more immoral! We did not accept any invitations for return visits to that parish. In most places we were well received and the audiences were enthusiastic and involved.

Others were not so fortunate. I heard of another amateur drama group performing a play in a small hall in a very Republican area of Tyrone. They were a visiting company from another parish and they were performing a melodrama based on the trial of Robert Emmet, the Irish patriot who was executed by the British for treason in 1803. The high point and climax of the play was intended to be Emmet's speech from the dock after he was found guilty and before he was sentenced. The play was performed with such enthusiasm and feeling that the audience became increasingly vocal and extremely hostile to the witnesses and counsel for the prosecution. So much so, that the jury, made up of members of the cast and fearful of the audience, under guidance from the producer off-stage, found Emmet not guilty instead of guilty; the stage manager pulled the curtain and the entire company beat a hasty retreat from the stage door at the rear of the hall. The unfortunate Emmet never had the opportunity to deliver his speech from the dock!

At that time, local amateur theatre in Ireland received great encouragement and stimulation from the Drama Festivals that were being held in various parts of the country. The Castlederg Players, green and inexperienced as we were, entered some of these festivals from 1958 onwards. We received wonderful encouragement and education in theatre from professional actors and directors like Micheál MacLiammóir, Barry Cassin, Ria Mooney, Tomás Mac Anna and many others who acted as adjudicators at these festivals. They were kind and tolerant, never patronising, and they were as anxious to teach, as we were anxious to learn. I will always remember an occasion when the players and myself spent an illuminating night from midnight until six in the morning with Micheál Mac Liammóir after a Festival performance in Ballyshannon. With great patience, he dissected each individual performance and each element of the production and taught us how it should have been done and how much we could improve on our performance. He interspersed his advice with an unending series of hilarious anecdotes. We went to many festivals all over the north and west of Ireland, often arriving home just in time to celebrate morning Mass, as people were going to their work. With hard work and much effort, we had improved the standard of our performances sufficiently to qualify for a place in the All-Ireland Festival in Athlone in 1961. We all enjoyed the experience immensely. As well as making some wonderful friendships I found the education in theatre to be an invaluable aid to my preaching, and later in my dealing with the media. It also provided me with a lifelong love of the theatre and motivation to attend the professional theatre in Dublin and London. I was surprised to find out that some statute or other prohibited Catholic priests from attending the theatre or theatrical productions in Ireland. The Abbey Theatre in Dublin kindly facilitated myself and other like-minded clergy by accommodating us backstage just inside the proscenium. Apparently some canon lawyer, with a delightful touch of casuistry, had determined that the statute only applied to viewing theatrical productions from the auditorium! That strange anachronistic law was wisely discontinued some time in the 1960s.

One of the more difficult and embarrassing tasks a priest was called upon to do at that time was the collection of funeral offerings. In some parts of Ireland, up until the early 1970s, this was an integral part of the funeral ceremony. I was familiar with the practice from my experience accompanying my father to funerals in my childhood. At one stage during the funeral Mass the funeral offerings were taken up. A table was brought out to the altar rails and people queued up and made their individual offering – a shilling, two shillings, half a crown, or five shillings. The priest called out the donor's name and the amount offered in a loud voice. When all the individual offerings had been made, the money was added up and the total amount of offerings was announced. People took a very careful note of the amount paid by the individual and gave even more careful attention to the total amount. Some parishioners could remember amounts of offerings paid at funerals for years back. Funeral offerings constituted an important part of the priests' income. At the end of each quarter, the amount paid in funeral offerings was added up, and the parish priest usually retained half of the amount, and the curates divided out the other half equally. Without this income, at that time, I could not have kept body and soul together. I do not know how or when this custom began but I do know that most priests breathed a big sigh of relief when it was finally abolished in the 1970s and a salary structure introduced. Apart from the embarrassment involved, for both priests and peo-ple, it led to great inequities and uncertainties in the already paltry income of priests. A three-month period without funerals meant that payments on the car and other items fell behind.

At the end of the 1950s, I was obliged to change 'digs' once again. To my great sadness, Mrs Peggy Gallagher, the lady of the house, became ill and died. She was a charming woman and it was a great joy to share Cherry Cottage with her husband, Joe, and her brother, James. I then went to another house where I happily spent the remainder of my time in Castlederg. I stayed in the Carlin household, where there were twin babies, two little girls, their par-ents and their grandparents. Again it was a wonderful home and each of these various 'digs' educated me in various ways.

Over the years, Father McMenamin became more and more frail. From 1960 onwards he was nervous about celebrating public Mass. Despite my reassurances, he was constantly anxious about having the funds necessary to pay for the secondary intermediate school, which had been under construction since late 1958 or early 1959. The school was eventually completed and opened for its first pupils in September 1961. The Urney parish had raised adequate funds to cover our share of the cost, much to Father McMenamin's relief. Bishop Farren performed the formal opening and blessing of St Eugene's Secondary Intermediate School in November 1961. It was a memorable occasion for everyone concerned and went without a hitch. With the people of the area, I felt a great sense of achievement.

There was nothing designed to raise Father McMenamin's blood pressure more than a pending visit from the bishop! He worried about it for weeks beforehand. Apart from special occasions, such as the opening of a new school or some similar event, the regular visits took place once every three years when the senior children in the primary schools of the parish would receive the sacrament of Confirmation. The Bishop, in addition to administering Confirmation, would inspect parish registers and parish plant, such as churches and houses. Father Michael asked me to organise everything for Bishop Farren's first visit during my term in Castlederg. All went smoothly. On the bishop's second visit for Confirmation three years later, I was again entrusted with the arrangements. I thought that I would be a little more adventurous on this occasion. There was an Italian lady, Mrs Coyle, living in the parish. She was married to the owner of the local fish-and-chip shop and was an excellent cook of Italian dishes. We became friends. We were both happy to have someone with whom we could have a conversation in Italian. From time to time, she cooked me an Italian meal, which I enjoyed with her husband, Pat, and herself. I thought that it would be a brilliant idea to have an Italian meal for the bishop and visiting clergy after the Confirmation. I had imagined that it would be a pleasant and interesting change from the roast beef or chicken and ham that, at that time, was the all too predictable fare for such meals. The meal was to be served in Father McMenamin's house. The cook, Mrs Coyle, and some of her assistants came early in the morning to start preparing the sauces, setting the table and other things. When Father Michael and his housekeeper eventually came downstairs and experienced the exotic and strange aromas that permeated the house and gradually came to the startling realisation that this was the 'Bishop's Meal' in preparation, they nearly went crazy. He sent for me and asked me what was going on. I explained to him and he was nearly out of his mind. To say that he was not

impressed by the whole concept would be an understatement! I told
him, admittedly with a certain degree of foreboding, not to worry;
everything would be alright. After the Confirmation ceremony
ended, the bishop and the clergy arrived at the parochial house. The
house was full of the fragrance of *ragú* and *saltimbocca* and other
Italian culinary delights. A few former Roman students among the
clergy became quite interested and excited by the surprise cuisine.
Magnifico! Most of the others became concerned and asked various
questions about Italian food. Several found sudden and unexpected
commitments that precluded attending the meal. Father Michael
decided that he was unwell and asked to be excused and went
painfully and fretfully upstairs. A few others and I thought that the
meal was delicious. Everyone else was very polite, including the
bishop. But during the subsequent inquest in the parish priest's bedroom late that evening, after I had served him with a few glasses of
what remained of the *Orvieto Bigi*, Father Michael declared, with a
twinkle in his eye, that I had lost marks that day. I had blotted my
copybook! We decided unanimously that it would be chicken and
ham next time around.

But sadly there wasn't to be a next time. In the early months of
1962, Father Michael became more and more frail. He only came
downstairs for a few hours in the afternoon. The doctor told me
that he was dying. I used to bring him Holy Communion each day.
I was very humbled when he asked to make his confession to me and
I gave him the last sacraments. In those last weeks, we joked and
laughed and reminisced about the famous Italian dinner and other
events that had occurred in the five memorable years that we were
together. He said that he was at the end of his life as a priest and I
was at the beginning. He was delighted about having the construction of the secondary school completed and the necessary funds
raised. The people and the parish were in good heart. Towards the
end, some parishioners would come to the house to sit up at night
with him. It was my custom to join them for part of the night.

During this period, one night at about 11 p.m., I brought Father
Michael a cup of tea to his bedroom. I was aware that his housekeeper, Sarah, who was in a bedroom close by, was a little jealous of
all the attention that he was receiving. She also was unwell. I called

in to her to ask her would she like a cup of tea. She said she would. So I brought her a cup of tea and a few Digestive biscuits. Sarah thanked me and said to me rather faintly and indistinctly, 'Couldya get me me "teeght" please?' I asked her what she wanted and I gradually realised that she was asking for her *teeth*. I looked around, could not see any teeth and asked her where they were. She said, 'They are in the sweetie tin', pointing to a redundant tea caddy that had found a new use. I opened the sweetie tin, and there was this enormous set of false teeth on top of a collection of Bulls' Eyes, Clove Balls and assorted other sticky sweets. I didn't know whether to hand the tin to her or reach in and hand her the teeth. I handed her the tin. Sarah took out the teeth, popped them into her mouth and then, whilst handing back the tin to me, said with a broad smile, 'Wouldya like to have a sweetie?' I declined, gently.

Father Michael got weaker and weaker. He died on 2 March 1962. He was eighty-one years old. He was buried in Castlederg. Shortly before he died, he gave me his well-thumbed prayer book that I still have. I was very privileged that he was my first parish priest. For better or worse, he gave me complete freedom and considerable responsibility, something few priests experience in their first years of priesthood. He allowed me to make my mistakes and learn from them. He lived very simply. He was quiet and shy but the people had great respect for him. He was serene and content and totally peaceful in the face of death. I learned a great deal about priesthood during my years with him. He and the people of the parish made my years in Castlederg just as important in my formation as my years in Rome.

I knew that, after he died, my stay in Castlederg would soon come to an end. I had been there almost five years and had been sent there to see Father Michael through his last years. At that time, priests did not retire; they died 'in harness', even if the entire parish was falling down around them.

There was great speculation among the parishioners as to who would be appointed as Father Michael's successor. About four or five weeks after the funeral, I received a phone call from the Vicar Forane of the deanery advising me that the new parish priest would be installed that day at three in the afternoon. The ceremony would be private. I was instructed to be present at St Patrick's church at that time and to have the main keys of the church available. I was silly enough to ask who had been appointed, only to be told that I would find out at three o'clock! I thought of Father Michael. I am sure that he would have considered that I had blotted my copybook once again!

The new parish priest, Father Tom Devine, was duly installed. On a Monday morning about two weeks later, Bishop Farren asked me to call with him in Derry. He told me that he was appointing me as curate in St Eugene's Cathedral in Derry City. I asked him when I would take up my appointment. He asked me to be there for Thursday!

CHAPTER 6

Hi Mister! Are You a Priest?

*The wonderful world of the Bogside – Rossville Street –
rounds men – St Eugene's cathedral and parochial house –
women of the Bogside – the scarf –
Gransha hospital*

St Eugene's Cathedral parish in Derry was a culture shock after
Castlederg. I was not prepared for the sheer numbers of people who
thronged the cathedral for weekend Masses and for the seemingly
endless hours spent in the confessional every week. I was not prepared for living in a house with four other priests, with a bishop living next door under the same roof; nor was I prepared for a
parochial house where the phone and doorbells rang incessantly
from early morning until late at night and often all through the
night. I was not prepared for the type of night duty, when one was
called out almost every night and frequently several times during
the night. But, most of all, I was unprepared for the housing conditions and overcrowding in which many of the people in the parish
were obliged to live.

About 16,000 people lived in St Eugene's parish in the early
1960s. The parish was divided up into districts. Each priest was allocated a district. Shortly after I arrived, Father John McNally,
administrator of the parish, designated me to look after the pastoral
care of the Bogside district. The Bogside today is perceived as a
much larger area than it was in the 1960s. Then it was confined to
the area bounded by William Street, Waterloo Street, the City
Walls, Westland Street and the Bull Park. About 5,000 people were
crowded into this small area. They were placed under my pastoral
care. They were my flock.

The Bogside district of Derry was a strange and intriguing place in the early 1960s. It was full of interesting contradictions. Despite the fact that the population was almost one hundred per cent Irish Nationalist or Republican, many of the principal streets were named after British military icons or commemorated triumphs from bygone wars, such as Wellington Street, Nelson Street, Blucher Street and Waterloo Street. It was an area where, contrary to the norm, the workforce was predominantly female. Whilst some of the men were dockers and others worked in the BSR factory, which manufactured record players, a very large percentage of the men were unemployed. Most of them had signed on the dole for years. There was poverty and overcrowding everywhere. Despite the poverty and the dreadful housing conditions, most of the people were incredibly good humoured and kind. They had brilliant, razor-sharp wit. It was a quintessential urban community, yet even in the early 1960s there were a few people who kept pigs or chickens in their backyards, somewhat to the discomfiture of their immediate neighbours. One of the more incongruous memories of early mornings in the Bogside was that of hearing a cock crowing in the middle of a city! Despite their poverty, they were by and large law-abiding people. Few doors were ever locked. Vandalism and criminal activity were insignificant. Most children were cherished, and there were many, many children. Anyone's problem was everyone's problem. There was a powerful community network of informal support in almost every situation that needed it – considerable emotional support, and as much financial support as could be afforded. Sickness, death and other family crises were occasions when such support would be gladly offered. There were even women in the community who washed and laid out the bodies of the dead, or 'stretched' them, as it was described. It was a Christian community in the real sense of the word.

One of the major arteries of the Bogside was Rossville Street. This was a street that could provide most of the staple needs of life. There were several grocery shops, many pubs, two small bakeries, a fish-and-chip shop, a newsagent, a confectionery shop, a very busy pawnbroker's shop and a lot of residential dwellings. At one stage, before I came to Derry, it had a bathhouse. There was the city cattle-market, just off Rossville Street and occasionally in the early 1960s the street would be filled with the chaos of cattle driven by shouting drovers on their way to the market or on their way to the nearby Glasgow or Liverpool boats which berthed about a half a mile away on the quays. Rossville Street embraced seven-day opening for pubs thirty years before it became legal! There was a hall, the Rossville Hall, where older men played cards, and discussed the affairs of the day; there were several bookies within easy reach. Rossville Street was always crowded with women and girls after the factory horns sounded at the beginning or end of work each day or at lunch hour. They stopped and purchased a bap or a turnover to eat at work, or something more substantial for the family meal on their way home for work. There was a cluster of large shirt factories nearby; the City Factory, Hogg & Mitchell's and Richardson's. Little streets led off Rossville Street, like branches of a tree – Pilot's Row, Eden Place, Joseph Street and Foxes Corner on one side and Union Street, Thomas Street and Bogside on the other.

Bogside was the name of a street as well as the name of the general area. It was an unlikely city street. At one end there was a large house, built in the style of a farmhouse. At the other end there was the city abattoir. The abattoir was a great place for men to gather to discuss football, horses or the news of the day. I do not know how any work got done there. There was just one pub in the street, Duddy's, and a grocery shop, the All Cash Stores. Houses of various sizes lined the street. None was similar to any other. There were single-storey, two-storey and three-storey houses of differing shapes and sizes. The area had many culs-de-sac. There was a cul-de-sac off the Bogside called Carlisle Place. On the other side Abbey Street linked the Bogside to William Street. Abbey Street derived its name from the medieval Dominican Abbey that was located in that general area of Derry.

Town gas was the main source of energy in the area. Whole families cooked on one gas ring and in some houses the lighting was also fuelled by gas. In some homes, there were hearth fires with a crook for pots and kettles, the same as houses in the country. In others there were black ranges. There were open coal or coke fires in most houses, and in the still, dark, cold days of winter, the entire area was shrouded in a pall of blue smoke, wisps slowly going up in a straight line from every chimney.

There were all kinds of men constantly doing the rounds of the streets and homes – coal men, gas men, brock* men, insurance men, bread men, debt men, cruelty men, post men, rent men, milk men, bin men, dole men, football pools men, lemonade men, sanitary men, Corporation men, school attendance men, wee Indian and Pakistani men selling clothes and there was me!

'Hi, mister, are you a priest?' called a small grubby youngster amid a group of children playing in a battered cardboard box. It was my first day in the Bogside. It was a whole new, fascinating world. This was to be my home and place of work for the next eleven years.

Life was hectic and exhilarating. I thought that I had been working hard in Castlederg, but I never dreamt that I could be as busy as I was in St Eugene's. For the first time, I was working as part of a team. The support of the other priests in the parish was reassuring and affirming. There were colleagues to share problems with. There were men of experience and some younger men like myself. The ministry was varied and always interesting and challenging. I learned a great deal about priesthood and about people during my first years in the Bogside.

St Eugene's Cathedral was built in the third quarter of the nineteenth century. It is a classic and beautiful Gothic cathedral, designed by the architect J.J. McCarthy, one of the major figures in the Gothic revival in Ireland. He designed many cathedrals and churches throughout Ireland. The tower and spire were added in the early years of the twentieth century. I became very attached to St Eugene's Cathedral. It was to be a central part of my life for more than thirty years. In the early 1960s, there were four daily morning Masses in the cathedral. There were also many evening devotions and sodalities. There were confessions for three and one half hours on a Friday evening, two and one half hours on a Saturday morning and three and one half hours on a Saturday evening. After hearing Confessions on a Saturday evening, one felt completely exhausted.

---

*   Leftover food, peelings etc. collected to feed pigs and other animals.

On Sunday mornings, there were six Masses. The attendances at ceremonies in the cathedral were amazing. People of all ages, men, women and children, attended Sunday Mass in huge numbers. Few people in the parish absented themselves from Sunday Mass. In fact, it must have taken enormous courage for anyone to absent himself or herself!

The accommodation in St Eugene's parochial house was basic but comfortable. I lived in two rooms on the top floor overlooking the busy crossroads of Creggan Street and the Lone Moor Road. The five priests shared one bathroom and two communal wash-basins. Few floors had carpets. There was no central heating, just open fires in the wintertime. Buckets of coal were carried up to the second and third floors. It was very cold and draughty in winter but it was a lot better and much more spacious than the accommodation that many of our parishioners had to put up with. The food was good and the craic was even better. We had a small oratory in the house where we could pray and reflect from time to time. There were two housekeepers – Maggie Doherty, who was to play a large part in my life for the following thirty years and Mary McDaid. With a large house to look after and five hungry men to be fed, they were greatly overworked. There were people at the door constant-ly seeking various things and sometimes late in the evening callers had over-indulged in alcohol and were abusive. There wasn't an office or secretary at that time. So the housekeepers answered the telephone. There were no phone extensions to the various priests' rooms; as a result, various people had to be called to the phone by a system of gongs, and in a three-storey house that was tedious. Maggie and Mary were wonderful and patient women. Maggie Doherty, who had been housekeeper there since 1938, was the love of my life, my second mother.

I began visiting the homes in the Bogside district the week after I arrived. Without a single exception, I received a warm welcome from the people. They were relaxed, easy and informal in my pres-ence. They did not make a fuss or try to put me on a pedestal as they did in other places. They took me as they found me. I liked that. They spoke their minds. They were amazingly open, down-to-earth people. Before I was an hour in their presence, they would be telling me their whole life history in great detail. Very often it was a history of hardship and struggle to survive. Their spirit, however, was incredibly strong. The women in the Bogside made a powerful impression on me. They possessed dignity and fortitude. They had a powerful sense of Christian charity. They had great character and had a tremendous influence on the community. The Bogside granny in her wraparound apron was marriage counsellor, social worker, peacemaker, child psychologist, family accountant, psychotherapist and spiritual director all rolled into one. What she said, was law! The typical Bogside mother insisted that daughters handed over their weekly wage packets unopened. If the wage packet was opened before being handed over to mother, it was considered tantamount to theft. If the daughter did not marry and still lived at home, she was expected to do this even if she was forty years old! The Bogside daughters were most often the breadwinners of the family. When I visited homes, I introduced myself, then met various members of the family who were at home, chatted about everything under the sun, took a census of the people living in the house, prayed for a short time with the people, and then moved on to the next home or the next room in the house where another family lived. Visits could be anything from fifteen minutes to three hours in duration. I visited homes in the district on three or four afternoons and two evenings every week. I often did not get back to St Eugene's until the small hours of the morning. During the home visits I noted people who were confined to the house for one reason or another, age, handicap or illness, and subsequently arranged to attend them monthly, if they so desired. I endeavoured to visit each home in the district at least once a year, but it was often much more frequently than that.

Most of the houses in the Bogside district at that time had four rooms, a kitchen and three other rooms. Some were smaller than that. Families had lived in the same houses in the same streets for three or four generations. Few of the homes had a bathroom; most had a cold-water tap and outside toilets in the backyard. In many cases, the rooms other than the kitchen were filled with beds, each room accommodating a separate family. They had to eat, wash, sleep and endeavour to bring up children in that confined space.

This shocked me. I had never seen anything like it before. When young couples married, they were faced with a dilemma as regards accommodation. Some emigrated to England or further afield. Some moved into sub-standard flats for which they were required to pay exorbitant rents. Many were accommodated in their parents' homes. The parents would give them a room in the house in the hope that they would get accommodation for themselves sooner rather than later. Years later, in many cases, they would still be in that room with two or three or more children. Often this process was repeated with another son or daughter, and so the house became grossly overcrowded. But there were few alternatives. Finding fifteen to twenty people in a four-roomed house was a regular occurrence. I remember one instance where more than twenty-five people endeavoured to survive in such accommodation, but this was exceptional. Such arrangements were not good for the health of the individual occupants or for the health of the marriage. Living in these conditions was claustrophobic and offered little opportunity for privacy. But most people coped remarkably well and with great stoicism. Before I went to Derry, I didn't realise that such housing conditions existed in Ireland. Gradually I came to understand that this situation was brought about by political corruption and injustice. It was a situation that could have been avoided with a less malign and more humane local political administration. The Derry City Corporation built and allocated housing in the city. They had complete control. To protect an artificial Unionist majority on the Corporation, and to rig the local government elections in an effective manner, they confined non-Unionists to certain areas of the city. By means of a notorious rigging and manipulation of electoral boundaries – a system that became known as gerrymander – they maintained absolute control of a city in which they were a minority. The Unionists had control and they were determined to maintain control.

When a priest arrives for the first time in a new parish, he is confronted with a whole variety of new people, new places and new customs. He is expected to come to terms with these very quickly. One of the things that struck me most of all was the manner in which funerals were conducted in the parish, and especially the ritual of the scarf. I was in the parish only a few days when I had to conduct my first funeral there. Before I was collected by the undertaker at the parochial house to go to the funeral house to bring the remains to the church, Maggie, the housekeeper, warned me, 'Don't forget your scarf!' It was a warm sunny morning in June. I thought that the housekeeper was joking or 'having me on'. However, I soon realised that this was not the case. The scarf was not really a scarf but a length of white linen folded over several times. It was more like a sash than a scarf. It was worn over the left shoulder and across the chest. At the shoulder there was a rosette, white for a single person, and a black ribbon was added to the rosette for a married or widowed person.

The priest wore this whilst accompanying the remains from the house of the deceased to the church and then from the church to the cemetery, walking ahead of the hearse. I had never before heard of this custom or experienced it in any other area. As far as I know, it only existed in Derry City. I remember making enquiries about its origins. Several elderly people told me that the custom went back to the end of the nineteenth century. At that time, the family of the dead person presented the officiating priest with a shirt length in white cotton and the priest in the funeral procession carried this. I do not know how many priests actually had shirts made from the cloth. However, with a couple of hundred funerals a year, I presume that large and unwanted amounts of white cotton or white shirts must have accumulated in various parochial houses, so the scarf was introduced as a substitute. Unfortunately, this custom of the funeral scarf seems to have died out in city parishes in the past twenty years or so. It was an interesting traditional custom. Speaking of funerals, it was a great relief to know that the custom of funeral offerings was not practised in Derry City.

Walking alone ahead of the funeral was an interesting experience for a new arrival in Derry who did not know his way around. I remember, at one of my first funerals in the parish, leading a funeral procession out of a side street on to Rossville Street and turning left. The funeral undertaker directed the hearse and funeral procession to turn right and travel via William Street! I did not realise this until a wee woman called on me and very diplomatically said, 'Is the funeral going to the Long Tower or the Cathedral, Father?' I took the hint and looked around. At that stage, I was walking along the centre of the street in lonely splendour, decked out in my scarf, with the funeral cortège proceeding in the opposite direction!

There were two nursing homes, a very large psychiatric hospital and a small specialist hospital* in the parish in 1962. A few months earlier, the City and County Infirmary, the main city hospital, just across the street from the cathedral, had closed and moved to Altnagelvin in the Waterside. The so-called mental hospital was known as Gransha. One of the cathedral priests celebrated Mass there for the patients and staff every Sunday morning at 9 a.m. I had never visited a psychiatric hospital before. This hospital was built in Victorian times. It was like something straight out of a Charles Dickens book. There were high ceilings, huge open fires, long corridors, large dormitories and an overwhelming smell of Jeyes Fluid disinfectant. Some of the elderly patients had been there for almost their whole lifetime. Some were merely suffering from a mild handicap and were hidden away in Gransha to avoid embarrassment for their family. They should never have been in such an institution. Others had psychiatric problems of varying degrees. Sadly many patients had few visitors. They were beautiful, simple people. From being nervous and anxious on my first visit, I came to look forward to each visit to Gransha. I developed great affection and respect for the patients. I witnessed in that hospital the relic of a cruel unchristian workhouse era of which society and the Churches could not be proud. The staff, however, seemed to treat the patients well and respectfully. Gransha Hospital in the Strand Road was closed down some time around the end of the 1960s with the advent of a new and more enlightened and, hopefully, more Christian understanding of this aspect of care of the sick.

For a priest full of energy and enthusiasm, St Eugene's parish was the ideal appointment. There were always new and interesting things going on. A cathedral is the centre of much of the ceremonial activity in any diocese. Every possible dimension of pastoral ministry could be experienced in the parish. The Bogside area was, in

---

*   This was called the Eye and Ear Hospital.

many ways, a world of its own within the parish and the city. It had its own particular culture and way of life. It provided a challenging, demanding and very fulfilling ministry for a priest. This ministry involved sharing the joys and the sorrows, the successes and failures, the impatience and frustration, the laughter and tears, as well as the doubts and questions of people. The Bogside people insisted you listen as well as speak. It was precisely such a ministry that attract- ed me into the priesthood in the first place, and serving in such a situation provided everything I could have asked or hoped for in priesthood.

CHAPTER 7

The Daily Pastoral Round

Father Tony Mulvey – weddings and breakfasts –
sailors and submariners – turning 'fellas' –
night calls

The early 1960s was a period of calm before the storm in Church and State. Pope John XXIII had announced an Ecumenical Council, but it was not expected to be anything more than the swansong of a saintly and much-loved elderly 'caretaker Pope'. Mass and the other rituals of the Church were celebrated in the Latin language as they had been for hundreds of years; exactly the same words were being used in the celebration of Mass from the Bogside to Bolzano to Bogotá. In the local political sphere, the Unionists reigned arrogantly and merrily in Stormont and in the Guildhall. Authority in both Church and State went unchallenged. People generally did what they were told to do. It was the period of certitude, where everyone was happy in the conviction that he or she and everyone of like mind were right and that all those who thought or acted otherwise were wrong.

One of my priest colleagues in St Eugene's was Father Tony Mulvey, a native of Omagh and son of a former MP. He had a very keen political mind. He also had a powerful social conscience. At lunch each day, the priests in the parish would discuss various problems encountered during the previous twenty-four hours. These problems could be pastoral, spiritual or social. I found this to be a great means of learning and becoming more aware of my responsibilities as a priest. Tony Mulvey had been in St Eugene's since the early 1950s. He knew the parish and its people like the back of his

103

hand. He was extremely exercised about the injustices and the circumstances under which many of the people were forced to live. In
1960, he had been instrumental in founding a branch of Credit
Union in Derry. Other people had collaborated with him in this initiative, including a young teacher called John Hume and Paddy
Doherty, a foreman in the construction industry. It was one of the
first Credit Unions in Ireland. Father Tony, on a visit to the United
States some time previously, had witnessed the work and social
potential of Credit Union. He had had first-hand experience of the
greed and exploitation perpetrated by the moneylenders who
preyed on people living in the parish. The main banks had little
time for little people like those in the Bogside. Credit was not available to them. Derry Credit Union was immediately successful and
ever since then it has provided a most important and valuable service to the community. It gave people a degree of dignity and an
opportunity to free themselves from exploitation. It was from
Father Mulvey, too, that I first heard about the work of the Catholic
Social Service Centre in High Street Derry. It was initially established by the Church in Derry in March 1947, after the introduction of social legislation initiated by Aneurin Bevan, to assist people
in receiving all the health and social benefits to which they were
entitled and to help them in their dealings with statutory bodies and
bureaucracy generally. It was funded by door-to-door collections
over the years, and directed by an amazing and dedicated man called
John Doherty; it provided a magnificent and invaluable service. It
was the forerunner of the multitude of agencies now in existence
that provide community services. When I arrived in Derry in 1962,
Tony Mulvey's primary concern was about how the housing conditions of people could be improved. He was not quite sure how this
could be done but he was convinced that, as priests, we had a
responsibility to address the problem and to do something con-
structive to give people the human dignity and rights to which they
were entitled. The injustices had to be addressed; it was not sufficient to moan and complain about them. Tony could be impatient.
He was stubborn as a mule; when he set his mind on an objective,
he could not easily be deflected. He had 'a short fuse', particularly
in the morning when someone else was trying to share the shaving

mirror! We had many heated arguments on various subjects over the years. However, friendship always predominated. Tony Mulvey was an outstanding example of practical priesthood and I learned more from him about the social responsibilities and dimensions of priesthood than from any other individual. I always treasured his friendship. Before I came to Derry, those responsibilities had not been a priority for me. I regarded politics like many other Irish people at that time – as something to be avoided. To declare oneself as non-political was perceived as virtuous. People who made such claims considered themselves and were generally perceived as occupying the high moral ground. It is a peculiar Irish trait. Tony Mulvey helped me to understand, in his own trenchant manner, that opting out of such responsibilities, as a priest, was simply a coward's way out and a dereliction of duty.

After the first year, I quickly became accustomed to the accelerated pace of life and ministry in Derry. I was at full stretch, working harder than I had ever worked and relishing the various new challenges with which I was confronted.

There was no fixed format for the day. Every day was different. But there were some constants. Each day began with the celebration of Mass. Mass was only celebrated in the morning at that time. Those going to Holy Communion or celebrating Mass had to fast from midnight. Weekday Masses were well attended. There were four Masses each weekday, 7, 8, 9 and 10 a.m. If there was a funeral or funerals, they always took place at the ten o'clock Mass – on occasions there were two or three or more funerals at this Mass. The priest who was on sick-call duty and who had been on duty the previous night always celebrated the ten o'clock Mass. Weddings, if there were any, were celebrated at 7, 8 or 9 a.m., and never later than 9. At certain times of the year such as St Stephen's Day, Easter Monday and the period at the beginning of the annual Derry factory holiday in the first week of August, there were often several weddings at the one Mass, which presented a considerable challenge for both priest and the parties concerned. There were also added pressures when weddings were at nine o'clock Mass. Steps had to be taken to ensure that the wedding party leaving the church did not meet a funeral cortège arriving for the ten o'clock Mass! Baptism was administered after the ten o'clock Mass. There was an average of four hundred Baptisms a year in St Eugene's in the early 1960s. There was a Baptism or Baptisms almost every morning. The infant was normally baptised on the day it was born or the day afterwards. Usually, its godmother and nobody else accompanied the newborn infant. The parents were never present at the baptism. If there was a wedding or weddings, the priest was expected to attend the reception. At that time, these were described as wedding breakfasts rather than wedding receptions. People went straight from the church and sat down immediately to the meal; there was no hanging around at the bar beforehand. There were about five venues, hotels and restaurants, for wedding receptions in the city and care had to be taken to attend the correct function, as, at busy times, there were multiple receptions in several of the venues. This could lead to problems. On one occasion, I arrived late, dashed into the dining room and sat in the first vacant chair I could find, then looked up at the newly wed couple. I had never seen them in my life before! I had crashed in on another couple's wedding breakfast! Most people getting married at that time in Derry went to Dublin for their honeymoon, and the time of the wedding and the duration of the reception was geared to enable the newly married couple to catch the early afternoon train to Dublin from the Great Northern Railway station in Foyle Road. The train left Derry around 2.30 p.m. – most of the guests went to the station to see the couple off. Wedding receptions were much simpler and much less costly in those times.

The morning period after Mass was normally spent attending the sick or visiting schools. I brought Holy Communion monthly to about 100/120 people in their homes in the Bogside district: these were people who were temporarily or permanently confined to the house because of age or illness, people whom I had identified during my home visitation. I also made daily visits to the dying or those who were critically ill. Ministry to the sick and dying is demanding but very fulfilling. I have always understood it as a ministry of accompaniment, endeavouring to offer spiritual support to a sick or dying person and their family during difficult and trying times and helping them to bear the burden of pain and anxiety. I consider it to be one of the great privileges of priesthood. At times, it is a very challenging ministry.

When the sick were attended, the cathedral priests visited the schools. I was chaplain to the Francis Street Schools. These were primary schools; one catered for Infants and the other for the upper end of primary education. They were located on either side of Francis Street. I was fascinated to watch and admire the expertise of good teachers, and the manner in which the learning and knowledge and personality of children developed from the day they first arrived at school to the day they left. I assisted in the preparation of children for First Confession, First Communion and Confirmation. Seasons like Christmas and Easter and the beginning and end of the school year were marked in special ways. Sister Cecilia, a Mercy Sister, was Principal of the Infants' School. She and her staff did much more than teach. They were enormously kind and generous to the large number of very deprived children among their pupils. This was done quietly and unobtrusively without in any way infringing the dignity of the child or its family.

When the school broke for lunch, it was time to go back to the parochial house where the priests usually had their lunch together. After lunch, we took a rest, read the newspaper or spent some time in prayer. Three afternoons and two evenings a week were spent in home visitation. Through this activity, I got to know the people of the Bogside very well and they came to know me. Home visitation was full of pleasant surprises. It was a regular experience to be asked by busy mothers with children to go to the shop for a message; now and again, an invitation to hold or feed the baby was extended when another child demanded attention. On one occasion an elderly lady animatedly beckoned me into her doorway and asked me could I go the bookies for her to place a bet on a horse. Her usual messenger hadn't turned up and race time was fast approaching and she had a 'certainty'. Although I cannot remember the name of the horse, I remember that the race was at Wincanton. Backing horses was a major activity in the Bogside almost every afternoon. The other great passion was football. Most men were at home in the afternoon. They would greet the children coming home from school and after school, the streets were soon filled with playing children.

Supper was at six and after supper there were various things to be done. There were meetings of various organisations like the St Vincent de Paul Society or Legion of Mary to be attended. Two evenings a week were spent on home visitation. There were evening devotions in the cathedral at various times of the year. Friday and Saturday evenings were reserved for hearing Confessions, and I usually spent a couple of evenings engaged in my activities in St Columb's Hall.

There were other evening duties such as instructing people and preparing them for reception into the Church. Many of these were members of the British or United States Navy. At that time, Derry was a big and important naval base. There were a large number of US Navy and Royal Navy personnel based in the city. The numbers were augmented from time to time by visiting naval ships and submarines. From time to time NATO exercises would take place in the Atlantic Ocean to the north or northwest of Ireland. On such occasions large numbers of ships and their crews would be in town and all would have a lively time. Apart from the naval craft and warships, there were a large number of merchant ships coming into Derry port at that time, including regular passenger sailings to and from Glasgow. A remarkable number of the United States personnel who arrived in Derry at that time as single men returned to their homeland as married men when their term of duty here was completed! There was romance in the Derry air.

A feature of life in St Eugene's at that time would be the arrival of a Derry girl with a somewhat bashful and embarrassed uniformed sailor on her arm. She would say, 'Father, I want you to turn me fella.' The first time I was confronted with that request, I didn't know precisely what service was being requested of me! I soon learned. At that time, no mixed marriages were permitted in Derry. So, if the sailor was not a member of the Catholic Church, the choices were stark for such a couple. The relationship would have to end, the marriage would have to be carried out in a registry office or the sailor would have to be instructed in the Catholic faith and received into the Church. If the latter option were chosen, I usually tried first to ascertain whether the candidate was engaging in this course of instruction knowingly and freely. In many instances, this was not the case and the process was taken no further. In many other cases, I was satisfied that he was sincere and had given careful consideration to the matter. The course of instruction lasted anything from four to six months and most of the priests in St Eugene's would have had two or three candidates at any time during those years. Whilst some of the marriages did not last, most of them subsequently turned out to be very happy and stable. I still exchange Christmas cards with a number of the couples whom I encountered in this way. Most of them live in various parts of the United States and some in Britain. Happy as many of those marriages turned out, I feel, in retrospect, that the Church put those young couples under very unjust pressure at that time.

It was not the only thing that was unfair and unjust. Single women who had children outside marriage were also treated cruelly. Parents could be quite ruthless with a daughter caught in this unfortunate situation. Society generally was not supportive or sympathetic to the single parent, at that time. I dreaded and loathed being involved in these situations. On a few occasions, thankfully not very often, I was called to a house to be confronted by such a situation. On arrival, I was told, usually by a distraught mother but sometimes by both parents, that they had just become aware that their daughter was pregnant. They had younger children at home and they did not want them or any of the neighbours to know of their daughter's dilemma. I was then asked to make arrangements for the daughter to go somewhere discreet where she and the baby could be cared for until and after childbirth. They almost always insisted that the baby be placed for adoption, or, at least, that it should not, under any circumstances, be brought back to the family home. The young woman herself was seldom consulted on these matters. It was a very difficult situation and any suggestion that the young woman might stay at home would be met with incredulity and anger. It was my practice to try to comfort and support the young mother as best I could, but usually she was so distressed and ashamed that she, too, at this stage, just wanted to get away from all the hysteria at home as quickly as possible. I felt quite inadequate in such circumstances. An order of religious Sisters would usually care for mother and child for as long as was necessary. In most cases, the

Sisters received no payment whatsoever for this from the State, the expectant mother's family or any other agency and, in my experience, looked after them with kindness and tenderness. Cruel cases have been highlighted in the media in more recent times, and I have no doubt that they existed. In a harsh society, religious Sisters often had to pick up the pieces. My experience, however, was that the expectant young single mothers placed in the care of religious Sisters received excellent and tender support and were able to pick up the threads of life afterwards although I am sure that they never forgot their child. Adoption arrangements and registration of such children were extremely slipshod at that time and were only brought into line properly in the 1970s. Efforts were made, in some cases at the direction of the natural mother's parents, to ensure that no link could be subsequently established between the adopted child and the natural mother. Thankfully, with new legislation in both the North and the Republic, it is now possible to trace most such cases, if the natural mother is willing to have her name revealed. One of the more troubling aspects of all this pain, was that one would never imagine that a man was involved; that there was a father in the background as well as the mother who was always placed in the foreground. The father of the child or the existence of such an individual was seldom mentioned. However, we must always be careful about judging issues that occurred a long time ago by the standards of today.

Once every three or four weeks, we had to take our turn for night duty. The priest on night duty covered the entire parish for night calls. Night duty in St Eugene's was interesting, to say the least. Whatever time of the night one was called out on sick calls, there would always be somebody walking or hanging about. I was convinced that a considerable number of male residents of the city lived in a different time zone than the rest of the population. They got up about 2 p.m. or whenever the first horse race would be starting and went to bed about 4 a.m. or later. I had always understood that the priest on night duty was there to be available to minister to the acutely sick and the dying. I didn't realise that Friday and Saturday nights would regularly be spent sorting out rows between drunken husbands and terrified wives. Early in my career in St

Eugene's, I spent a considerable time one night trying to push a radiogram, a rather elaborate record player and radio popular in the 1960s, in through the window of a small house whilst a drunken husband inside tried to push it back out. From time to time, we had to accommodate women and young children in the parochial house after a drunken thug of a husband had arrived home in the small hours and thrown them out. There were no women's shelters in Derry at that time. I remember on one occasion, rather nervously, going in to an intoxicated man in his kitchen during the small hours and pleading with him to let his wife and children back into the house. They had arrived earlier at the parochial house in their night attire. I got them into my car and then brought them back to their home. I left them sitting in the car outside while I went in to confront the man. When I made my way into the house, I found him sitting on a sofa, scowling. After staring at me for some time, he picked up a little kitten, which was playing around the kitchen, snapped its neck and threw it into the corner and said to me, 'You're next', colourfully decorated with expletives. I am not a hero, and I made sure that I placed myself between him and the door. Shortly after this, to my considerable relief, another man came into the house, called by the wife. Between us, we removed the drunk from the house, took away his key, and let the woman and children back into the house. I once got a call around 4 a.m. on a Sunday morning. When I arrived the lady met me at the door. She wanted to know if I thought she was well enough to go on an excursion to Bundoran later that day! When I assured her that I considered that she was extremely fit and able, she asked me could I give her the loan of five shillings to help her get through the day.

Some people sent for the priest for everything. He seemed to be the cure for all insoluble problems or else the ultimate sanction. Some parents in Derry used to say to a disobedient or rebellious child, 'I'll send for the priest for you.' It was the ultimate yellow card! I continually protested about such practices and refused to go if I perceived that the summons was sent in that context. I am sure that there are some adults today who are antipathetic to priests because of that, among other things, because a parent called a priest to the home and said 'Father, will you talk to him/her!'

There were always those who were going through a black period and contemplating suicide, people who were frightened or fearful for various reasons. They usually came to the parochial house late at night. They may have felt abandoned, alone, marginalised. There was no Samaritans organisation in those days and there were not many telephones either. In a close-knit claustrophobic society such as existed in Derry at that time, with limited privacy, anyone who stepped out of line could easily find himself or herself in real or perceived difficulties. It could be something trivial, the way one dressed, or an unusual hairstyle. It could be something more substantial like a marriage or relationship breaking down. Sometimes, people got themselves into dreadful situations of debt. It could be a sexual tendency or orientation different than the accepted norm. The feeling of fear or desperation or depression or insecurity was the same. They wanted someone to talk to, someone who would listen, a shoulder to cry on and, often, someone who would pray for them or with them. The first solution that people usually considered in such situations was to emigrate to England. It was the solution, despite pleadings to the contrary, which many opted for. I expect that it was the same in every large urban parish in Ireland at that time. Derry was no better or worse than anywhere else.

I considered it a powerful source of affirmation of priesthood that people sought out the ear or the assistance of the priest when they were troubled or distressed. I was glad to offer them a listening and sympathetic ear and whatever small comfort I could. If I was able to offer support to the people, it was nothing as compared with the inspiration and example that the people offered me. I have always had great affection and respect for the people who lived in the Bogside at that time.

CHAPTER 8

No Business Like Show Business

Bingo – concerts – pantomimes –
Abbey Theatre – friendships

About two months after arriving in St Eugene's, Bishop Farren asked me to take over the administration of St Columb's Hall, in addition to my other parish duties. St Columb's Hall was a substantial building near the city centre, built in the 1880s by the Catholic people of Derry. It consisted of a large auditorium seating about 1,000 people, a smaller Minor Hall and various other rooms and facilities. The large hall had been used as a cinema since the 1920s, but in the early 1960s the movies were having a bad time. The new phenomenon of television had drastically reduced the numbers attending the cinema. Besides, it was proving difficult to get first-run films when competing with the big multi-national cinema chains. St Columb's Hall had closed as a cinema a few months before I came to Derry. It cost a lot merely to maintain the fabric of the building. Bishop Farren asked me to organise functions there and to try to keep it viable. He told me that he had heard about my activities in this field in Castlederg.

This request was to give an added dimension of enjoyment to my years in Derry. St Columb's Hall provided a completely different challenge to St Patrick's Hall in Castlederg. It was much bigger, a theatre rather than a dancehall, and an urban environment rather than a rural environment. The activities there afforded a welcome counter-balance to the often harsh realities of pastoral ministry in the Bogside.

The building had been neglected for many years but it was a beautiful old building and it had great potential. Some activities had to be devised that would attract audiences, despite the counter-attraction of television. I talked to a number of people and sought advice how we could bring St Columb's Hall back to life. Among those I talked with were James MacCafferty and Donald O'Doherty. James was a singing teacher, a superb pianist and accompanist, choral arranger and musical genius. He taught singing to many generations of Derry children and adults and was greatly respected in the city. Donald had been associated with entertainment in Derry for many years. I also consulted with other people and drew from my previous experience in Castlederg.

I settled for a twin strategy – a series of concerts of high quality with top-class performers from Ireland and abroad, and Bingo! The more glitzy presentation of this much-slandered pastime had not reached Derry. I borrowed a few ideas on presentation from elsewhere and launched Bingo in Derry in September 1962. I was completely stunned by the response. Within a few weeks, the main auditorium in St Columb's Hall was unable to accommodate the crowds and, within a couple of months, every available space in every room in the building was occupied on two nights a week. The attendances were regularly in excess of 2,000 people. Little old ladies who had not been seen out for years attended, with their hair newly done. People dressed up for the occasion – men and women, young and old; they came from the Bogside and Waterside and from outside the city, Protestant and Catholic. This continued for years.

Twenty years later, someone who was castigating me about something or other, was running out of ideas and invective and then made the ultimate allegation, 'Aye and it was you who introduced Bingo to Derry and nearly wrecked the town!' People often criticise Bingo but they are usually people who have never played it or attended a Bingo session. In the 1960s, it certainly gave people in Derry an opportunity to get out of their homes and offered them a social outlet. They enjoyed themselves. They made new friends. There was a good package on offer. As well as the game, there was some good live musical entertainment and it constituted for many a relaxing and enjoyable night out at relatively small cost. Besides there was always the possibility of winning something. I did not witness much overspending. Most of the people who attended were conservative and prudent in their expenditure. Like everything else, people can abuse it. But on the whole, Bingo is a relatively harmless and pleasant pastime that a lot of people enjoy and many charities have hugely benefited from it.

In October 1962, a series of Sunday-night concerts was initiated, which continued for the next eight years. Considerable investment was made in stage lighting and sound systems and other equipment that would enhance optimum presentation. James MacCafferty was resident musical director, Donald O'Doherty was resident compere and Frank Carson, a young man from Belfast, was the resident comedian. Frank was booked for three shows and stayed for six or seven seasons! We also had a resident chorus and small orchestra directed by James. The concerts featured some of the biggest names in show business at that time. We had American and British entertainers as well as almost all the leading Irish performers of the time. People like Jim Reeves and Roy Orbison, Milo O'Shea and The Dubliners, The Seekers from Australia and Moira Anderson from Scotland, Val Doonican, the Clancy Brothers and Tommy Makem, classical singers like John Holmes from the Sadlers Wells Opera were all featured. We catered for a wide range of tastes. The big show on television on Sunday nights at that time was *Sunday Night at the London Palladium*. Our concerts began at the same time, eight o'clock on Sunday evening, had an unashamedly similar format and, on more than one occasion, the star who topped the bill in the television show on one Sunday, topped the bill in Derry on a subsequent Sunday. I learned that many of the big name artistes were free and anxious to have bookings on Sunday nights. It was the age of the Beatles and a very exciting time in the history of popular music and entertainment. I had an excellent agent in London who booked artistes for me and he managed to get some wonderful performers to come to Derry. Several of the artistes became my personal friends. The inclusion of local Derry or North West performers on every bill was a policy that was always adhered to. I believed that it offered good experience for promising young artists to appear on the same bill as big established stars. At the very first concert in October 1962, Phil Coulter, a young Derry pianist, appeared down the bill as a supporting act. It was one of his first ever concert appearances. Dana also performed on several occasions as a child and teenager in the Sunday night concerts. There were fifteen to twenty of these concerts each winter in the season between October and Easter. After the first series, season tickets were introduced, and more than seven hundred season tickets were made available and sold for each of the subsequent series. Scarcely any of the concerts played to an empty seat in the 1,000-seat auditorium. Almost without exception, the concerts and various stage shows in St Columb's Hall in the 1960s were sold out.

As well as concerts, there was an annual pantomime, which was staged for the three weeks after Christmas. These, too, were very successful and attracted capacity audiences. Friendships were formed that have endured down through the years and a number of couples who met through participating in the concerts or pantomimes were subsequently married. Speaking for myself, I have always treasured the long-lasting friendships that were made at that time. There are few better ways of getting to know anyone, warts and all, than to be involved with them in a theatrical production.

As well as concerts and pantomime, plays were also staged in St Columb's Hall. At my invitation, the Abbey Theatre Company from Dublin graced us with visits on two memorable occasions. They first presented *The Enemy Within* by Brian Friel in October 1962. This was Brian Friel's first play. It was about St Colmcille and set in the island of Iona. It had an all-male cast. The late Ray McAnally played the part of St Colmcille in a memorable production that was performed to full houses. It was the Abbey Theatre Company's first visit to Derry. A large number of members of the Abbey Company, directors, actors and wives of the cast members came to Derry for the first night performance. This unexpectedly led me into an embarrassing situation. After the performance, many members of the cast expressed the wish to go somewhere for a drink. Being a teetotaller and rather new to the business, I had not anticipated this. In the 1960s there were no pubs open in the Six Counties on a Sunday night; hotel bars were closed, even to guests, after 9 p.m. I didn't know where I could bring them and suddenly got the bright idea of going to a private club, known as the Derry Catholic Club. I had never been there, but I had heard about it and knew that it was open on Sunday nights. A number of cars were organised and the entire party arrived at the Catholic Club. A white-coated steward opened the door. I explained the situation to him and asked him if we could come in, and he agreed, until the first female appeared. He said, 'I'm sorry, this Club is for men only!' I didn't know what to do when, fortuitously, a member of the Club, James Doherty, appeared on the scene and said, 'Bring them all to my house.' James lived nearby and, thanks to his generous hospitality, a very good night was had by all. I made sure that I was never caught out like that again.

The Abbey Theatre Company paid us a second visit in November 1964 with Seán O'Casey's *Juno and the Paycock*. This visit occasioned a letter from Seán O'Casey to the Abbey Theatre, which Ernest Blythe, managing director of the Abbey, was very excited about, as there had been a coolness between O'Casey and the Abbey for many years. Blythe spoke at length about this letter in his curtain speech after the first night. I had an interesting correspondence with Ernest Blythe about these two visits. Those performances by the Abbey Theatre in Derry were memorable.

Derry is rightly noted for its music and musicians. Feis Doire Colmcille, held annually at Easter, and the Londonderry Feis, held a month earlier, provide wonderful platforms for young people to perform at an early age. A large percentage of children in Derry have the opportunity to perform at one or other or both of these festivals and most children with promising talent are identified at this early stage. The city has been blessed over the years with many inspiring teachers of music, dance and singing, such as the aforementioned James MacCafferty. When I first went to Derry, I remember being struck by the quality of singing at wedding receptions and other family and community celebrations. Most people knew which key they wished to sing in, and their breathing, phrasing and interpretation of songs were impressive even when they had over-indulged! I used to sit terrified on such occasions, fearing that I might be asked to sing. In contrast, many Derry people would be highly offended if they were *not* asked to perform.

The years in St Columb's Hall provided me with some of the most enjoyable experiences of my career and life-long friendships. At many times, happy though I was as a priest, I was tempted to dream of being a full-time impresario! There is great thrill and satisfaction to be derived from staging and presenting successful shows. I found it particularly exhilarating to stand on a theatre stage just before curtain-up, listening to the buzz of excited anticipation from a packed audience. Indeed there is no business like show business! As noted earlier, it was a much appreciated counter-balance to the harsh realities of the time. It was an added bonus that those years provided a handsome income for the Derry Catholic Building Fund and funds to carry out some necessary maintenance and refurbishment to St Columb's Hall itself.

CHAPTER 9

Seeds of Unrest

Education reform – university for Derry – Lockwood –
housing injustices and Derry Corporation – Housing Association –
Gaudium et Spes *– 1968 and the international scene –*
protest – civil rights and the RUC

Derry people are very conscious of their city's position as the second city of the North. During the early 1960s, the city began to feel
more and more isolated. Railway and shipping lines out of Derry
were under threat and several were closed down. The Stormont
Government made no secret of its wish to build and develop a new
city between Lurgan and Portadown, and this confirmed the view
of most Derry people that, if Unionists had their way, their city
would soon become the third city of the North.

The Catholic people of the North have always been acutely
conscious of the importance of education; they perceived it as a
most effective way out of the ghetto. The 1944 Education Act in
Britain was brought into effect here by the 1947 Education Act
(Northern Ireland). This Act transformed the Catholic community
in the North. Suddenly every young person had the opportunity to
be educated to the limit of his or her potential. Before 1947, sec-
ond- and third-level education was the preserve of those with financial means and a few others who were fortunate enough to win
scholarships. Now second-level and third-level education was open
to everyone who had the potential to avail of it, irrespective of
financial means. This changed everything.

The Catholic Church poured a huge amount of its energy and
resources into providing schools and school places so that Catholic

children could take full advantage of this new opportunity. New second-level schools, secondary intermediate schools and grammar schools sprang up all over the North in the late 1950s and 1960s. Parishes had to raise 35 per cent of the capital expenditure and a considerable share of the current expenditure and maintenance. This amounted to vast sums of money at that time. Priests and religious sisters and brothers taught in some schools and their full salaries went towards the further extension and provision of educational facilities. In earlier chapters, I outlined some of the efforts made to raise funds to provide these schools. Lay members of the Church realised that this was something really worthwhile and even those with meagre means responded most generously. There was a degree of competition between parishes to have secondary schools located within their boundaries. As a result of this over-enthusiasm, in my view, too many of these schools were built in the Derry diocese and some of them were sited in unsuitable locations. But the huge efforts and sacrifices made to provide these schools should not be underestimated. Nor should the impact of these schools on the social and political life of the North. From the late 1950s onwards, large numbers of young people began to emerge from these second-level schools and go on to third-level education.

By the mid-1960s, the first batch of these young people was graduating from the universities. Many of these young people had grown up in deprived areas and they were able to air their grievances and highlight the perceived injustices in an effective and articulate manner, which both the international media and the people living in the deprived areas could understand. They and their generation were to have a profound and radical influence on our society during the next thirty years.

With the dramatic expansion of second-level education in the North, it was obvious that university provision would have to be similarly expanded to accommodate the increasing demand for university places by the young people emerging from these new second-level schools. The North would need a second university. It was believed, indeed assumed, that even the Stormont Government could not be so arrogant as to locate such a university anywhere but in Derry. After all, Derry was the second city and it already had the nucleus of a university in Magee College. Such a decision could be the springboard for a renaissance of the city.

That feeling of confidence was further strengthened when, in 1963, the Derry Corporation made a submission in support of the location of the North's second university in Derry. Terence O'Neill was Stormont Prime Minister and he gave the impression of being less bigoted than his predecessors. As in the case of the foundation of Derry Credit Union, John Hume, the young teacher from St Columb's College was prominent in the university campaign and was eventually its leader. The four main Churches also supported Derry's case. The issue seemed to be cut and dried. Derry would be the location for the North's second university.

The Stormont Government appointed a committee, chaired by an English academic, Sir John Lockwood, to study the entire university issue, and asked the committee to report on it. In early 1965, leaks suggested that the Lockwood Committee was going to recommend somewhere other than Derry for the second university. There was a packed public meeting in the Guildhall in early February 1965. It was my first time ever at a public meeting of that nature. Both sides of the Derry community were in there in force and all were at one. There were passionate speeches. There was an intense feeling of disbelief that Lockwood could come to the conclusion he reportedly had reached. A University for Derry Committee was formed and this committee decided to organise a motorcade to parliament buildings at Stormont on Thursday 18 February. Thursday was the half-day for business in Derry at that time. Most shops and offices closed at lunchtime. More than 20,000 people and most of the cars in the city made that journey over Glenshane Pass. It was my first time at Stormont. The huge building on the hillside with the long drive leading up to it was impressive. Equally impressive on that day was the sheer number of people gathered before the Parliament building. It was a very powerful protest, but the allegedly liberal Terence O'Neill rejected it.

After some toing and froing, the Stormont Government formally accepted the Lockwood Report and decided to site the North's second university in Coleraine. It subsequently emerged that several prominent Unionist figures, leading citizens in Derry, had not supported the city as the site for the second university. They were described as 'the faceless men'. There was outrage among much of the Derry population. The die had been cast. Things would never be the same again.

There was a concatenation of significant events both locally and internationally in the mid-1960s. BBC television was first introduced into the Six Counties in the late 1950s. Ulster Television came a few years later. By the mid-1960s there was a television set in almost every home in Derry, however deprived. Television made a considerable social and political impact. People in deprived urban areas became aware that twenty people sharing a four-roomed house without running water was not the norm elsewhere in the Western world. They also became aware of the manner in which people in other countries were countering State injustice. Suddenly there was a new window on the world.

The mid-1960s was a traumatic period for the Catholic Church. The Second Vatican Council turned out to be a major watershed for the Church. It was a time of great hope for many of us and of considerable apprehension for others. Those of us who studied our theology prior to the Council suddenly experienced things being turned upside down. The use of Latin in the liturgy, upon which so much emphasis had been placed, was being phased out. The liturgy of the Mass was being dramatically changed. In the wake of the Council, there was widespread speculation that the Church's regulations on priestly celibacy were about to be reviewed. It was a very unsettling time for priests. We had grown up with the idea of an unchanging, unchangeable Church and suddenly everything was changing or being reviewed. Feelings of insecurity were widespread. Those who wished for progress were discontent because things were not moving quickly enough; and those who wished that everything should stay as it was, felt that things were moving out of control. The reality was that changes were gradually embraced and introduced and, generally, found to be good. My view is that, by and large, the pace of change in the Irish Church at that time was reasonably well judged. Changes were introduced gradually but surely. There were no major divisions created in the Irish Church at that time. The situation was quite different in many other countries.

Nevertheless, it was a very unsettling time for priests and people, particularly for younger priests. Virtually everything had to be unlearned and learned again in a new context.

The idea of a Housing Association was the brainchild of a young Irish priest who was working with Irish emigrants in London. His name was Father Eamonn Casey, subsequently Bishop Eamonn Casey. He was a Maynooth classmate and friend of Father Tony Mulvey. He came to Derry at Father Mulvey's invitation and spoke to various people about the idea. As a result, in 1965, Father Tony, with John Hume and Paddy Doherty and others, founded the Derry Housing Association. This Association had, as its primary aim, a determination to do something of a practical nature about the dreadful housing conditions in which many Derry people were forced to live. On the one hand, there was gross overcrowding in primitive housing conditions. This was the direct result of political discrimination and a vital element in the effort to retain power in the hands of the Unionists. It was a cynical, cruel and uncaring political policy. On the other hand, there were flats being let at exorbitant rents. Young newly married Catholic couples experienced enormous difficulty in acquiring or affording accommodation of any kind. The Derry Housing Association initially purchased properties and converted them into flats and rented them at a reasonable rate. Then, within a few years, the Association succeeded in acquiring land and building houses outside the designated areas, thereby threatening the Corporation's stranglehold on house building and the allocation of houses. The Association repeatedly highlighted the immorality and injustice of the Derry Corporation's housing policies. The Corporation did its utmost to make life difficult for the Association, but they were meeting a more determined, able and intelligent group of individuals than they had ever encountered before.

One of the most notable documents to emanate from the Second Vatican Council was the Pastoral Constitution on the Church in the Modern World, *Gaudium et Spes*. It highlighted the social teaching of the Church and the rights and responsibilities of individuals and societies in the profoundly changed world that existed twenty years after World War Two. Right at the beginning of the document, the dignity of the human person is emphasised and it goes on to teach about the responsibilities of the Church and individuals within the Church towards society. This document was discussed and studied in detail at two of our Conferences of Priests in Derry in 1966 or 1967. It had a profound impact on all of us who ministered among people who had been deprived of their dignity and their rights and it fuelled our desire to do something to improve the living conditions of the people. Up until then, most priests were reluctant to rock the political boat. But this document called on all members of the Church to challenge injustice, especially when people were being denied their rights and dignity. We were challenged to do this in a non-violent manner. Few of us, however, were very sure about how we could go about it. Everyone was a little fearful about stepping out of line.

On a bleak Monday in January 1967, the spectre of ever-increasing male unemployment became a reality. There was a dispute between management and workers at the Monarch Electric factory in Bligh's Lane in Derry. Monarch Electric, manufacturing record players, was the major employer of men on the west bank of the city. Workers returning after a break found themselves locked out. About 850 workers, mostly male, were told that the factories were closed permanently. Few enough men in the Bogside were in full-time employment. And now this small number became even fewer. The closure of Monarch Electric had a devastating impact on the morale of the community. In its wake, emigration from Derry intensified, and I recall an atmosphere of depression and almost despair in many homes and in many families.

1968 was a momentous year on the international scene. The Vietnam War was at its height. In January, the Tet offensive by the Viet Cong, perhaps the turning point of that dreadful conflict, took place. In March, Martin Luther King, the American civil rights leader, was murdered in Memphis, Tennessee. Two weeks later, Enoch Powell, with impeccable timing, chose to make his infamous 'rivers of blood' speech on race relations in England. In May, the students' uprising took place in Paris and continued for most of the month, causing the National Assembly to be dissolved and threatening the presidency of Charles de Gaulle. In June, Senator Bobby Kennedy was murdered in Los Angeles, whilst campaigning in the California primary election. In July, Pope Paul VI published an encyclical entitled *Humanae Vitae*, which was to generate more controversy and discussion and pain than possibly any other papal document in the modern history of the Church. In August, the Red Army tanks rumbled into Prague to crush the quest for freedom of the Czech people in a ruthless manner. It was a year during which people lost whatever inhibitions they might have had about protesting against the status quo. All of these events received worldwide media coverage. But most people in the world were still unaware of Northern Ireland and its problems.

However, the victims of the various injustices, which underpinned the very existence of Northern Ireland, were very aware of what was happening in other parts of the world. Catholic people, Irish Nationalists, who suffered cruel discrimination in the allocation of housing and in employment, watched these events in faraway places on television with particular interest. They were also keenly aware that few people outside Northern Ireland knew of or were interested in their problems. The perceived lack of concern or interest from their compatriots across the Irish border was particularly frustrating.

People here became conscious of the fact that unless we could somehow get our problems highlighted on the international media, especially television, like Martin Luther King's people in the United States or the students in Paris or the Czech people in Prague, that nobody outside Northern Ireland would show much interest. Many people noted that, although they were countered by violence, the protests of the Civil Rights Movement in the United States were non-violent. The power of non-violent protest became more and more obvious. The moral high ground of non-violence was clearly a very powerful position from which to launch any campaign. In Ireland, protest against the establishment had historically been realised in the context of violent armed struggle. The time had come to approach this problem in a different way.

Until then, only a handful of Westminster MPs showed any interest in Northern Ireland issues, notably Stan Orme and Paul

Rose and a few other Labour MPs. Gerry Fitt, the West Belfast MP, had made them aware of our problems. Northern Ireland, however, was still not considered newsworthy by the international media, nor was it considered worthy of concern or of serious debate by either the Westminster Government or the Government in Dublin. The rule of the Stormont Government was rubber-stamped. There are few things more frustrating and infuriating for a victim of injustice than the realisation that nobody seems to care. It was considered essential, if our problems were to be resolved, to make people outside Northern Ireland aware of these problems and then to get them interested in helping us to resolve them.

Somebody who had no doubts or inhibitions about the way ahead was Eamonn McCann, a young political activist from the Bogside. He was able, intelligent, witty, very articulate and a powerful public speaker. Eamonn stood in a number of elections but he never succeeded in being elected. He assembled a group of young like-minded, left-leaning, bright people around him. They produced some of the most original and best political posters and slogans ever seen in Derry. They created a new political vocabulary. McCann's influence in the evolving situation should not be underestimated. With others, he founded the Derry Housing Action Committee. Right from the beginning, Eamonn McCann was more aware of the influence and power of the media than many of his contemporaries. The Derry Housing Action Committee began a series of high-profile protests at Corporation meetings and on the streets highlighting the injustices of the housing situation in Derry.

Around the same time, NICRA, the Northern Ireland Civil Rights Association, came into being. NICRA did not have a significant presence in Derry in early 1968. They held meetings in Belfast and Armagh. In June 1968, Austin Currie from East Tyrone, the youngest MP in Stormont, was enraged by the allocation of a house to a single Unionist lady, aged 19, in Caledon, County Tyrone. She was the secretary to a local Unionist big-shot. She had been allocated the house, despite the fact that there were Catholic families with young children desperately in need of housing on the waiting list. Austin Currie squatted into the house and stayed there for some time before being evicted by the RUC. Austin Currie's action, however, received substantial media coverage and served to highlight powerfully and effectively the shameless political corruption that permeated the North at that time.

It was from this background that the idea of Civil Rights demonstrations or marches took root. Whilst there had been a large Civil Rights march in County Tyrone from Coalisland to Dungannon and some other small demonstrations elsewhere, there had not been protest marches of any great significance in Derry prior to October 1968. A march in Derry was planned for Saturday, 5 October. The organisers were a somewhat eclectic mixture; as well as the Northern Ireland Civil Rights Association, there were also some radicals like Eamonn McCann and his Derry Housing Action Committee, some veteran Republicans like Sean Keenan. Supporters included John Hume and the local Stormont MP and the veteran leader of the Nationalist Party, Eddie McAteer. There was no sinister plot or cunning master-plan to exploit the march as an instrument in overthrowing the northern state, as some commentators would have it. The leadership was not made up of 'reds under the bed' or the IRA. The civil rights demonstrators merely sought to highlight injustice and seek reforms. They highlighted housing, employment and local government as areas of concern.

The 5 October march planned to start at Waterside Railway Station and to proceed via Duke Street, Craigavon Bridge, Carlisle Road and Ferryquay Street to the Diamond, where there would be a meeting with speeches. The fact that the march passed inside the city walls and that a meeting was planned in the Diamond was too much for the local Unionists. They regarded the centre of the city as their exclusive preserve. They used their influence to have the parade banned by William Craig, the Stormont Minister for Home Affairs. Craig duly obliged.

NICRA decided to oppose the ban. The Catholic community in Derry was not sympathetic to mass demonstrations at that time. There was no culture of protest here. Originally very few local people planned to attend the march on Saturday, 5 October. The ban possibly doubled the numbers taking part. However, in the event, a relatively small number of people actually took part in the march, hundreds rather than thousands. As is the case with all historic events, many more claim to have been present there than actually attended. I have to confess that although I thought about attending the march, I chose instead to do what I did on most Saturday afternoons at that time, attend a football match!

The RUC enforced the Stormont ban with enthusiasm and extreme brutality. Despite the fact that, apart from a few chants of 'Sieg Heil', no violence was used against them, the police used their batons with rare abandon and obvious enjoyment, attacking many people, including Gerry Fitt and the elderly Eddie McAteer. A large number of the marchers were injured and almost all of them were drenched by water from water cannons. The police, including senior officers, were patently out of control. One senior police officer was even seen on television hunting down a terrified young man with his blackthorn stick and striking him on the ground. A water-cannon vehicle was driven wildly around. The batons continued to be used. All of these events were covered graphically by one television cameraman from RTÉ, the late Gay O'Brien, and subsequently received widespread coverage here and abroad.

As news spread in Derry of the events in Duke Street, local people were infuriated. As on every Saturday night, I spent from 6.30 until 10 p.m. in the confessional. When I was finished and came over to the parochial house, the civil rights march and the actions of the police were the only topic of conversation. The pictures on the television news were dramatic and had a powerful impact.

About 11.30 p.m., I was having a cup of tea with the other priests in the parochial house. People came to the door to tell us that there were disturbances around the edges of the Bogside. They asked that some priests go there to try to restore order. It was my first time to experience a riotous situation. It was disorganised chaos fuelled by anger. Young people were very angry about the events in the afternoon. When we reached the scene, the young people were about to break up and go home. They had made their point. After we had a short chat with them, they dispersed.

But things were never to be the same again. Everything had changed.

The genie was out of the bottle.

1 Tom & Susan Daly 1933.

2 1939.

3 As first year seminarian 1951/2.

4 First Year Class, Irish College, Rome, 1951/2. *Standing* (l. to r.)
Christy McLaughlin, Tom Egan, Seamus Casey, Martin O'Grady,
Niall Molloy. *Sitting* (l. to r.) Michael Walsh, John Hanly,
Tommy O'Reilly, Seamus Creighton, author.

5 Ordination to Diaconate, Basilica of St John Lateran, Rome, 1956,
Father Dominic Conway, Spiritual Director, Irish College, centre.

6 Ordination to Diaconate, Basilica of St John Lateran, Rome, 1956.

7 (*avbove*) Ordination to Priesthood, St Patrick's Church,
Belleek, 16 March 1957, with mother and family (l. to r.)
Marion, Anne, Dympna and Tom.
8 (*below*) Ordination to Priesthood, 16 March 1957, with
Bishop Neil Farren, clergy and altar servers.

9 (*above*) Father Michael McMenamin, parish priest in Castlederg.
10 (*below*) Father McMenamin and Bishop Neil Farren.

11 A wedding in St Eugene's Cathedral, Derry. Owen Dawson and Patricia MacCafferty, October 1970. Patricia's photograph was used extensively by Aer Lingus at the time in their promotional campaigns.

12 (*above*) Speaking at the final performance of a pantomime in
St Columb's Hall, Derry, 1966.
13 (*below*) Presentation to group in St Columb's Hall, late 1960s, includes
Eamon Gallagher, Donald O'Doherty, author, Eddie Friel.

14 St Eugene's Cathedral.

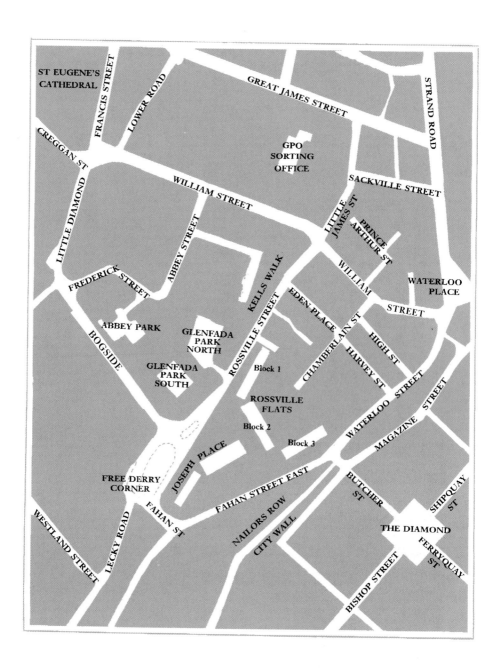

15 Map of the Bogside area in the early 70s.

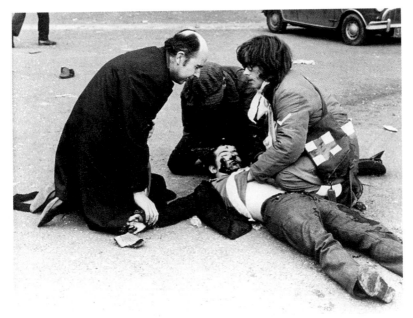

16 (*above*) Ministering to Jackie Duddy, with Charles Glenn
and Liam Bradley in car park of Rossville Flats, Derry,
Bloody Sunday, 30 January 1972.
17 (*below*) 13 Coffins of the Bloody Sunday victims in the sanctuary
of St Mary's Church, Creggan, Derry, on the night of
Tuesday, 1 February 1972.

18 Audience with Pope Paul VI, March 1972.

19 Cartoon by Terry Willers, presented by colleagues in RTÉ Religious Affairs Department on appointment as Bishop, February 1974.

20 Family group after Ordination as Bishop of Derry, 31 March 1974.

CHAPTER 10

Marches and Protests

Derry Citizens Action Committee – We shall overcome –
an ecumenical vigil – the impossible happens –
'Ulster stands at the crossroads'

Photographs and stories of the events in Derry were on the front pages of all the newspapers on the morning of Sunday, 6 October 1968. The events in Duke Street formed the only topic of conversation among the crowds chatting after Masses outside the cathedral on that Sunday morning. Such events might be expected elsewhere, but were something quite dramatic, sensational and frightening in Ireland. I had booked the folk group, The Dubliners, to appear as top of the bill at a concert in St Columb's Hall that night. They were at the height of their popularity and the concert was completely sold out. Their manager called me early on Sunday expressing anxiety for the safety of the performers travelling to Derry. He hinted, not very subtly, that it might be best to cancel or postpone the concert. I would not agree to that. The concert must go on as planned.

On that Sunday afternoon, there were more disturbances, this time in the city centre. A few shop windows were smashed. Skirmishes between the police and rioters went on until late at night. The Dubliners, who were extremely nervous, performed to a full house in St Columb's Hall. They tailored their repertoire to suit the circumstances. They gave a great performance but somewhat more restrained than usual. After the concert, I went back to the streets, trying, with others, to bring calm. There were quite a number of injuries, none serious. A number of properties in the city centre suffered damage, largely of a superficial nature. The rioting, however, was more intense and widespread than it had been the previous night.

When Monday came, it was obvious that the events and the pictures of the events in Duke Street had generated concern in Dublin and Westminster, as well as Stormont. William Craig denounced the Civil Rights march, suggesting that it was an IRA ploy. He praised the actions of the RUC and denied that they had been brutal. British Prime Minister, Harold Wilson, summoned the Stormont Prime Minister, Terence O'Neill, to London to discuss the situation. Derry people in the Nationalist areas of the city were quietly satisfied that their problems were, at last, being noticed and acknowledged by people in high places. Their problems were now on the front pages, like those of the American blacks and the people in Czechoslovakia.

During the week after the events of 5 October 1968, Derry was a centre of frenzied activity. It was a situation that demanded leadership if all this frustration was to be channelled and harnessed in a positive manner. A meeting attended by representatives of many organisations in Derry took place in the City Hotel on Wednesday 9 October. As a consequence, a group, which described itself as the Derry Citizens Action Committee (DCAC), was formed. This group was to have a powerful influence on events in the coming year. The members of the committee were as follows: Ivan Cooper (chairman); John Hume (vice-chairman); Michael Canavan; Claud Wilton; John Patton; Paddy L. Doherty; Paul Grace; Billy Kelsall; Campbell Austin; Frank O'Doherty; Eamonn Melaugh; Willie Breslin; James Doherty; Dermot McClenaghan; Brendan Hinds; John White. Most members of the committee were relatively young. There were a few business people, teachers, workers and unemployed people. Significantly, several of the members were Protestant. Eamonn McCann chaired the meeting at which the DCAC came into being, but would not accept membership of the committee. He thought that it was too conservative. He described it, rather unfairly, as 'middle class, middle aged and middle of the road'. He seemed unable to conceive of any role for what he described as 'middle-class people' in the civil rights campaign.

On Saturday, 19 October, the DCAC organised a mass sit-down protest in Guildhall Square. This led to the resignation of Campbell Austin from the committee; he could not agree to this type of demonstration. Thousands of people, however, took part in the sit-down on a wet and dreary afternoon. It was my first personal experience of a civil rights protest. My lasting memory of that occasion is hearing a few people in the crowd tentatively begin to sing the American Civil Rights anthem 'We Shall Overcome', and gradually the singing being taken up by more and more people, and soon the entire square was enveloped in song. It was a very powerful and moving moment. There were several speakers who explained the plans of DCAC. Claud Wilton, a Protestant member of the DCAC, addressed the crowd and made the most memorable speech of the afternoon. Claud was a much-loved and respected figure in Derry, part of Derry folklore. He was a solicitor, an able sportsman in his youth and a friend of the poor. Among other things he said, 'The time has come for people of my religion with courage to stand up and be counted. If we stand together we can make our beloved city a place of which we shall all be proud. Despite bans and Rachmanism,* right is on our side.' His speech was greeted with thunderous applause. There were no problems at the meeting. The RUC were not visible to the demonstrators and there were no scenes of confrontation or violence. The demonstration was a triumph for the DCAC. They had channelled the people's frustration in a positive, effective and non-violent manner.

On Saturday, 2 November, the DCAC asserted their right to march peacefully by walking the original 5 October route, from the Waterside Railway Station to the Diamond in the city centre. Thousands took part. There was a token counter-demonstration by Loyalist groups. The march passed off peacefully. The clear message was that the RUC was the primary reason and source for the violence on 5 October. If civil rights marches were left alone, they would be orderly and there would be no violence.

---

* Rachman was a notorious London landlord who charged his tenants exorbitant rents for substandard accommodation. Such nefarious activity became known as Rachmanism.

All the while, more and more interest was being generated in the political problems here. Journalists and television news crews from many countries began to arrive and to take an interest in the Northern Irish situation and report on it. The Stormont Orange Curtain was being penetrated effectively for the first time.

The DCAC announced a major march in Derry for Saturday, 16 November. Once again William Craig banned it and, into the bargain, banned all other non-customary parades or processions in Derry for a month. This would have meant that the Apprentice Boys' Lundy's Day demonstration could take place in December, but the Nationalists could not have their Civil Rights march. The DCAC decided to defy the ban. The banning of the march infuriated people. There was considerable fear in the community.

Representatives of the various mainstream Churches and others in the city interceded with Terence O'Neill to have the ban revoked, but O'Neill refused to take any action. Outside the North, in my view, Terence O'Neill was much over-rated as Stormont Prime Minister. His record would suggest that he was as partial as many of his colleagues when the chips were really down. Whilst he may not have had much scope for movement, he was not, in my view, the liberal he purported to be. The Churches responded to the fears of the people and the refusal to remove the ban by organising an all-night vigil in both of the city's cathedrals on the night before the march. This was a remarkable and unprecedented event. Both cathedrals remained open from 10 p.m. until 6 a.m. St Columb's Cathedral and St Eugene's Cathedral received large crowds throughout the night. The prominent figures in DCAC came to each cathedral. Many Derry people stayed up all night. The sound of footsteps echoed in the streets around both cathedrals in the small hours of the still, dark and chilly night. Protestants and Catholics visited the two cathedrals. There was a short Prayer Service each hour on the hour in each cathedral. It was my first ever visit to St Columb's Cathedral and it was the first public act of ecumenical worship in the city. Many people felt awkward about it. Crowds of people genuflected on entering St Columb's Cathedral and the quiet rattle of Rosary beads was clearly audible. Whatever about the niceties, people derived great comfort from this first exercise in public ecumenism.

The Church of Ireland demonstrated great courage. Some days later I wrote to Bishop Charles Tyndall congratulating him on his courage. I came to know him through our common interest in music and theatre. He replied on 24 November as follows:

> My dear Father Daly
>
> I am very thankful for your letter and I was deeply moved at the support you gave us in the Cathedral. Whatever happens one feels that a Presence was with us that night. Indeed we must all pray for the full potential of happiness, prosperity and Christian charity. It is something rather wonderful to feel a transcending power of unity in this matter.

Whilst there was tangibly a Presence with us, there was also an underlying fear and tension throughout that cold, dry night. Nobody was quite sure what the morrow would bring.

A massive crowd attended the march on the afternoon of Saturday 16 November. The Cameron Report,* which covered this period, estimated that at least 15,000 people took part in the march. The crowds were optimistic and determined. Most people walked from the city centre to the assembly point at the Waterside Railway Station. The spirit was good humoured. The sheer numbers of people walking across Craigavon Bridge reassured everyone. The crowd encompassed all ages and classes and there was a substantial sprinkling of Protestant people there as well. Nobody was in any doubt about the justice or the reason for the march or the injustice of the banning of the march. The RUC informed the assembled crowds by loud hailer that the march was banned. A spokesman for the DCAC responded, amongst cheers, that the march would go ahead. There was a huge media presence to cover the event. The police, who were there in great numbers, formed a cordon and set up barricades on the west end of Craigavon Bridge. The march set off and soon the whole length of the bridge was filled with marchers

---

* *Disturbances in Northern Ireland. Report of the Commission appointed by the Governor of Northern Ireland* (HMSO, Belfast, 1969).

singing their civil rights anthems and chanting. It was heady stuff. There was a token breach of the police barricade by some of the DCAC leaders, and gradually the sheer numbers of the crowd swept the RUC to one side and poured through the police lines. Loyalists stoned the marchers at various points, but over the next thirty minutes the crowd, all 15,000 of them, had made their way by various routes to the Diamond. The police, showing good sense for once, pulled back. Craig's ban was irrelevant. There are two excerpts of speeches, which I still remember from that day. The first was from Finbarr O'Doherty, a Civil Rights spokesman, who announced that, 'he was from a long line of butchers but he never minced his words!' and John Hume invited Craig to arrest all those who had taken part in the illegal march. It was obviously not an occasion for profound political oratory, analysis or ideas, more an occasion for dramatic political gestures and action, and in front of the world's press. People did not want to leave the area. The atmosphere was festive. It became a celebration rather than a demonstration. People stood around excitedly chatting in groups until the late evening. They were satisfied that they had made their point, and made it effectively.

On the Monday and Tuesday afterwards, there were spontaneous marches by all kinds of groups: factory workers downed tools and marched, dockers marched, the unemployed marched, and the women marched. All of these protests were illegal but all of them proceeded. The marches were short and peaceful but a very powerful expression of the frustration and anger of the people.

However, the situation was threatening to get out of hand. There were marches taking place all over the centre of the city at all times of the day. The message was being delivered loudly and clearly to William Craig. The DCAC appealed for an end to unplanned marches.

Then on the following Friday, 22 November, the big news came. The seemingly impossible happened. Terence O'Neill, obviously after intolerable pressure from Westminster, announced a five-point reform programme:

1. A points scheme for housing.

2. The appointment of an Ombudsman.
3. The abolition of the company vote in local government elections.
4. A review of the Special Powers Act.
5. The setting up of the Londonderry Development Commission to replace the old Derry Corporation.

This was stunning news. Virtually all of the main civil rights demands had been met in one fell swoop. It was more than anyone could have expected. The corrupt Derry Corporation was dumped, as was the business vote. The housing allocation system was to be radically reformed.

On Monday, 9 December, Terence O'Neill made his 'Ulster stands at the crossroads' speech on television. He explained to Unionists that Harold Wilson, the British Prime Minister, had made it 'absolutely clear that if we did not face up to our problems, the Westminster Parliament might well decide to act over our heads'. The following day William Craig said that the financial pressure from Westminster was blackmail, which a strong Unionist Party would not tolerate. O'Neill asked him to resign as Minister of Home Affairs, which he did. There were few tears shed over his disappearance in Nationalist circles. But, in a perverse way, he was the person who made the progress of the past few months possible!

1968 was a truly memorable year. It is often forgotten and should be emphasised that the Civil Rights Movement ultimately achieved all of its objectives and achieved them through non-violent mass popular protest and the highlighting of injustices. Local government in Northern Ireland was reformed. The Derry Corp-oration was prorogued. The construction and allocation of public housing was taken out of the hands of local government and made the responsibility of an independent statutory body. Housing was subsequently allocated on the basis of need, rather than political patronage.

CHAPTER 11

Burntollet and Its Aftermath

Students on the march – Paisley holds a rally in the Guildhall –
RUC invade St Columb's Wells – redevelopment in the Bogside –
a dramatic election – Sammy Devenney

Christmas 1968 and New Year 1969 was a strange time. It was a restrained celebration. People in Derry looked back with a sense of achievement and looked forward with a degree of concern. The civil rights marches, the civic disturbances and O'Neill's speech were the main topics of conversation in the homes I visited in the Bogside over the Christmas period. I went to visit my mother briefly in Belleek after Christmas. Down in tranquil Fermanagh, there was little indication of the turbulent events in Derry. For the first time in many years, there was no pantomime in St Columb's Hall. It had to be cancelled. It would have been irresponsible to ask young people to come out to attend rehearsals in the prevailing tense atmosphere. There were special prayers for peace in all churches in the diocese on 1 January. There was a large congregation for a New Year Vigil and Midnight Mass in St Eugene's Cathedral.

Many people in Derry, including many members of the DCAC, felt that the civil rights marches had made their point and that there should be a cooling-off period. However, a few days before Christmas a group of students at Queen's University in Belfast, styling themselves as People's Democracy, announced that they were planning to have a civil rights march from Derry to Belfast, beginning on Wednesday, 1 January 1969. Like many others, I was not happy about the announcement. I have to admit that my initial reaction was that the proposed march was simply providing an opportunity for a group of students to have a bit of craic during the Christmas holidays and, as a bonus, to get in on the civil rights 'act'. I expected that it would be banned in any case. I was wrong on all counts.

The People's Democracy, which came into being during October 1968, consisted, in the main, of intelligent, politically committed young people, many of whom were to distinguish themselves in various fields in later life. Some, but not all of them, were Young Socialists. Planning and organisation were not their strong suits, but they were not lacking in courage or commitment. Their proposed march from Belfast to Derry was not banned and it set out from Belfast as scheduled on New Year's Day 1969.

During the first three days of their march from Belfast to Derry, the students were attacked and harassed by various groups of Loyalists at various predictable places along the route. They were diverted here and there but, by and large, the march was free of serious incident. On the night of Friday, 3 January, the marchers reached the village of Claudy. They planned to stay there overnight before the last stage of their journey to Derry, about eight miles away. The march had been receiving extensive media coverage.

As the group of marchers was resting in Claudy, Ian Paisley was holding a meeting for his followers in the Guildhall in the heart of Derry city. As the word spread that Paisley was holding a meeting, crowds of people began to assemble in Guildhall Square. In the highly charged atmosphere of that time, it did not take people very long to come to the conclusion that Paisley was organising his own 'welcome' for the student marchers. He and his followers had confronted civil rights marchers in many places and organised counter-demonstrations in the previous months. One of his most ardent henchmen at that period was a fanatic called Major Bunting. It became known that he was among those assembled in the Guildhall. Regular reports or rumours percolated to the gathering crowd outside in the square. As time went on, people emerging from pubs some of whom were the worse for drink joined the crowd. There were people coming home from the cinemas and Bingo and other social activities. There were always large numbers of people socialising in the centre of town on Friday nights. There were relatively few taxis in service in the city then. Guildhall Square was the departure point for buses to all the outlying areas. The last buses left around 11 p.m. As a result, the square was particularly crowded at that time. Only the prudent and timid went home on that Friday night. Those who were more curious stayed. The crowd quickly built up. The RUC were there in force standing by. There was also the somewhat incongruous sight of local people in evening dress and all their finery on their way to a dinner dance in the nearby City Hotel. They mingled with the spectators waiting to see what would happen. A large cohort of media who were covering the march was staying in the City Hotel. The journalists, photographers and camera crews were also waiting to see what would happen. A fairly lethal cocktail was being created. John Hume and some of the civil rights stewards arrived on the scene and tried to cool things down, but to little avail. I went there from nearby St Columb's Hall and joined the stewards in their efforts. But tempers were too high at this stage. Some rioting and stone throwing broke out between rival factions. Major Bunting's car was identified by the mob and set on fire to the accompaniment of raucous cheering. A few stones were thrown at windows in the Guildhall. Then Paisley's audience in the Guildhall, understandably fearful and armed with chairs and any other improvised weapons they could acquire, suddenly charged out of the main door into the square. The police tried to offer them cover. There was a fierce confrontation for a few minutes; fortunately there were few injuries. The burning of Bunting's car served to defuse the anger of the crowd. It was the first time that I witnessed a violent sectarian confrontation with my own eyes. It was not a pleasant sight. The ugly sectarian atmosphere that was prevalent that Friday night on both sides did not bode well for the following day.

On Saturday, 4 January, Bunting and a large number of his cohorts attacked the People's Democracy marchers at Burntollet Bridge. Burntollet Bridge was on the main road from Claudy to Derry, the main Belfast to Derry road. (The original bridge is bypassed now and a new bridge was built about twenty years ago, but the original bridge is still there.) A number of the students were quite viciously beaten and injured but they continued their journey to Derry. Meanwhile, stories were circulating in Derry about the events at Burntollet. Some people decided to travel out there to join the marchers, others awaited them in Guildhall Square. There were further attacks on the marchers by Loyalists in the Waterside area of Derry. When the marchers arrived in Foyle Street and approached the Guildhall, they were greeted and applauded by large numbers of people. Some of the marchers were bloodied. My lasting memory of that afternoon is Bernadette Devlin's speech. I had heard of her, but it was the first time I saw her in person. She was a tiny, dynamic figure and a captivating and articulate public speaker. After the speeches had ended, people gathered in small groups and discussed the events of the past twenty-four hours. I do not recall any rioting or disorder at this juncture. However, everyone was agreed that the local situation had become more polarised than ever before. It was not a good twenty-four hours for people with moderate views and worse was to come.

In the early hours of Sunday morning, 5 January, RUC officers in uniform, without any provocation whatsoever, invaded the St Columb's Wells area of the Bogside. They smashed many windows and doors, beat up local residents and terrorised the people of the area, many of whom were elderly. It was an outrageous attack accompanied by loud and ugly and repeated sectarian taunts. As was to be the case in similar and even more serious offences perpetrated by the RUC in the years to come, no individual or group of individuals was made amenable for this disgraceful attack on defenceless people. People coming to Mass in St Eugene's that Sunday morning were furious at what had happened. These events, allied to the events of the previous forty-eight hours, caused people in their thousands to attend a meeting in the Bogside that afternoon. John Hume and Ivan Cooper were aware of the highly inflammable atmosphere and tried to cool things down. They led a procession down to the nearby RUC headquarters in Strand Road to deliver a message there, protesting at the events of the previous night, and then led them back again to the Bogside, appealing that there should be no violence. Despite their pleas, there was some rioting and sporadic violent confrontations between young people and the RUC in the Fahan Street area. But it was not on the scale that it might have been, thanks to the appeals and leadership of Hume and others.

On Monday 6 January, a holyday, the feast of the Epiphany, a statement from Bishop Farren was read out at all Masses in Derry. It stated:

> I ask you in making your legitimate protests to continue to act with the dignity and restraint, which you have exercised in the last few months.

> I will ask the civil authorities to consider the validity of the protests that have been offered, whether about civil rights in general or the abuse of authority in particular.

After the events in October and November, the Nationalist community in Derry did not hold the RUC in high esteem. They had carried out their duties in a clearly partisan manner. Generally speaking, there was, up until then, no deep animosity towards the police. However, after the events of 4/5 January, attitudes changed radically. The RUC, to this day, have never succeeded in gaining the trust and respect of many in the Nationalist community in Derry.

By early 1969, many of the liturgical changes proposed by the Second Vatican Council were being introduced. The Holy Week liturgies were radically changed. I was saddened that the beautiful atmospheric Tenebrae liturgy of the early days of Holy Week was completely dropped. Tenebrae in St Eugene's was always particularly beautiful and an ideal preparation for the ceremonies later in the week. By and large, I welcomed the liturgical renewal, but it was a major adjustment ten years into priesthood to unlearn virtually all that had been learned

All the other pastoral duties continued and I enjoyed them as much as I ever did. I particularly enjoyed visiting the homes and being with the people in their good days and bad. During those years, a major housing construction scheme was taking place in the Bogside. Even more people were being squeezed into the area by the construction of huge blocks of multi-storey flats on Rossville

Street in the late 1960s. Some of the old streets were being demolished and disappearing. Locals described the activity as 'the Redevelopment'. The plan was to house more people in the area by building vertically rather than horizontally. There was a political purpose in this. But, to be fair, a lot of people living in the Bogside did not wish to be re-housed outside the area either. The Bogside was very convenient to the city centre and to the factories, and shops; families had lived there for many generations. But in addition to building new housing, the redevelopment was also wiping out longstanding communities. Old streets like the Bogside itself, and places like Walker's Square, Nailor's Row, Adam's Close and Foxes Corner were all being demolished. Old and familiar neighbourhoods were being dismantled. People were being moved from small houses, which were almost a century old and unfit for human inhabitation, into flats in a multi-storey environment. Initially people were delighted with the new accommodation and especially with the hot and cold running water and other facilities, which they had not had before. For many families, it was the first time that they had exclusive tenancy of a property for themselves and their children. Many of them had previously been obliged to live with in-laws or parents. Most of the flats were quite beautifully and tastefully furnished and decorated. Tenants were, however, obliged to live in very close proximity with other occupants and the dividing walls were thin and certainly not soundproof. A small, insignificant family row could be heard in three or four adjacent units. There was little privacy. Shortly after the flats were opened, I was called one night to curb the enthusiasm of a budding Benny Goodman who chose to practise his clarinet at 2 a.m. His musical gifts were not greatly appreciated by neighbours over a wide area. Then after a few months, the lifts began to break down, forcing young mothers to try to manage prams and their small children up long flights of stairs and confining elderly people to their flats. Despite the best efforts of tenants, the stairwells and other enclosed public areas of the flats attracted crowds of young people late at night, and rowdy, noisy and drunken behaviour resulting in vandalism was often the consequence. I visited each flat shortly after the family or individual moved in and blessed their home. Almost without exception, the families were initially delighted with their new homes.

Visitation of the sick and elderly continued. It was quite a task keeping up with people when their homes were demolished and they were allocated new accommodation. As a lot of old neighbourhoods disappeared, people were moved out of the parish. The old Bogside was changing.

In St Columb's Hall, the usual activities, concerts, theatre shows and Bingo, continued. After the initial scares, people began to go out socially in the evening as they did before.

The topic on everyone's lips was 'What is going to happen? How are we going to get through the summer?' People were soon going to have plenty of opportunity to play their part in major political developments, which would irrevocably break the traditional political moulds of Nationalism in Derry.

Towards the end of January 1969, a commission, called the Londonderry Development Commission, was appointed to replace the old Derry Corporation. People generally welcomed the membership of the commission, but the prevailing attitude was 'Wait and see'. There had already been too many false dawns.

Then in February 1969, there was an unexpected election to the Stormont Parliament. For Terence O'Neill, it was a last throw of the dice. Brian Faulkner and other Unionist party luminaries had deserted him. In Derry, the stage was set for the transfer of political leadership from the old brigade to the new able and articulate young leadership thrown up in the university and civil rights campaigns. There was a contest between Eddie McAteer and his followers and John Hume and Eamonn McCann and their followers. Eddie McAteer was greatly respected in Derry and was a very fine person, with great integrity. He had fought many political battles for the Nationalist people of the city and had experienced years of frustration from Unionist government. But he was a politician of the old school and lacked the attraction of the young and articulate rising stars like Hume and McCann, who had received massive media exposure and who had used the media quite brilliantly. It was an election that was notable for the quality and the wit, sometimes cruel, of the brilliant posters and graffiti, which the McCann camp, in particular, created. There was one graffito in a very prominent place in Derry, in William Street, as far as I can remember, which simply stated 'Let's face it, Big Eddie's past it'. It accurately and succinctly reflected the feelings of the electorate. People respected Eddie McAteer and were grateful to him for what he had done in the past, but they believed that new faces and new minds were required for the new task now in hand. It was time to move on. There was no love lost between the Hume and McCann camps either in a fiercely contested election campaign. The result of the election was a stunning victory for John Hume. That election marked the political demise of Eddie McAteer. Eamonn McCann, despite a brilliant campaign, got 1,933 votes to Hume's 8,920. It was a fascinating election and highlighted the manner in which the civil rights campaign had captivated the electorate. Ivan Cooper also won a seat in the Mid-Derry constituency. It was a brilliant election victory for the civil rights leaders. They now had a powerful electoral mandate. John Hume was to be a central figure in almost every positive development in Derry and one of the major figures in the politics of the North during the following thirty years. He has never lost an election since that ballot in February 1969. He is now an internationally respected figure and a deserved Nobel Peace Prize recipient.

The Civil Rights activists had another stunning election victory in April 1969 when Bernadette Devlin won a seat in Westminster in a by-election in the Mid-Ulster constituency. Bernadette Devlin and John Hume were, by now, household names throughout the North and further afield.

Sammy Devenney was less well known. He was a family man who worked for a funeral undertaker driving a hearse and carrying out all the various tasks that funeral undertakers do. Sammy was well known to myself and all the priests of the city because we met at many funerals. He lived in a house on William Street near the cathedral and was not involved in any kind of political activity. His primary interests were his work and his wife and their six young children. He was an inoffensive man who did not enjoy robust health. He was married to Phyllis, a well-known and very popular woman in the area. Phyllis was a devoted wife and mother, lively, good humoured and great fun.

On Saturday 19 April 1969, there was to be a civil rights march from Burntollet to Altnagelvin outside Derry. The march was banned once again. There were sit-down protests by young people against the ban in Guildhall Square and other locations in Derry, and then a group of Paisleyite supporters appeared nearby in Shipquay Street and in the Diamond. Despite the efforts of many people, including John Hume, there was an ensuing violent confrontation. Gradually the RUC was drawn in and the worst rioting yet seen in Derry ensued. Whilst the confrontations began in the city centre, gradually the rioting moved to the familiar battleground of William Street and Rossville Street. There were many casualties, among them Sammy Devenney.

He was in his own house late that afternoon whilst there was rioting in the street outside when a small group of rioters, pursued by police, ran through his house, in through the front door and out through the back door. The police raced into the house but rather than pursue the rioters they attacked the helpless Sammy in his own home in full view of some of his children. He was subjected to a savage beating without any reason whatsoever. He was severely injured. One of the first people in the Devenney home after this incident was Father Tony Mulvey. He was incensed by what he witnessed. I also visited the house shortly after Sammy had been removed to hospital and I can recall that there was blood visible everywhere. Sammy was, perhaps, the most seriously injured of the many casualties on that day. There were shots fired by the police at one stage and the rioting continued until well into the Saturday night. None of us had previously witnessed anything like the intensity and ferocity of that rioting and police action. At times, members of the police seemed to be completely out of control. Their behaviour was despicable. Whilst I and other priests were on the streets endeavouring to calm the rioters, I have to admit that I was as angry as the rioters at what was happening. There were times when one was severely tempted to join the rioters rather than attempt to quell them.

On the Sunday morning, riot police, who had been moved in force and large numbers into the Bogside/William Street area, accosted people coming to Mass. People alleged that they were subjected to sectarian jibes and taunts. The city was, as ever, awash with rumours about the death of some of the previous day's casualties. The presence of the police in such force on a Sunday morning was deeply resented.

By lunchtime on Sunday, things were at a boiling point and a major confrontation seemed inevitable. Once again, John Hume demonstrated his brilliant leadership qualities. He, assisted by others, persuaded the residents to evacuate the Bogside before 3 p.m. and go to Creggan for a public meeting. Apart from the very elderly and housebound, the entire population of the Bogside and William Street was evacuated and the area left to the RUC. The mass movement of people from the Bogside to Creggan that Sunday afternoon was a stunning sight to behold. Eastway, at one stage, was filled with people. Meanwhile Church and civic leaders joined with Hume in asking the Minister of Home Affairs, Robert Porter, to withdraw his police from the entire Bogside area before 5 p.m., when the people would return. Porter eventually acceded to the request and withdrew the police. After the Creggan meeting, attended by a huge crowd and addressed by Eamonn McCann and others, the people returned to their homes in the Bogside. The police were gone and peace was once again restored. The idea of evacuating of the Bogside, whether John Hume or others thought of it, was ingenious. It was a powerful example of non-violent protest that effectively defused a very dangerous situation.

Sunday, 20 April, was a most dramatic and eventful day. I remember going around the Bogside late that evening and people were gathered in groups outside their houses discussing the day's events. A few days later I accompanied Bishop Farren, Bishop Tyndall and the leaders of the Presbyterian and Methodist Churches in a walking tour around the Bogside and the Fountain, an inner city area populated almost exclusively by Protestants. The bishops saw at first hand some of the worst housing conditions in the city. I brought them to several homes in the Bogside where the conditions were particularly bad. People in both areas were welcoming and discussed the current situation with the Church leaders. With the events of the previous weekend fresh in their memories, most people had the view that worse was to come but they felt relieved that a potentially fierce and bloody confrontation had been averted or postponed.

The soothsayers in the community had a field day when a piece of a meteorite fell in County Derry later that week!

CHAPTER 12

Mayhem

Death of Sammy Devenney – Apprentice Boys parade –
the battle of the Bogside – almost an uprising –
resultant destruction – the Home Secretary pays a visit

The summer of 1969 brought the events of the previous nine momentous months to a climax.

In most parts of the civilised world, people look forward to summer. It is a time of long days and reasonably fine weather. Children are on holiday from school and things are relaxed. People go to the seaside or parks and, in areas like the Bogside, people took chairs from inside their houses and sat at their doors on sunny afternoons and evenings. In Derry, however, the pleasure of summer is annually blighted by the Apprentice Boys' parade on 12 August. There is a period of escalating tension beforehand, and, on the day itself, many Nationalist people simply leave town and go elsewhere as the city echoes to the thunderous beat of the Orange drums, the local tom-toms. The city is invaded by thousands of Apprentice Boys ostensibly demonstrating who is really in control in Northern Ireland. In 1969, this was particularly offensive to the majority of citizens in Derry. Whilst in previous years, local Nationalists were prepared to tolerate this march, and had tolerated it, the mood in 1969 was different. The Civil Rights marches had been banned by the Stormont Government, and marchers had been beaten and hosed off the streets by the police, yet this parade in our city would be backed up and forced through and supported by thousands of police.

For a few weeks after the weekend of 19/20 April, there was a period of relative calm, but everyone was concerned about the marching season. There were disturbances in Derry on the evening and night of Saturday, 12 July. Orangemen returning from a demonstration in Limavady were confronted by Nationalist youths. There were subsequently violent clashes with the police. People living in the city centre area telephoned the cathedral and asked for some priests to come and try to calm things down. Shops were being looted by teenage youths. I was appalled by the sheer wanton vandalism and theft, which I witnessed that night in the Diamond, Butcher Street and Shipquay Street areas. This was not an action in support of any worthy cause; it was criminal activity. Things had taken a new turn. I scarcely got to bed that night and at Mass on the following morning in the cathedral, I scrapped my planned sermon and spoke instead of my experiences during the previous hours. Among other things, I said:

> The activities of last night amounted to sheer hooliganism. They have no connection with civil rights or religion. There is no excuse for the extent of destruction to property wreaked by 200-300 young people, many of them armed with bricks. Their conduct was absolutely disgraceful. Whilst there may have been some provocation earlier in the day, the young peoples' behaviour last night was of a type that cannot be excused by any amount of provocation.

I added:

> Priests were insulted when they tried to remonstrate with the young people and prevent the damage to property. Parents have an important responsibility in all of this. Boys and girls of 10, 11 and 12 were running around the streets at one o'clock this morning.

Unknown to me, there was a journalist in the congregation, and extracts from the sermon appeared in the national press the following day. Most of the reaction to what I said was positive. The DCAC in a statement said, 'We strongly condemn the wanton hooliganism and looting which took place in our city.' The *Derry Journal*, in its editorial on 15 July, described the events as a 'Weekend of Shame'. The looting and vandalism in the city centre shocked people. But these young people had now got a taste for blood and the influence of people, like us, was having little impact on them. Late on Sunday afternoon, 13 July, there was further rioting in the Bogside and the Rossville Hall, a noted landmark at the William Street end of Rossville Street, was burned down. We were on the slippery slide.

On that same Sunday night, there were disturbances outside the Orange Hall in the town of Dungiven, about 20 miles from Derry. A number of people were injured. On the following day, one of those injured, a man in his late sixties, Francis McCloskey, died. It was believed that he was struck on the head with a police baton during a baton charge. That night, Father George Doherty, curate in Dungiven, courageously confronted a crowd intent on again attacking the Orange Hall and persuaded them to disperse. Francis McCloskey was the first person in the Derry diocese to lose his life as a direct result of the civil conflict.

Within the same week there was a second fatality. Sammy Devenney, beaten in his home on William Street in Derry by police on 19 April died in a Belfast Hospital on 17 July. He had never fully recovered from his multiple injuries. He was only forty-two years old. His funeral took place to the City Cemetery on Sunday, 20 July. It was attended by one of the largest crowds ever to attend a funeral in the city. The *Derry Journal* estimated the attendance at over twenty thousand. His wife, Phyllis, made a moving appeal for calm.

That same weekend, the world was enthralled, as Neil Armstrong became the first man to walk on the moon. This event was hardly noticed in Derry. We were too preoccupied with events on this planet.

Despite a protracted investigation, nobody was ever made amenable for the fatal assault on Sammy Devenney. The RUC, as ever, closed ranks. A celebrated detective from Scotland Yard, whose name I cannot recall, was sent over subsequently to investigate the case. He was a key member of the team of crack Scotland Yard detectives who investigated the 1963 Great Train Robbery when £2.3 million was stolen from a mail train by a group of London's top gangsters, among them Ronald Biggs. This detective became well known in the Bogside and a celebrity in the area. It was said that he frequented the Grandstand Bar in William Street, just across the street from the Devenney home, and regaled the locals with colourful stories of his experiences. He may have tracked down and arrested the Great Train Robbers but, despite his best efforts, he failed to find the culprits within the RUC who were responsible for the death of Sammy Devenney. He was reported as commenting that he was meeting 'a wall of silence'.

The first few days of August were spent in Lourdes on pilgrimage with a group of people who worked voluntarily for me in St Columb's Hall. It provided a pleasant change of atmosphere and pace from Derry. It was a timely interlude for prayer and reflection and a preparation for the events that lay ahead. I have always experienced great calm and peace in Lourdes.

Towards the end of July and during the early days of August, local representatives met everyone from James Callaghan, the British Home Secretary, to the local Governor of the Apprentice Boys, expressing concern about the Apprentice Boys march in Derry on 12 August. There were appeals to ban the march and appeals for people to stay calm. Apprehension was heightened when the Stormont Government announced in late July that it was mobilising the hated B Specials. The place was now a tinderbox. Many families with young children began to leave the city to stay with relatives in Donegal and elsewhere as 12 August approached. There was a distinct impression that a juggernaut was fast heading in our direction and nobody could stop it.

On the Sunday before the march, 10 August, a letter from Bishop Farren was read at all public Masses in Derry and there were prayers seeking calm. In his letter Bishop Farren stated:

> Realising the serious dangers threatening our community at the present time, I appeal to all to do everything they can to maintain peace.

On that same afternoon, at a meeting in Celtic Park in Derry, an organisation called Derry Citizens Defence Association (DCDA) was set up. It was a practical expression of the peoples' desire to defend and protect themselves from attack in the wake of the experience in St Columb's Wells and in the Devenney household in previous months. The DCDA was made up of people from a wide spectrum of Nationalist opinion from all over the city. Many of those who had previously been in the Derry Citizens Action Committee, now overtaken by events, were members. While there may have been well-intentioned pleas for calm, nobody was expecting calm. Most people, with any first-hand experience of the previous nine months, were expecting mayhem.

During my formal education, like many in my generation, I had learned comparatively little about twentieth-century Irish history. We were taught all about Napoleon and the War of the Roses, the Franco-Prussian War and the Magna Carta; but virtually nothing was taught about the War of Independence, the setting up of the Irish State, the Boundary Commission or how the Six Counties came into being. It did not seem to figure on the curriculum. Most of my knowledge of Irish history in the early part of the twentieth century was garnered from folklore and oral tradition. I was about to get a grandstand view of some of the events that would have a profound influence on the history of the latter part of that century.

The morning of Tuesday, 12 August 1969 was a glorious, warm and sunny morning. It is remarkable that the major events of the Troubles in Derry were usually accompanied by dry, bright weather. No major confrontations or atrocities seemed to take place when it was raining! Derry Catholics feigned doubts about the goodwill of the 'man above' because the Apprentice Boys and Orangemen always seemed to enjoy good weather for their marches! The sound of drums and flutes provided background music during the early morning. It could be clearly heard all over the Bogside and around St Eugene's. Women rushed to get their shopping done early. After the ten o'clock Mass, people, who had already been in the city centre, remarked that the place was 'hiving' with police. In the Bogside, where I attended and visited a few sick and elderly people that morning, things were calm but tense. There were not many people around, and the usually ubiquitous children were notably absent; many families had prudently moved out.

The first violent confrontations took place at a predictable place – Littlewoods Corner, at the junction of William Street, Waterloo Street and Waterloo Place. The Apprentice Boys march passed through Waterloo Place in the early afternoon. Crowds of youths from the Bogside assembled at the mouth of William Street and Waterloo Street at Littlewoods Corner. The police formed up in between. There were catcalls from one group at the other and then there were missiles thrown. John Hume, Eddie McAteer and DCDA stewards endeavoured to calm the situation down but they were eventually overwhelmed by the numbers and the intensity of the anger and frustration with which people were seized. The crowds got bigger and more dispersed. With other priests from the parish, I spent that afternoon going around the area on foot trying to calm things down and reassure the many elderly who lived there. Around 5 p.m. the police baton-charged the crowd in William Street and in the next two or three hours, things gradually descended into chaos. Barricades were being built across streets throughout the Bogside. Crates of petrol bombs appeared and were carried along Rossville Street. People of all ages arrived in the Bogside from all over the city. Bernadette Devlin was there, addressing the crowds with a loudhailer. The Bogside prepared for an invasion and built defences accordingly. A huge barricade was built across Rossville Street where it joined with William Street. There was much construction work going on in the Bogside with the redevelopment at this time. Materials were conveniently at hand – scaffolding poles, timber, concrete blocks – any thing and every thing. At one stage, the police led a charge into the Bogside through Abbey Street followed by a large group of civilians. These were believed to be Apprentice Boys or their supporters. They penetrated into Rossville Street by this flanking operation. Before being driven out by the locals, they succeeded in breaking windows in peoples' homes. The obvious collusion between the police and the Apprentice Boys' supporters, though not a surprise, further inflamed the situation. As Lord Scarman wrote in his report:

the entry of the armoured cars and foot police, closely followed by Protestant civilians throwing stones, appeared to many as the embodiment of their worst fears (11.29).*

Father Bennie O'Neill, administrator of St Eugene's, and Father Tony Mulvey both protested vigorously to the police on the street about this particular incursion. They then proceeded immediately to the RUC headquarters at Victoria Barracks in Strand Road and demanded that the police be withdrawn from the area, to no avail. By this time, the residents and others had converted the roof the Rossville Flats, ten storeys high, into a strongpoint, a place from which to throw or launch missiles at the police and an observation point from which the entire area could be monitored. There was no talk of calm or restraint now. Even we, as priests, had given up on that particular effort. A lot of elderly people wanted to get out of the area, and we now concentrated our efforts in facilitating them, by getting them, by various means, to the cathedral grounds, and then taking them in our cars to relatives and a convent in other parts of the city. In the course of these journeys, it was rather uncanny to note that whilst the Bogside area was in complete turmoil, other areas of town were perfectly normal. As darkness approached, it was obvious that this was not going to be just another riot. This was now a battle, almost an uprising.

The night that followed provided a whole series of new and very unpleasant experiences. A number of large buildings, including the huge Richardson's Shirt Factory on William Street and the Methodist Church Hostel for Men near the Long Tower church were set alight. I can remember some of the women who worked in Richardson's looking on hopelessly and helplessly in disbelief as their workplace and their jobs were destroyed. They were greatly distressed. CS gas was used for the first time in the North. I heard gunfire for the first time on the streets of Derry; in this case, it was almost certainly fired by the police. The rioting died down significantly for a time after the CS gas was used. But it was not long before people realised that it could be coped with by soaking cloths

---

* *Violence and Civil Disturbances in Northern Ireland in 1969. Report of Tribunal of Inquiry*, vol. 1 (HMSO, Belfast, 1972).

in vinegar and wearing the cloth like a mask over the nose and mouth. This served a double purpose and became standard gear for the subsequent riot situations. The fish-and-chip shops in the Bogside soon ran out of supplies of vinegar! The rioting continued until the small hours of the morning, largely along the William Street/Rossville Street axis. But when it eventually petered out, nobody on either side believed that it was over. People merely wished to rest and re-assess the situation. The noxious odour of CS gas mixed with the smell of burning permeated everywhere, even my bedroom, where I snatched a couple of hours of fitful sleep.

During the following morning, there were remarkable scenes in the Bogside. Barricades were being built on almost every street in the area, and built with great skill and ingenuity. There was an assembly line in Nelson Street for the manufacture of petrol bombs, sourced from a hijacked petrol tanker. This gave cause for one of the more memorable graffiti of the period, '*Throw well, throw Shell*'. How a major conflagration was avoided, I will never know. People, as was their wont, were smoking cigarettes everywhere, even as milk bottles were being filled with petrol nearby! There were television crews and other journalists and photographers of many nationalities wandering around. In the afternoon, the rioters regrouped and took the initiative attacking the police. It was announced on the radio that the police had brought in reinforcements during the night. Once again combat was joined. Petrol bombs and stones and missiles from catapults were thrown at the police. A heavy-duty metal catapult was erected on the roof of Rossville Flats that had the capability of projecting petrol bombs over a long distance – without great accuracy, it must be said. Anywhere within a radius of hundred yards was a potentially dangerous place to be when it was in use. Bernadette Devlin and Paddy (Bogside) Doherty were everywhere, organising and encouraging. The battle ebbed to and fro, easing at teatime, when the rioters stopped to have refreshments and to have the thrill of viewing themselves being featured on the evening television news.

There was a dramatic radio broadcast around 9 p.m. that night on RTÉ from Jack Lynch, the Irish Taoiseach. I listened to Mr Lynch with dozens of others, outside McClenaghan's house in

Wellington Street, on a car radio with the volume turned up full. There was loud cheering everywhere after the broadcast; the impression given being that Irish Army troops were about to enter Derry to come to the aid of the local residents. This was a false impression. But the atmosphere was so charged that night in that particular area that people only heard what they wanted to believe. Some time after this broadcast, somebody came to me and told me to get back to St Eugene's Cathedral as it was about to be attacked by police and Paisleyites who had gathered in Great James Street. Cars with loudspeakers circulated in Creggan and other Nationalist areas with the same message and more people were mobilised and drawn into the Bogside and, in particular, the area around the cathedral.

Whilst there was certainly a crowd of Paisleyite types assembled in the lower end of Great James Street with police, I have never been persuaded that they ever really intended to attack the cathedral. They did try to force their way up Great James Street. However, the large crowds, now assembled around the cathedral perimeter, were prepared to defend it, if necessary. There was intensive stone throwing, petrol bombing and dozens of CS gas canisters were fired. At one stage an ice cream van was set on fire and pushed downhill in Great James Street towards the assembled police and Paisleyites. As it careered blazing down the street towards the police lines, the chimes on it were playing 'The Teddy Bears' Picnic'. It was one of the more surreal moments of a bizarre night. Then there was gunfire that seemed to come from where the police were assembled. Two people in the crowd at the back of the cathedral in Great James Street were hit by this gunfire. I remember that one of them was called McDaid. Both were taken to a first aid station at a sweetshop called Candy Corner, in West End Terrace, one of the several hastily equipped first aid stations in the area. Doctors and nurses and members of the Knights of Malta staffed these stations. They did incredible work and tended dozens of casualties. After the gunfire the Nationalists withdrew slightly and the police advanced up to the corner of Infirmary Road and Great James Street at one stage, but then were driven back again. It was a fierce battle and it spread right across the area. In the meantime, buildings were being torched, some accidentally some deliberately, and the rioting spread to other areas. Rosemount police barracks, a few hundred yards up the hill from the cathedral, was attacked. A lot of people had gathered in the parochial house for safety. The place was crowded. Everyone was fearful of what might happen. Whilst the rioting subsided between 3 a.m. and 4 a.m., nobody in our house went to bed. I remember, with others, dragging a young man who had been overcome by CS gas in Windsor Terrace through the back door of the parochial house sometime in the early hours of the morning. We were tending to him on the floor and glanced up only to see the elderly Bishop Neil Farren standing looking down at us in a bewildered fashion. He did not say anything; he just shook his head in disbelief. He was not the only one to be bewildered and perplexed by it all. Few people in Derry got to bed that night.

On Thursday morning, the disturbances continued sporadically. There were several fires and there were sectarian confrontations in the Fountain Street/Bishop Street area where Catholic homes were set alight. Then the radio reported that the B Specials were being sent in and this further poisoned the atmosphere. As ever, rumours were rife and when it was suddenly reported that the British Army were coming in, it was not believed at first. However, in the late evening, there they were in Waterloo Place erecting barbed wire barricades, with their helmets and guns just like in World War Two movies. Eddie McAteer and Paddy Doherty spoke to the crowd and tried to persuade them to disperse and return home. As far as I can recall, the speeches were given at the corner of Rossville Street and William Street. Bernadette Devlin did not seem to agree with them and, as ever, made her views known. However, everyone was exhausted and extreme fatigue and a gradual realisation of the enormity of what had occurred served to encourage people to follow the more moderate advice.

The area was a mess. The streets were strewn with stones and broken glass and all kinds of debris and blocked by barricades. Many buildings were still burning because the fire brigades were unable to come in to deal with some of the fires. The smell of burning was everywhere. People wandered around the William Street area in the quiet of the late evening, dazed and bewildered by the experience of the previous twenty-four hours. It may have been exhilarating whilst it was in progress, but many were shocked when they realised the full consequences of the activities they had engaged in. The destruction was widespread. Many individuals and families were homeless. Places of employment and business had been destroyed. William Street and Little James Street bore the brunt of the damage. Amazingly, despite the large numbers involved and the intensity of the confrontations, there had been no fatalities on any side.

The night of 14 August in Derry was a night during which most people got to bed and slept soundly. This was not the case in Belfast and other parts of the North. What had begun in Derry ...

The North woke up on the morning of 15 August to horrendous reports of the sectarian confrontations in Belfast. Several people had been killed. In subsequent days, whole streets of houses were burned down and many Catholic residents fled south.

After the days and nights of manic activity, a relative calm descended on Derry. Some of those who had left the city began to return. The DCDA was very active. Whilst debris was cleared from some streets, the main barricades remained intact and, in some cases, were strengthened. I watched in puzzlement, one morning, as a group of men painted a white line across the Lone Moor Road, just below my window at the intersection between Lone Moor Road and Creggan Street. The same thing was happening on all streets on the periphery of the Bogside. This was to define and delineate an area subsequently declared a 'No Go Area' for RUC and British Army personnel. This area had been proclaimed as 'Free Derry'.

The St Vincent de Paul Society in Derry did Herculean work in the weeks after the August riots in assisting the many victims of the conflict and particularly the homeless. They visited the large number of families whose homes had been damaged and helped them with cash and furniture and other needs. Pope Paul VI sent £1000 to Bishop Farren to assist victims, and many other individuals and groups also sent financial assistance. Members of the St Vincent de Paul Society distributed this to people who had suffered. Some people, whose homes were badly damaged, were given temporary accommodation in caravans in Brandywell and other areas of the city. Some went to live with relatives.

To give an idea of the extent of the suffering of residents of the area, it is interesting to look at just one contemporary record of people who suffered damage. There are several similar records of the damage sustained during the Battle of the Bogside. These records, drawn up by the St Vincent de Paul Society and parish clergy, would suggest that the prime losers in this battle were the local residents. The little community that had lived for generations near the intersection of Rossville Street and William Street was literally destroyed. This record is dated 8 September 1969.*

- Mrs & Mrs Charles Harkin and one child of William Street, burned out completely. In new flat at 17 Meenan Square.
- Mrs Vincent Doherty of 80 William Street, burned out completely. Now living with relations at 17 Garvan Place.
- Mr & Mrs John Harkin of Bishop Street, burned out completely. Now living with relations at 1 Eastway.
- Mr & Mrs Burns of 80 William Street, burned out completely. Rehoused.
- Mr & Mrs Lynch of 49 William Street, burned out completely, rehoused in Creggan.
- Mr & Mrs P.T. Carter of 41 William Street burned out completely. Rehoused at 91 Cloneen Drive.
- Mr & Mrs McConomy of 47 Bishop Street, burned out completely. Rehoused at 22 Tremone Gardens.
- Miss Margaret Friel of 49 William Street, burned out completely. Living with friends.
- Miss Monaghan of 49 William Street, burned out completely. Living with friends at Limavady Road.
- Mrs Coghlan of 78 William Street, burned out completely. Living with friends.
- Mrs Mary Gallagher 29 Rossville Street, burned out completely. Living with relations at Circular Road.
- Mrs Devenney of William Street, widow with six young

---

* Derry Diocesan Archive.

children, living in rented house in Buncrana. [This was the family of Sammy Devenney, the first fatal victim of the Troubles in Derry City. After losing her husband a few months earlier, Phyllis Devenney and her children lost her home and all its contents during the riots in August 1969.]

- Mrs Sarah Harkin of 25 Rossville Street, house and contents destroyed by water. Now living in flat at 12 Lislane Drive.
- Mr Michael Lynch of 82 William Street, house destroyed with most of his clothes and furniture. Now living at 4 Ramore Gardens.
- Mr & Mrs Patrick Doherty of 98 William Street, burned out completely. In new flat.
- Mrs Hazlett of 1 Little James Street, burned out completely. Now living with relations at Maybrook Park.
- Miss Sharkey of 27 Rossville Street, burned out completely. Living with relations.
- Mrs & Mrs William J Molloy of 193 William Street, burned out completely. Present address unknown.

On Thursday 28 August, James Callaghan, the British Home Secretary, visited Derry. The DCDA announced his arrival and schedule in its newsletter, the *Barricade Bulletin*:

> Seamus O'Callaghan [sic] is to arrive in our area at 3.00 p.m. via the main Army barrier, Waterloo Place – William St – Rossville St – Free Derry Corner. His visit is expected to last approximately 45 minutes, after which he will proceed to Fountain St via the Long Tower. John Hume MP will also have talks with him.

James Callaghan first visited the Guildhall and then he walked to the Bogside accompanied by John Hume and Ivan Cooper and thousands of local people as well as a posse of journalists and camera crews. It was the first time that most of us had seen a British Cabinet Minister in the flesh. He afterwards described it thus:

> There were many people who wanted to shake my hand and touch me; it was a rare experience in a politician's life, a great

and dramatic moment which brought home the awful responsibility I carried for their hopes and fears.*

Indeed people in the Bogside placed great hopes in James Callaghan. He met community leaders in Mrs Diver's house on Lecky Road. Subsequently he addressed the huge crowd by poking his head rather incongruously out of a tiny upstairs window and speaking through a loud hailer, an article that was in plentiful supply in the Bogside at that time. He said that he would endeavour to ensure that there was justice and equality. He promised to do his best, although he qualified it by saying, 'I am not going to promise you the earth.' He then left to visit the Unionist community in the Fountain area, where the welcome was somewhat more restrained.

On the previous day Mr Callaghan had announced the establishment of a Tribunal of Inquiry under Lord Scarman to investigate the dramatic events of 1969 in the North. During subsequent months Lord Scarman and his colleagues were kept busy as people willingly gave evidence of their experiences. The tribunal held many hearings in the courthouse in Derry and were the focus of much public interest. Scarman was an astute, impartial and witty chairman.

After the summer mayhem, the remaining months of 1969 were relatively quiet on the streets of Derry. There were visits by many prominent British and Irish politicians and delegations from here and there. The Bogside was the focus of much media attention. The redevelopment of the Bogside resumed. Many new homes were under construction and other old Bogside streets with their tiny overcrowded houses were disappearing forever. People got on with their lives as best they could. However, the events of August were always on people's lips and in their minds. In the course of pastoral work in the Bogside area, it was the only topic of conversation. Cultural activities had virtually come to halt. Whereas in the past, when on sick calls, I would meet people around the streets at all hours of the night, the streets were now empty late at night. The

---

* Rt. Hon. James Callaghan M.P., *A House Divided* (Collins, London, 1973), p. 85 .

Army kept a high profile presence around the city centre. They did not attempt to come into the Bogside area or the area now known as Free Derry, however. The DCDA were in control there, had checkpoints and manned them, kept good order and continued issuing their bulletins and newsletters

Most ominously of all, in the very last days of 1969, it was reported that the IRA had split, and a new organisation that called itself, the Provisional IRA, had emerged. Although, this development did not get much media coverage or attract much attention at the time, this fledgling organisation was set to take centre stage in many of our lives for next quarter century.

CHAPTER 13

All Kinds of Everything

Dana – a priest departs – Colmcille Choir and the '71 Players –
the guns come out – internment – to Letterkenny by ambulance –
death of first IRA volunteer – tea chests and clothes-lines –
death of Annette McGavigan – tarring and feathering – Long Kesh –
Army conversations

When the British Army first arrived in Derry in August 1969, soldiers were welcomed. They were certainly preferable to the RUC and their arrival implied defeat for the police. For the first few months after they arrived, they acted very passively and received a degree of hospitality from the local Nationalist population. A number of soldiers regularly attended Sunday Mass in St Eugene's in uniform. Some soldiers socialised with local girls and several of these couples subsequently got married. People were courteous and correct and kind to soldiers who had the unpleasant duty of standing for hours in cold and exposed checkpoints around the city centre. However, the enthusiasm and depth of that welcome have been much exaggerated by some chroniclers of that period. It is not pleasant, in any community, to have helmeted soldiers in full battledress armed with machine guns at the end of your street. People were uncomfortable with this presence and hoped and presumed that it would be a very temporary and short-lived arrangement. I think it was General Freeland, Commander of the British army in the North, who described this period as 'a honeymoon period'. It was a perceptive observation.

Visiting people in prison was a new dimension of pastoral ministry during the early months of 1970. I had only occasion to visit a parishioner in prison once prior to 1969. Before the civil turmoil, the Bogside was a very law-abiding community and very few of my parishioners had been in prison. But suddenly now there was a number of young people from the parish in prison in Crumlin Road prison in Belfast as a result of convictions for riotous behaviour. Thus began a ministry that would take up a considerable amount of my time during the following twenty-five years.

Dana (Rosemary Brown), representing Ireland, won the Eurovision Song Contest in Amsterdam in March 1970. She was from Derry, and was the first person representing Ireland to win the contest. She sang a song called 'All Kinds of Everything'. She was still at school in Thornhill College at the time and she lived with her parents in the multi-storey flats in Rossville Street. She had appeared and performed on many occasions at concerts and pantomimes in St Columb's Hall. On the Monday after the contest, she was flown in triumph back to Derry. The Aer Lingus Boeing 727 with its distinctive green markings swept in low over the city before landing at Ballykelly RAF base. On her arrival back in town, the City Commission honoured her by giving her a civic reception in the Guildhall. Eventually she made her way home to the Rossville Flats and a tumultuous reception there. Her family was well known and popular. Everyone in the city was excited and pleased for her and for her family. Derry celebrates and enjoys the success of its own. Dana's triumph and subsequent celebration were pleasant and enjoyable interludes and provided a small chink of light in the gathering gloom that prevailed in those early months of 1970.

There was sporadic rioting in the William Street area in the weeks after Easter that year. As the summer months approached the intensity and frequency of the rioting increased. During that same period there were increasingly frequent reports of gunfire being exchanged between the British Army and the Provisional IRA. It was repeatedly emphasised that there was no tradition of guns being used in civil conflict in Derry. People said, 'That only happens in Belfast. The IRA won't get any support in Derry. There'll be no guns here.' It was not an accurate historical observation. There were several fatalities from gunfire in Derry during civil conflict in the early 1920s. But most local people were confident that whatever happened elsewhere, Derry would not succumb to guns being used. Rioting, yes; petrol bombs, yes; but guns, no. That was the conventional wisdom.

Then towards the end of June, there was a dreadful tragedy in Dunree Gardens in the Creggan area of Derry. Three adults and two young children, aged four and nine, asleep upstairs, lost their lives when an explosive device prematurely detonated. There were gruesome accounts of this fire. I did not know any of the victims nor was I on the scene. There was intense speculation as to whether the conflagration was caused by petrol bombs or something more powerful like nitro-glycerine. Whatever the cause, this was a dramatic wake-up call that something more sinister was going on behind the scenes in our community. This tragedy was followed by several days and nights of intense rioting.

One of the many incongruities associated with the rioting in Derry in the early years was the fact that many of the rioters wore suits and shirts and ties when rioting. The dedication of joggers was particularly striking. Very often during a riot in Rossville Street or William Street, a jogger would come running along and would pick his way through the rioters, soldiers, barricades, rubble and the other detritus of such activities and continue on his merry way, oblivious, as if nothing were amiss. On the sombre side, more and more buildings were set on fire, some accidentally, others deliberately. The unfortunate residents of the area suffered intensely. CS gas, which was now being used with increasing frequency by the Army in riot situations, was a most unpleasant irritant, and much more than an irritant for people with bronchial problems. Rubber bullets also made their appearance, around this time, as a riot control weapon. The 'honeymoon', to which General Freeland had referred, was coming to an end. The Army was increasingly being drawn into the conflict. They were being asked to carry out policing duties. Soldiers are not good at that. The Army commandeered schools and halls and other buildings, some of them in the Bogside, in which to billet their soldiers. Several of these buildings were Church property.

The Apprentice Boys' annual celebration in August passed off without any major incident or confrontation. There was a ban on all marches at this time. Instead of a march, a rally was held in St

Columb's Park in the Waterside. All the public houses in the city were closed and the city side of Derry was relatively quiet. Conor Cruise O'Brien, the Dublin politician and writer, made a much-heralded appearance at the demonstration either as an observer or as a gesture of good will or both. The impression given was that this broadminded liberal Dubliner would show narrow-minded Northern Nationalists that the Apprentice Boys were really 'jolly nice chaps'. For his troubles, he was physically assaulted by some of the Apprentice Boys, an event that generated little sympathy and a certain amount of mischievous glee in local Nationalist circles. Fortunately he was not seriously injured.

In Belfast, there was a prolonged curfew on a large area of the Lower Falls for some days in early July. There was no confrontation of similar magnitude in Derry. However, there were ominous rumblings. As the year went on, the frequency of rioting increased and it appeared to be more organised than heretofore. Several customs posts along the border were damaged or destroyed by explosions. In early November, Sir Arthur Young, the Chief Constable of the RUC, announced that the inquiry into the attack on Sammy Devenney had been fruitless due to a 'conspiracy of silence' on the part of the police officers involved.

At this same time, priests were struggling with radical changes in the liturgy of the Mass, which we celebrated every day. We had been carefully trained to celebrate Mass in Latin with our back to the people. During the previous few years, the changes in the liturgy in keeping with new norms laid down by the Vatican Council had been gradually introduced. It was a completely new experience. Now the changes were being finalised; the entire liturgy of Mass was to be celebrated in the vernacular language and facing the people. These changes were difficult and even traumatic for both priests and people. At the beginning of Lent 1970, Bishop Farren issued a pastoral letter on the changes in the liturgy of the Mass, reassuring people and encouraging them to accept the changes.

The speculation that there would be changes in the rules of clerical celibacy in the wake of the Vatican Council proved to be unfounded. For some reason, it was widely and erroneously assumed among some sections of the younger clergy that some changes would take place. They looked forward to the changes. Others felt uncomfortable with the very idea of change. As priests, we found ourselves under increasing pressure in a society that was literally falling apart and a Church undergoing radical change. We were in great need of support. It was a very unsettling and difficult time for priests. Eventually these various pressures took their toll on some priests. Two diocesan priests, including a wonderful colleague who served with me in St Eugene's parish, resigned from the ministry in 1970. We had heard of this happening in the United States and Britain, but it was an entirely different experience when it involved a colleague whom one knew and admired. We did not know how to handle it. The priests in St Eugene's always had a meeting and had a cup of tea together late on Saturday night after hearing Confessions to make arrangements for duty rosters and other matters for the following week. It was at such a meeting, on an unforgettable Saturday night, that our colleague informed us that he was leaving the following day. None of us had an inkling that this was going to happen. We were devastated. Initially he left temporarily to give the matter thought. None of us, however, believed that he would be back. We knew the woman with whom he had fallen in love. We knew and respected his family and her family. I have to admit that, in the years since then, as priest and bishop, I have always had considerable difficulty in coming to terms with the departure of a brother priest from the ministry. There has been much study and consideration given to the impact that such an event has on the priest who has left the ministry. But such a departure also has a considerable impact also on those who have been left behind, priests and people. When you serve through situations of conflict with an individual, a very close bond of loyalty and friendship develops, and the sudden departure of a loved and respected colleague is quite shattering. The pain, in a small way, must be similar to that experienced by the partner left behind when the other partner walks out of a marriage. Many of the same emotions are experienced – initial feelings of anger and betrayal and subsequently a deep sense of pain and loss. The priest or priests left behind in the diocese or parish have to try and make sense of the departure to bemused parishioners whom the departed priest has baptised, married and whose Confessions he has heard. In our diocese, during the years since then, we lost some wonderful priests who had so much to offer in the priesthood. They have all been greatly missed.

But life had to go on. All through 1970, people were being moved to new accommodation after they had lost their homes, as a result of the rioting. The priests assisted the members of the St Vincent de Paul Society in this work. The number of people who lost their homes and property during the conflict has almost been forgotten. It was very significant, and people like the SVDP and other social services, statutory and voluntary, did great work in addressing this difficult problem. All through 1970, the redevelopment in the Bogside went on. People were being allocated new homes and the old streets and neighbourhoods, which had existed for years, were disappearing. However, the new homes were welcome and long overdue. But the bonds developed over many generations, which had cemented these communities together, were beginning to loosen and disappear. The new communities never acquired the solidarity or cohesion of the communities they replaced.

In the course of visiting families, I became aware of the social impact of all this upheaval on people, and especially on women. As a result of the rioting and unrest, virtually all social life had largely come to a standstill. For married women and young parents, social life outside the home had ceased to exist. They were worried about their children, especially their teenage sons. They feared that they would get caught up in rioting and suffer injury or imprisonment or worse. It was a difficult time to be a parent of a young family in Derry, especially in the troubled areas of the city. Children coming home from school were often caught up in riots. There was the discomfort caused by the frequent use of CS gas. I was anxious to create some type of social outlet for these women. In speaking with many women, I found that a great number of them had an interest in music, so I decided to try to start a Ladies' Choir. As a result, I advertised a public meeting in St Columb's Hall on 21 September 1970, with this purpose in mind. I was quite surprised when there was a huge attendance at the meeting. As a result a female choir was established. It was called the Colmcille Ladies Choir. It was incredibly successful not just as a means of social activity but also aesthetically as a choir. It is still flourishing, thirty years on. The Choir has travelled to many parts of Europe and to the United States, performed for Pope John Paul II in private audience in the Vatican and for the US President in the White House. It has won trophies at choral competitions in many International Festivals, including the Salzburg Festival in Austria, and the International Eisteddfod in Llangollen in Wales. At that same meeting in September 1970 a Drama Company called the '71 Players was formed. To provide a venue for their performances, a small one-hundred-seat theatre was constructed in the Minor Hall of St Columb's Hall. It was named the Little Theatre. The '71 Players performed successfully there during some of Derry's most difficult years and provided a major recreational and cultural interest for many people. The company staged about four or five productions a year covering a wide Irish, English and European repertoire and played to capacity audiences in the Little Theatre during the 1970s, at a time when no professional company would contemplate coming to the North. Their success and the success of the Colmcille Ladies Choir exceeded my wildest dreams. In the midst of conflict, I believed that it was important to keep cultural activities alive as far as possible. Cultural activity is an important constituent of the cement that holds civilised life together.

The '71 Players were so named simply because their first production was staged in 1971. This was the year in which the gun began to play a major part in the unfolding drama that was taking place on the streets of Derry. The rioting became fiercer and William Street, the street linking St Eugene's Cathedral to the city centre, was at the eye of the storm. Prior to the conflict, it had been a street of shops and tidy homes and industries, including a shirt factory and large industrial bakery. The first British soldier killed in Derry during the conflict met his death in Westland Street when his Land Rover was petrol bombed by youths late on the night of 28 February. Early in the year, gunfire could be heard sporadically, and, gradually as time went on, it became more frequent. There were rumours of men training in the use of firearms at camps in the more remote areas of Donegal. Then the bombing began in earnest.

First there were nail bombs, which were lethal weapons; then parcel bombs, and incendiary bombs in business premises. The cauldron first bubbled; then it overflowed.

July and August 1971 were dreadful months. The weather was fine but nobody had much chance to enjoy it. The schools were off. There were lots of young people with nothing particular to do and rioting was exciting. Young people had now got a taste for it. It was cowboys and indians with real 'indians'! They could riot in the afternoon and go home for tea and watch themselves featuring on the television evening news. There was rioting in Derry virtually every night and some afternoons in July 1971. The honeymoon with the British Army was certainly over now. The Army bore the brunt of the rioting. After spending many hours on the streets on the evening of Thursday, 8 July, I returned home and was just in bed when I heard shots. Shortly afterwards there was a frantic ringing on the doorbell of the parochial house – a man had been shot in Abbey Street. The priest on duty went to attend him. The victim's name was Seamus Cusack. He was bleeding profusely. After first aid was rendered and the last rites administered, he was taken to Letterkenny Hospital. Those injured in rioting feared that if they were taken to Altnagelvin Hospital, they would be arrested. As a result, many riot victims were transported to Letterkenny across the border in Donegal. The Army claimed that he was seen to aim a gun at soldiers. All who were on the scene vehemently denied this. Seamus Cusack was not believed to be in the IRA. I was present in those streets up until shortly the shooting and I could not recall seeing any civilians carrying firearms or hearing any gunfire previously that evening. He was the first civilian to be shot dead by the British Army in Derry. Worse was to come early the following afternoon. About half a mile from where Seamus Cusack was shot, at the corner of Westland Street and Lecky Road, another civilian met his death at the hands of the Army during a confrontation. His name was Desmond Beattie. The security authorities alleged that he was about to throw a nail bomb when he was shot. John Hume protested vehemently at these shootings and insisted that the victims were not carrying firearms or bombs. On the day of the funerals of Cusack and Beattie, I joined a group of priests meeting senior police and Army officials to protest at the fabrication in the official version of events. The rioting in Derry now became more widespread. It spread to the Creggan area in particular.

The Apprentice Boys march on 12 August was approaching once again. In the prevailing atmosphere, it was a highly explosive situation in every sense of the word. A group of priests serving in city parishes met in St Eugene's parochial house on the afternoon of Saturday 7 August. All of us were concerned about the potential of this situation. We decided to draft a letter and send it to the leaders of the Apprentice Boys appealing to them to call off their march for this year. The statement was as follows:

> The situation in our city is worse today than it was two years ago. After the August disturbances of 1969, it was said that it was easy to be wise in retrospect and that the parade of August 12 of that year would have been banned had the consequences been foreseen.
>
> As priests who are working in the parishes in this city we would earnestly appeal to the leaders of the Apprentice Boys to make the magnanimous gesture of calling off the parade on Thursday next in the interests of Christian charity and peace. The parade is held to have a religious significance and for that reason we would direct our appeal also to clergymen of Protestant denominations. It has been our pleasure to co-operate with them on matters of common concern and we would ask them to use their leadership amongst their flock to avert the cloud that hangs over our city. Such a responsible decision will command the respect of all, except those who will not listen to or consider others. We all look forward to a time when any parade may be held in any of our streets. No one deludes himself that at the present time we enjoy such a climate, and we would point out that Catholics in this city, in which they form the majority of the population, do not hold religious processions in the streets.
>
> We feel that we would be failing in our responsibility as priests if we did not speak for those on whose behalf no voice has been raised. Too little thought and consideration has

been given to the residents, especially the elderly residents, of areas that regularly have been plagued by disturbances. In the coming week many will have to leave their homes to stay with friends; others will have nowhere to go, and once again will have to endure the anxiety and fear that accompany such occasions. There is also the demoralising effect of violence on the young and the very young. It is surely a Christian responsibility to consider the possible effects of any public action, especially one that will bring crowds to the streets. There are on all sides people who are prepared to use violence and intimidation for private ends. Human life is sacred, but in recent weeks we have seen deaths, explosions and destruction in our city. We abhor and condemn this, and consistently in our churches over the past three years we have tried to promote peace. We have condemned violence whether it be the violence of riot and destruction or the violence of injustice and abuse of authority. We have gone on the streets during riots and endeavoured to calm situations with varying degrees of success. We have never before, however, made an appeal in public such as this, but we feel that in this grave situation it would be wrong to be silent.*

The letter was signed by thirteen priests in parishes in Derry and the Waterside viz. Eugene Boland, Denis Bradley, Edward Daly, James Doherty, Liam Donnelly, John Irwin, Stephen Kearney, Edward Kilpatrick, Patrick Mullan, Anthony Mulvey, John McCullagh, George McLaughlin and Henry O'Kane. The letter was posted that Saturday afternoon and a copy issued to the media. It was significant in the sense that it was the first joint statement, which priests serving in the troubled parishes had issued. In view of coming events, unfortunately, it proved to be irrelevant.

On Monday, 9 August, I was awakened before 5 a.m. by a commotion on the street below my bedroom window. I pulled back the curtain and looked out. There were people in the street below in a state of panic. I asked them what was the matter. They told me that just a few minutes before, police and army had raided nearby homes

* Derry Diocesan Archive.

and arrested people. All the other priests were awake at this time. The doorbell and phones were ringing. As I was dressing, another priest called me to his room at the front of the house and together we watched a number of huge helicopters flying in formation from the southwest over the city centre. They seemed to come from the Strabane direction and were flying towards Limavady, along the Foyle, south to north. It was like a scene from the Vietnam War, or a scene from the movie *Apocalypse Now*. We quickly got dressed and went out to the streets. Few people in the area were in bed at this stage. They were all out in the streets, some of them still in their night attire. There were no army of police vehicles or personnel on the streets around the cathedral at that time. The rumours flew. It was obvious that something very dramatic had happened and that a number of men had been taken in. We knew some of those who had been 'lifted'. We were puzzled because there was no obvious reason for their arrest. There was a mixture of panic and fear on the streets on that bright sunny August morning. It was not until mid-morning that Brian Faulkner, the Stormont Minister of Home Affairs, announced that internment without trial had been introduced.

There followed a day and night of community unrest and alarm and the fiercest and most intensive rioting since August 1969. The barricades went up again and the sound of gunfire accompanied the rioting from time to time. A substantial number of individuals and families fled the city and went across the border. The families of the interned were endeavouring to find out the whereabouts of their men who had been taken away. Little information was forthcoming. Whilst, remarkably, there were no fatalities on internment day in Derry, more than twelve people lost their lives in various parts of the North, mostly in Belfast. Amongst the fatalities in Belfast was a priest, Father Hugh Mullan, shot dead when he was endeavouring to administer the last rites to a victim.

The days immediately following internment were frenzied. There were demonstrations, marches, riots, shootings, protests, explosions, refugees, destruction; people were seeking comfort, reassurance, and advice. We lived amidst chaos and extreme anger. It was clear that internment had been used merely against the

Catholic community and in many cases people were interned simply because of their interest in Irish culture or language. There were others who were detained, for no discernible reason, fair or foul. Internment was perceived as yet another instrument of repression. Cardinal William Conway, Archbishop of Armagh, condemned internment unequivocally and also claimed that the internees had been maltreated. Archbishop Simms of the Church of Ireland said that internment was the lesser of two evils. Many Catholics in positions of public office resigned as a protest against internment.

Around this time, in the crazy summer of 1971, there was an interesting, if frightening, incident. In the heady days of 1969, there were great promises of reforms in the RUC and there were many appeals made to Catholics to join the RUC. Some Catholics joined the RUC at this time, in good faith, including at least one man from the Rossville Flats in the very heart of the Bogside. This young man, called Danny Barr, was home in the Bogside visiting his family on the weekend of 15 August 1971, the weekend after internment. He attended the 7.30 Mass in St Eugene's Cathedral on the Sunday evening and then decided to visit his grandmother who lived a short distance away in Westland Street. He was in civilian clothing, of course. I celebrated the 7.30 Mass that Sunday evening. Shortly after I returned to the parochial house after Mass, there was a frantic caller at the door saying that this young police officer had been attacked by a crowd, who had ambushed him at Laburnum Terrace a short distance away. I immediately went there and saw a crowd gathered in front of a house. I pushed my way through the crowd and this man was up against the front door of a house and was being viciously kicked and beaten. My colleague, Father Bennie O'Neill, was already there, endeavouring to protect the man. We managed with the help of a few reasonable people to position ourselves between him and the crowd and to plead with them to stop. There was an elderly lady in the house. She was terrified and wisely refused to open the door. After what seemed an interminable period of time, another priest, Father Joe Carolan, came along in a Volkswagen, and by general persuasion and cajoling we persuaded the crowd to let us bring the injured man to a first aid post. We brought him in Father Joe's car to St Mary's School in Creggan where there was a first aid post and nurses treated him there. However, the crowd followed us up to Creggan and assembled outside the school demanding that the police officer be handed over to them when he had received first aid. He was badly injured and terrified. We hid him in an obscure room in the school, a kind of cupboard. Eventually a local GP, Dr James McCabe, arrived on the scene. He had been a member of the old Derry Corporation. He contacted somebody in Stormont by phone. Whilst he was on the phone, three masked civilians carrying pistols arrived in the school, stating that they were members of the Provisional IRA. They demanded that the police officer be handed over to them immediately. It was the first time that I had come face-to-face with a group of masked men carrying firearms, the first time that I knowingly saw an IRA unit. We were fearful at first, but they were so nervous and inexperienced that the people staffing the first aid post felt that they did not pose a real threat. They were only a few minutes in the school, when most people had a good idea of their identities. As time went on, they became increasingly edgy and insecure. We eventually persuaded them that we would try to embarrass the Stormont Government by demanding that the police officer be taken to Letterkenny Hospital for treatment. (A few days earlier the Stormont Government had strictly banned the removal of riot victims from Derry to hospitals in Donegal.) Eventually, after much haggling, Dr McCabe and others persuaded the Stormont authorities to allow the police officer to be taken to Letterkenny in a Knights of Malta ambulance. It was agreed that the ambulance would be permitted to drive non-stop at speed through an army checkpoint on the Letterkenny Road *en route* to the border. It was a checkpoint at which all vehicles were required to stop. The deal was that Dr McCabe, Attracta Simms, who was a young nurse, and myself would travel in the back of the ambulance with the police officer, as security! Everyone, including the masked men seemed to be satisfied with the deal. Nobody lost. All the time, we were worried lest the British Army would storm the school. However, around midnight, Father Martin Rooney, the parish priest of the area, and others managed to calm the crowd outside. We took the police officer from his hiding place and Dr McCabe, Attracta and myself and another man, unknown to any of us, boarded the ambulance. The ambulance driver, Hugh Deehan, flew through the Army checkpoint at about sixty miles per hour with all of us lying flat in the back of the ambulance saying our prayers! We hoped that the soldiers manning the checkpoint had got the signal from their authorities! We eventually arrived safely with our patient at Letterkenny Hospital. Danny Barr was moved by helicopter to a hospital in the North shortly afterwards and eventually recovered from his injuries.

An interesting aside – the next time I met the 'unknown man in the ambulance' was six months year later in Washington DC in the US Congress where he appeared to be very much at home. I do not know to this day what his precise role was in Creggan on that night. He was one of several mysterious and sinister people from various parts of the world who circulated in Derry during those years. I was once loudly and severely reprimanded by a pony-tailed young German hippy, when I interrupted him preparing petrol bombs in Colmcille Court. He told me that he knew the people of the Bogside and I did not! In the summer of 1971, a large number of students from continental Europe came to Derry seeking excitement. It was the place to be, 'the scene' during that particular summer. Most of the locals would have been happier, if they had chosen to stay at home.

Wednesday, 18 August 1971 is one of the days that stand out in my memory for several reasons. During the early morning, the movement of Army vehicles awakened me. There was a substantial Army presence in the street outside. They were moving into the Bogside to remove barricades. In the immediate vicinity of the cathedral, there were not any confrontations, but accompanying the sound of the Army vehicles was the din of bin lids being rattled. After Internment Day, this became the form of alarm used by the Bogsiders to indicate the presence of the Army in the area. Whilst few homes in the Bogside had telephones at that time, there were metal garbage cans at every home and backyard in Derry. Once the Army was spotted moving into an area, people would take the lids of their bins and bang them on the pavement or on the wall of their backyard. This would be taken up in the adjoining street and so on. It was the Bogside version of bush telegraph – and it was very effective. The din was horrendous. After Mass on that morning, Father Bennie O'Neill received a phone call from a priest in Creggan informing him that a young man from our parish had been shot dead. His name was Eamonn Lafferty. He had been shot dead in a confrontation with the Army in Creggan near the City Cemetery. Father George McLaughlin, a curate in Creggan parish, risked his life to administer the last rites to him. Father Bennie asked me to accompany him to the Lafferty home in Creggan Road, just up the hill from the cathedral, to inform his parents and break the bad news to them. We both knew the family very well. Eamonn's parents were both very good people whom we greatly respected. Father Bennie and I walked together up Creggan hill to the house. There was not much conversation on the way. We were not quite sure what to say to the family. We were not sure of the circumstances of his death. We only knew that he was dead – shot by the Army. Breaking bad news to an unsuspecting family is one of the most difficult things that a priest is called upon to do. When the person has met a violent death, it compounds the difficulty. People immediately ask how did it happen, why did it happen. There is no reasonable or cogent answer that makes sense in such circumstances. The messenger just endeavours to comfort and console and pray with them and ensure that all the family members are informed as soon as possible. People very often wish to be brought to the scene immediately. In cases where the British Army shoots someone, this is not possible. The area is usually cordoned off and access is impossible. When we reached the Lafferty family home in Creggan Road, we realised that a family nearby was already aware of the death but the members of the Lafferty family were unaware of anything. It was a difficult duty, because they were a loving and devoted family. The parents were devastated. Father Bennie dealt with the situation as best he could. There is no easy way of doing this. The priest who had responsibility for that district of the parish then arrived and he took over the ministry to the family at that stage, and Father O'Neill and I departed from the scene. By now, relatives and friends of the family were gathering. News spreads quickly in Derry. Although we did not know it at the time, later on in the morning we became aware that Eamonn was an IRA volunteer, the first member of the Provisional IRA to die at the hands of the British Army in Derry.

The Army were very heavy-handed throughout that day and there were many protests against the Army's intrusion into the area. It was a very hot day. I remember taking part in one sit-down protest early that afternoon on a street in the Bogside. The occasion stands out in my mind because my trousers got stuck to the molten tar boiling up in the street. I had to go home and change! Two MPs in the Stormont Parliament, John Hume and Ivan Cooper, were arrested in another sit-down protest in Laburnum Terrace during that afternoon. They were hosed with purple-dyed water from water-cannon, and eventually arrested and taken to Victoria Barracks, the RUC headquarters. It was initially thought that they had been interned. As word spread of these and other arrests and their possible internment, people were outraged and a huge crowd converged on Victoria Barracks. John Hume was already hugely respected in Derry. I joined the crowd and we chanted and protested outside the barracks on Strand Road, one of the main city thoroughfares. Apart from the verbal protest, there was no violence at that stage, as a far as I can remember. Hume and Cooper were released about 8.30 p.m. and were carried shoulder high to the entrance to the Rossville Flats where both addressed the crowd to loud cheering and acclaim. After the speeches, I was chatting with Ivan Cooper on Rossville Street, when a man approached us. He told us that there was an unexploded bomb in a small tea chest in a children's playground in Gartan Square, about half a mile away. He said that the IRA had left it there as a booby trap for the Army, but the Army didn't come or rise to the bait. His story was that the IRA was concerned that the Army had spotted the bomb and had staked out the area, and that if IRA personnel were to remove or attempt to defuse the bomb, they would be either shot dead or arrested. He was concerned that the bomb be removed before the morning and the arrival of local children to play in the area. He wanted us to defuse the bomb and remove it! He told us the details of the fuse and how to make the device safe. We were not exactly brimming over with enthusiasm. Ivan and I discussed the matter for some time and we decided the best thing to do was to go to the police. So we

went to Victoria Barracks and, without stating the exact location of
the device, asked the police if they were aware of the presence of a
bomb or booby trap in the area. They assured us that neither they
nor the Army were aware of such a device anywhere in the city. We
told them that we were prepared to make the device safe and then
advise them of its location. They weren't very happy about this proposal, but allowed us to proceed. They had a lot on their hands that
night and would have agreed to most anything. We went to an area
near Gartan Square. It was after midnight at this stage. We looked
around the area for police or Army and, after satisfying ourselves
that they were not present in the area, sought the tea chest. Sure
enough we discovered the small box covered by some undergrowth
precisely as had been described by our informant. There was a wire,
covered up with grass, leading from the box, which we followed up
an alley behind some houses, and at the end of the wire was a car
battery covered in sacking. One of the terminals had already been
connected. We disconnected this and then pulled the wires with the
fuse out of the device, as instructed. It was a rather crude device.
The device was safe. As a concluding flourish, Ivan thought that it
would be 'good craic' to leave the car battery outside John Hume's
house in West End Park nearby. This we did. Then we telephoned
the police to tell them where the tea chest bomb could be found. I
do not know what happened after that. I never heard of the matter
after that night. I have to confess now that the entire exploit was
crazy and juvenile and utterly irresponsible. If truth were told, both
Ivan and I found it wildly exciting and derived considerable enjoyment from it.

Shortly after this, I had another experience of 'defusing' a
device. After I had finished hearing Confessions one Saturday
morning, a woman, Mrs Bryson, who lived nearby in the Little
Diamond was waiting for me in the parochial house. She was in an
anxious and distressed state and told me that she had discovered
what she described as 'an extra clothes-line' across her backyard.
She asked me to accompany her back to her home. I went with her
and sure enough just a few inches from the clothes-line was another similar wire running across her backyard. I climbed up on the
wall to see where it went. It seemed to run across another couple of

backyards down to a lane or alley between her house and houses in Eglinton Terrace. At the end of the alley, there was a car battery, hidden under sacking. Once again one terminal was connected. I disconnected it and replaced the sacking. I was, by now, becoming familiar with the procedure. I followed the other end of the wire to an abandoned and derelict house at the corner of Little Diamond and Eglinton Place, formerly occupied by a family called Doherty. I had attended two elderly handicapped brothers, known locally as the twin Dohertys, in that house years before. In what had been the kitchen of the abandoned house were two large sacks full of material, presumably explosives. They were placed against a wall. (I didn't examine the contents; I guessed they didn't consist of potatoes or coal!). I left the house quickly and went back to Mrs Bryson. I asked her if she had a pair of scissors. She did some dressmaking. Then, while she held it, I cut the 'clothes-line' across her backyard and got two stones, which held the separated wire in place on the wall. The device could no longer be detonated, although that was not apparent from the detonation point. I assured Mrs Bryson that all would be well. Although she never mentioned the word 'bomb', she knew quite well what the 'clothes-line' really was. That afternoon, there was rioting in the area. A troop of soldiers, as was their wont, took cover at the very gable wall of the house inside which the bomb was planted. Nothing happened, thank God. A third party advised the Army not to take cover in that particular place in future. The reason was not given. But they took the advice. The house was subsequently demolished as part of the redevelopment.

There was rioting virtually every afternoon and some evenings for several months after internment. Exchanges of gunfire were now an everyday event. Bombs were being detonated. I spent every afternoon and most evenings in the Bogside with the residents. The area had become like a war zone. Helicopters were constantly overhead. CS gas was regularly in the air. There was a mixture of fear and tension and also a certain measure of the excitement, which accompanies danger. This excitement attracted many spectators to the area when rioting was in progress. These were mainly, although not only, young people. Monday, 6 September 1971 was a typical afternoon at that time. There were initially skirmishes between young rioters and the Army in William Street. Gradually the rioting progressed up William Street towards the Little Diamond and the gates of the cathedral. Then it progressed over Little Diamond towards Eglinton Place and the corner mentioned earlier. At this time, on this particular afternoon, I happened to be in Eglinton Terrace, which adjoins Eglinton Place. I was calling on an elderly lady called Mrs Houston, who lived there. Suddenly there was a fierce burst of gunfire nearby. People scattered in all directions and sought cover. I went to the door to see what had happened. Then I was told that somebody had been hit. The victim was lying on the ground at the bottom of a lamp-post at a corner where three streets meet – Eglinton Place, Lisfannon Park and Blucher Street, outside the home of the Meenan family. The victim tragically was a lovely young girl called Annette McGavigan. She was 14 years old. She had been eating an ice cream that she had purchased in a nearby shop moments before. She was killed instantly. I administered the last rites to her. I was deeply upset. It was my first time to see a victim of gunfire immediately after being hit by a high-velocity bullet. It was not a pleasant sight. Annette was, like many others, a spectator, fatally attracted by the excitement of the rioting. She was an innocent caught in crossfire, an exchange of fire between the Provisional IRA and the Army. I had no idea, at the time, about which side fired the fatal shot. From where she was lying, it would appear that the more likely party was the Army. The rioters had obviously, either by design or accident, drawn the Army into a situation where an IRA ambush had been set up. After Annette's body was taken to hospital by ambulance, I had the task of informing her mother and family. Many people in the vicinity of the shooting knew her and, as far as I remember, she was accompanied by another girl of similar age. Her home was in Drumcliffe Avenue in the Meenan Park area. I made my way there and knocked on the door. Her mother opened the door and greeted me warmly and pleasantly. At times like that, I just wanted the ground to swallow me up. I gradually broke the terrible news. Then other members of the family had to be located and told. As ever in Derry, kind neighbours came to the house and endeavoured to support those who were devastated by grief. Even now, all these years later, I remember that afternoon and that family clearly – the tears, the disbelief, the heart-break, the anger, the questions – why, why, why? Annette McGavigan's death had a considerable impact on me.

Other young women, at this time, were the victims of a particularly crude and humiliating form of punishment. The Provisional IRA decreed that local girls should not befriend or socialise with British soldiers. They added that anyone disobeying this ruling would 'be dealt with'. A few young girls, who dared to disobey their dictum, were seized, had their hair violently cut off and, after being tied to a lamppost, had wet paint or tar poured over them. Sometimes feathers were also dumped over them and a sign hung around their neck with 'Brit lover' or something similar written on it. One of the sadder aspects of this disgusting, cruel and humiliating activity was that women often enthusiastically participated in these punishments that were harshly meted out. Newspapers and photographers were usually alerted and summoned to the scene by the media-conscious IRA to ensure that the message would go out to the general population. I happily never had first-hand experience of seeing a victim of 'tarring and feathering'. However, I did know one young woman who was made to suffer this experience. I knew her well. She was very vulnerable. Picking her or anyone out for this treatment was a cowardly and despicable act.

Neighbours called one of my colleagues to the scene after one of these incidents in Westland Street. He had to cut the girl free himself, because local people were afraid to do so. He was infuriated by the experience. The following Sunday, we preached at all Masses in the cathedral about the evil of this practice of tarring and feathering and all forms of intimidation. The idea that neighbour could perpetrate such atrocities on neighbour was appalling and an indication of where our society was going. Large numbers of our people were becoming brutalised.

In mid-November 1971, I wrote the following letter on this issue to the *Derry Journal* and several other newspapers:

As a priest who has spent almost ten years working in the Bogside area of Derry, I would like to express my condemnation and abhorrence of what has happened there over the past few nights. The haircutting and tarring of young girls is abominable and abhorrent and has shocked and saddened the vast majority of the people of the area.

Over the past three years, many terrible things have happened here. When people are just recovering from one horror they seem to be confronted by something even worse. We have seen 4 men, a young girl of 14 and several soldiers murdered. We have seen business premises and industries burned down and damaged needlessly, with all the resultant loss of possessions, homes and jobs. We have seen an evil and partial law of internment deprive innocent men of their freedom.

I am convinced that at least two of the Derry internees were cruelly tortured. I have visited the Derry internees at both Long Kesh and Crumlin Road prison. I hope to visit them again in the coming week. I know that some of them and others here in Derry believe that several men were interned as a result of information given by girls fraternising with soldiers. I am not in a position to determine the truth of this but, even if it were true, it does not justify the barbaric treatment handed out by self-appointed judges on recent nights. To cut off a young girl's hair, pour tar or paint over her head and publicly humiliate her four days before her marriage is really sinking to the depths of humanity. People like this have no right to call themselves Christians.

It is to be hoped that this kind of exercise that is carried out in the middle of the night when few people can intervene will come to an end at once. Derry people, Bogside people are basically decent, upright, kind and fair-minded people ... they seek equal rights for all. They find themselves trapped in an impossible situation resulting from the fumblings and manipulations of politicians over the years. I am confident that they will not allow defenceless young girls to be treated in this way ever again.

On returning to the parochial house after particularly awful experiences, and there were many such occasions, there was a mixture of emotions. With other priests, I was always extremely tired, and sad and angry too. There was a feeling of helplessness. I wondered where Jesus Christ fitted into all of this. It drove me to my knees and the oratory was a place where I could have a quiet period of prayer and reflection in the late evening or early morning and endeavour to put the situation in context and try to find some meaning or purpose in it. It was difficult to find meaning or purpose in the madness that had engulfed the community that I served. Prayer was a source of comfort.

There were no days off. We were on duty seven days a week and twenty-four hours a day. I scarcely got home to visit my mother in the last months of 1971. Previously, I had tried to get to visit her once a week. We talked regularly on the telephone and she was very understanding. She was concerned for my safety. Belleek was still relatively quiet at this time and far away from the bedlam in Derry and Belfast.

I was so demoralised in late August 1971 that I wrote to my Irish College Rome classmate, John Satterthwaite who was, by now, Bishop of Lismore in New South Wales in Australia. I discussed with him the possibilities of ministering in his diocese or somewhere in Australia for a few years and explained my frustrations to him. I longed for new pastures. John kindly answered me. However, by the time he had answered, I was feeling somewhat better and decided to hang on in Derry for another while.

In the weeks after internment, a new place or name suddenly found its way into the lexicon of the North – Long Kesh. Previous to 9 August 1971, Long Kesh, outside Lisburn in County Antrim, had been an unknown disused RAF airfield. Now it had become an internment camp. It was a place where a number of our parishioners were held without charge or trial. We regularly visited parishioners in hospital or prison. I remember my first visit to Long Kesh in October 1971. It was the first of many visits there. Long Kesh was a strangely familiar place. There were clusters of two or three Nissen huts surrounded by barbed wire. The internees ran the show inside the wire and aptly called their accommodation 'cages'. Their guards stayed outside. The familiarity came from old war films about German prison camps, especially escape films! The internees were very welcoming. Many of them were angry and frustrated.

They had no idea why there were interned or how long they would be held for. Almost all of them had been badly maltreated and some were systematically tortured after they had been arrested. They were worried about their families, their jobs, their farms, their businesses. They were anxious for news of home. They were anxious to know what was being done on their behalf and anxious that the injustice of their internment and maltreatment be highlighted. On one of my visits, the idea of a concert party from Derry to perform in Long Kesh was suggested by one of the Derry internees who knew of my interest in music and entertainment. I took up the idea and was advised to write seeking permission from the authorities. In the meantime, I set about getting a group of local entertainers to make up the concert party. There was no scarcity of volunteers.

There was light relief and black humour in the midst of all of the terrible things that were going on.

In the early years of the Troubles, many people in the Bogside area of Derry, including myself, had a little electronic gadget that could be attached to a transistor radio to enable the listener to tune in to the Army communications network. A local enthusiast manufactured these and offered them for sale. They sold like hot cakes. I am sure that they were illegal. They were very useful when a bomb or shooting was heard. You could tune in and find out immediately where the incident had taken place, as the Army rushed to the scene. The Army network was, perhaps, the most listened-to radio station in the Bogside at that time – the first local radio! Some of the discussions overheard on this network were highly amusing and illustrated the culture gap between the locals and the Army. An incident on an Ash Wednesday morning in the early 1970s provided a very good example of this.

At that time, the Army had observation posts on many of the taller buildings, the city walls and various vantage points around the Bogside. The soldier on observation duty reported back to his base commander on any unusual events or developments occuring in the surrounding streets. On the morning of Ash Wednesday about 10.30, the soldier on duty there was codenamed Delta One. He reported back to an officer whose codename was Charlie Oscar.

The soldier had a Geordie accent and the officer had a 'plummy' public school accent.

The following is a paraphrase of the conversation, as I remember it.

Delta One – 'Delta One here to Charlie Oscar. There are large crowds emerging from St Eugene's Cathedral with strange marks on their foreheads. Over.'

Charlie Oscar – 'Charlie Oscar to Delta One. Are these people carrying weapons of any kind? In which direction are they proceeding? Over.'

Delta One – 'I do not observe any weapons. They are dispersing in all directions – some are going in the direction of the Little Diamond, others are proceeding towards William Street. Over.'

Charlie Oscar – 'Are these people all yobboes?* Over.'

Delta One – 'Negative; there are adults, men and women, some elderly, some not so elderly and some are wheeling prams. Over.'

Charlie Oscar – 'Could you describe to me in more detail the marks on their foreheads, which you mentioned? Over.'

Delta One – 'There is a strange little black or dark mark. They all have it. Over'.

Charlie Oscar – 'Roger. Just leave that with me. Delta One. I'll get back to you in a moment. Over'.

A few moments later Charlie Oscar came back on air.

Charlie Oscar – 'Charlie Oscar to Delta One – re that matter about the marks on the foreheads – don't worry about that. I have just been advised that the padres do that to the Romans on this day each year'.

Delta One – 'Roger'.

Charlie Oscar – 'Over and out'.

* Army slang for young boys and rioters.

Later in the 1970s, the British Army changed their radio frequency to a band that could only be overheard on very sophisticated equipment. Thus they lost people like myself and the mass audience of eavesdroppers that they previously had, but 'interested people' were still able to overhear them. The Army was incredibly careless about their use of the radio and some of the sensitive matters they discussed on their networks.

There had to be some light relief from what was going on around us. Whatever happened, the sharp Derry humour prevailed. I found that my interest in and involvement in theatre served to bolster my morale. I had some small involvement with the '71 Players and their activities during that autumn. Despite the troubled background, the company managed to present a number of fine productions and had good audiences. Unfortunately a cloud was cast over this activity when two firemen lost their lives in a huge blaze in the Melville Hotel just across the road from the Little Theatre.

1971 was a wicked year. Internment was a major benchmark.

CHAPTER 14

A Defining Moment

The Paras – an anti-internment march –
fear and terror in Rossville Street – the death of Jackie Duddy –
bodies everywhere – Mrs McDaid and her family

In the days after Christmas 1971, I took the opportunity to have my first break for a considerable period of time. I went and stayed with my mother in Belleek for a few relaxing days. I also spent time with my brother, Tom, and his wife and family, who also lived in Belleek. I took the opportunity to join my mother in visiting my three sisters and their families – Marion in Belcoo, Dympna in Mountcharles and Anne in Lisnaskea. It was good to get in touch with the family once again. I had seen very little of them in the previous year. People from outside Derry had become frightened to visit the city since the Troubles began. My family were apprehensive about coming to visit me in a troubled city.

Returning to Derry after the short break, I decided to revive a few of my earlier interests. I offered to produce a play for the '71 Players. The three-act play I chose was *The Righteous Are Bold*, a melodrama by the playwright, Frank Carney, and set in the West of Ireland. I cast the play and began rehearsals in mid-January.

I also got cracking on the Long Kesh concert party, but a letter to me from the Secretary of the Ministry of Home Affairs in Stormont, dated 24 January 1972 put paid to that project. The letter read:

> I refer to your recent letter about the possibility of entertaining internees at the Internment Centre, Long Kesh.

You may be aware that a number of concerts were staged at Long Kesh at the end of last year. However, it was never intended that this arrangement would extend beyond the Christmas season and I regret that it is not now possible to allow 'live' shows to be staged at the Internment Centre.

Permission was refused. The refusal was not altogether a surprise.

Rioting, gunfire, arson and bombing punctuated early January 1972. Resentment against internment continued and deepened in the Catholic community. On Saturday, 22 January, there was a march on Magilligan beach near Derry. All marches were illegal and banned by the Stormont Government at this time. It was a protest against internment in general and the opening of a new internment camp in Magilligan in particular. It was one of a series of similar marches around the North. There was a heated confrontation between protesters and members of the Parachute Regiment. Such a confrontation on a beach was rather incongruous in the middle of January. Although not apparent at the time, it was a hint of the disaster that lay ahead. NICRA had planned a protest march against internment in Derry the following Sunday, 30 January.

The week before the march on Sunday, 30 January, was a bad week. Loyalists threatened to attack or disrupt the march. On the Thursday of that week, two RUC officers were cruelly murdered in a fierce IRA ambush just up the street from the cathedral. Police and Army saturated our entire area for many hours after the ambush. The atmosphere became very ugly and frightening. I was deeply disturbed by the fact that some people, who should have known better, were jubilant after the deaths of the two policemen. People were becoming more and more hardened by the constant violence. We waited for the weekend with a little foreboding, but no more than usual on the eve of a big march. We felt that we had been through all this before. My main concern was to have a good rehearsal of the play with my cast late on Sunday evening when, hopefully, all would be over.

Sunday, 30 January 1972, was a cold and crisp day, a beautiful invigorating winter's day with a clear blue sky. I assisted at the various morning Masses in the cathedral, did door duty, helped at

Communion and spoke with people as they came and went. On an average Sunday at that time, five or six thousand people attended Mass in St Eugene's. People talked about the usual things. Some mentioned the shooting of the police officers. Some talked about the weather, some talked about football and a few, very few, talked about that afternoon's march. It was not foremost in the minds of people. I was scheduled as celebrant for the 12 noon Mass. After the Communion ended and I was preparing for the concluding prayers of the Mass, Father Bennie O'Neill, administrator of the cathedral, came to me on the altar. He told me that, within the previous fifteen minutes, large numbers of heavily armed paratroopers had moved into position around the cathedral and into all the adjoining streets. He asked me to appeal to the people to remain calm and to make their way home without getting into any confrontation with these new arrivals. I made the appeal, as requested.

We had our Sunday lunch together as usual. At this time, due to the arrival of the paratroopers, we were becoming a little worried about confrontations at the march. Other priests, who had seen them, described the paratroopers as being gung-ho and quite aggressive. However, we were not unduly worried. Around 2.15 p.m., I left the parochial house to go to Abbey Street, to take a funeral to the City Cemetery. A lady called Mrs Organ had died. I had attended her during her illness. The funeral left Abbey Street about 2.30 and I led the funeral cortège, which made its way to the City Cemetery, which lay between the Bogside and Creggan. By this time, large numbers of people were making their way to join the march. The march was to set out from Creggan at three o'clock. The paratroopers were less visible than they had been earlier. In fact, I cannot recall seeing any soldiers on the way to the cemetery. I conducted the burial service, spent some time with the family at the graveside and then the undertaker drove me back to the parochial house some time between 3 and 3.30 p.m. The head of the Civil Rights March then was proceeding down Creggan Street from Lone Moor Road, past the Cathedral on its way to William Street.

When I returned from the funeral, I decided to go to the Rossville Street area to ensure that the elderly and housebound were alright. This was my usual practice when there was a possibility of serious confrontation or of CS Gas being used. On my way down William Street, as I walked along with some of those in the march, my attention was drawn to some marchers ahead who were jeering and looking to their left. I looked in that direction and saw a soldier with a rifle on a wall or roof at the rear of Great James Street Presbyterian church across the waste ground where Richardson's Shirt Factory used to be. I had never seen a soldier in that particular location before. At the corner of William Street and Rossville Street, most of the crowd turned right to go over Rossville Street; some people proceeded further down William Street. I went on past the junction of William Street and Rossville Street. The crowd had built up. The Army had erected a barrier further down William Street at the bend in the street, between the junction with Chamberlain Street and Waterloo Place. There was a crowd backed up some distance from the barricade. I went to the doorway of Porter's radio and television shop and observed the situation for a few moments. I was on the point of going back to Rossville Street when there was an outbreak of jeering and catcalling. Originally it was good humoured, and then, after a short time, missiles were thrown by some members of the crowd in the direction of the Army barrier. The firing of the missiles intensified and the Army respond-ed with water-cannon and CS gas. The people nearest the barrier tried to get away and there was a moment of panic as people at the back of the crowd tried to push forward; but then the crowd thinned and dispersed, apart from a hard core of rioters. Some of the crowd eventually dispersed along Chamberlain Street, some went through an alley at Macari's fish-and-chip shop, and the biggest majority went across Rossville Street with the main body of the march.

I then moved to Rossville Street, and stopped between the junc-tions with Pilot's Row and Eden Place. When I reached this point, I noticed a fair-haired man with glasses, whom I later knew to be Kevin McCorry, a leader of the Civil Rights Movement. He was using a loud hailer asking the crowd to leave the William Street area and go to Free Derry Corner where there was going to be a meet-ing. Most of the crowd paid attention to this and the crowd gradu-ally started to disperse, most of them moving towards Free Derry Corner.

I decided to stay where I was so that I could be available, if required, to the elderly people living in nearby Kells Walk and Glenfada Park. I did not intend going to the meeting. There was still some CS gas being fired and a greatly reduced number of young people were throwing stones at the Army barriers in Little James Street and William Street. I spoke with a number of people who were passing by. Some were discussing the march, expressing relief that it had passed off relatively peacefully. I spoke to Stephen McGonagle, former vice-chairman of the Derry Development Commission, and subsequently Ombudsman for Northern Ireland. Then I met Patrick Duffy (known to local people as 'Barman'), a Civil Rights steward, a very much-respected man in the Bogside area. I was concerned about some of the young people who were behaving rather suspiciously at the rear of some shops in William Street, adjacent to the waste ground. These shopkeepers had suffered a lot of vandalism and destruction at that time. I asked 'Barman' to keep an eye on them lest they do any further damage to this property.

Some time after this, I heard two or three shots ring out. I knew that these were gunshots and not rubber bullets, because the report of a live round is much sharper and louder than the report of a gas grenade or rubber bullet. These sounded to me like the sharp cracks of a rifle. With others, I moved close to the wall at the end of Kells Walk to take cover. There were two or three shots. They were single shots, with a momentary pause between each. I formed the impression that they came from the Great James Street area. Certainly most of the people present looked in that direction and took cover as if the gunfire was coming from there. There was a moment of panic and then things settled down again. Shortly after this, a person came rushing up to me and said to me that two men had been shot in the vicinity of the Grandstand Bar, which was located in William Street. I moved into the passage between Kells Walk and Colmcille Court to make my way to the scene, and I met people who told me that two priests were already on the scene attending to the two casualties. They said that the casualties were being taken to hospital. One of these priests was Father Joe

Carolan. I then made my way back to my original position in Rossville Street.

On my way, I spoke to some of the residents in Kells Walk. They opened their windows and spoke to me. They were concerned about the gunfire. I assured them that all was well and that there was nothing to fear. Within my sight, there were still a number of people in the vicinity, stragglers at the end of the march, people chatting, and a number of young people were still throwing stones sporadically at the Army. But most of the people had, by this time, made their way or were making their way to Free Derry Corner.

Some minutes after I returned to Rossville Street, the revving up of engines, motor engines, drew my attention. I looked across towards Little James Street. I noticed there or four Saracen armoured cars moving towards me at increasing speed, followed by soldiers on foot. I observed them for a few moments. Simultaneously everyone in the area began to run in the opposite direction – away from William Street and across Rossville Street towards Free Derry Corner. I ran with the others but veered to my left towards the courtyard of Rossville Flats. I was running and, like most of the crowd, looking back every few moments, to see if the armoured cars and soldiers were still coming. They kept coming. Around this time, I remember seeing someone thrown in the air by a Saracen. This happened somewhere on the waste ground to the east of Rossville Street.

As I was entering the courtyard, I noticed a young boy running beside me. I was running and he was running and, like me, looking back from time to time. He caught my attention because he was smiling or laughing. I do not know whether he was amused at my ungainly running or exhilarated by nervous excitement. He seemed about 16 or 17. I did not see anything in his hands. I didn't know his name then, but I later learned that his name was Jackie Duddy. When we reached the centre of the courtyard, I heard a shot and simultaneously this young boy, just beside me, gasped or groaned loudly. This was the first shot that I had heard since the two or three shots I had heard some time earlier in the afternoon. I glanced around and the young boy just fell on his face. He fell in the middle of the courtyard, in an area, which was marked out in parallel rectangles for car parking. My first impression was that he had been hit by a rubber bullet. That may be because the noise of the shot had been masked by the general din and chaos, which prevailed at that time. The shot seemed to come from behind us, from the area in which the Saracens were located. I thought initially, that the shot had been the report of a rubber bullet gun; I could not imagine that he had been struck by a live round.

I ran on still looking back. Some or all of the Saracens were still progressing towards the Rossville Flats. I looked at the passageway between Blocks One and Two of the Flats, the exit I had intended and hoped to use to escape from the courtyard. It was jammed by a mass of panic-stricken and frightened people. A woman was screaming. The air was filled with the sound of panic and fear. With considerable apprehension, I realised that there was no way out of the courtyard. Then there was a burst of gunfire that caused terror. I could not be sure whether they were shots from several weapons simultaneously or from one weapon. These were live rounds – there was no doubt any more. I then sought cover behind a low wall at the rear of the garages at the foot of Block Two of the Rossville Flats. There were about twenty or thirty people already taking cover there. There was no room for anyone else. So I threw myself on the ground at the end of the wall. All the shots seemed to come from the location of the Saracen armoured cars between Pilot's Row and the courtyard of the Flats. During this period of time, I was not aware of any shots being fired towards the soldiers' position or of shots being fired from the upper floors of the Flats or from any-where else.

During a lull in the firing, I looked over from where I was lying and saw Jackie still lying out in the middle of the car park where he had fallen. He was, at this time, lying on his back with his head towards me. This puzzled me. I had distinctly remembered him falling on his face. I thought that, perhaps, he had managed to turn himself over. I subsequently learned that Willie Barber, who was running behind me, had turned him over. I then decided to make my way out to him. I took a handkerchief from my pocket and waved it for a few moments and then I got up in a crouched posi-tion and I went to the boy. I knelt beside him. There was a substantial amount of blood oozing from his shirt; I think it was just inside the arm, on the right or left side, I cannot remember which. I put my handkerchief inside the shirt to try and staunch the bleeding. Then a young member of the Knights of Malta, Charles Glenn, suddenly appeared on the other side of this boy. He immediately set about treating the wound. I felt that I should administer the last rites to the boy and I anointed him. The gunfire started again around this time. We got as close to the ground as we could. Then there was another lull; a group of two or three people came out and stood behind us. They offered help. We asked them to go back – we felt that we were safer on our own – so they went back.

After some time, a tall young man with long, fair hair dashed past us. Just in front of us, a little to our right, he began dancing up and down and screaming at the soldiers. I thought that he was shouting, 'Shoot me, shoot me', or something of that nature. He had his hands raised over his head, waving them around. He had nothing in his hands. He appeared to be hysterical. We shouted at him to clear off and then a soldier stepped out from the gable end of Block One of the Rossville Flats, went down on one knee, took aim and fired at him. The young man staggered and then he started running around crazily for a few moments. I do not know exactly where he went to or whether he fell but I did not see him afterwards. I knew, however, that he had been struck by a shot from that soldier whom I saw taking deliberate aim. The soldier stepped out from the corner of the Rossville Flats, near the access door. I subsequently came to know that this man's name was Michael Bridge. He was hit in the leg, and fortunately, survived. It was the one occasion in my lifetime when I witnessed one human being deliberately shoot another human being, both of them being close to me and within my vision. One was armed, the other was unarmed. This occurred as I was kneeling beside another young boy whose lifeblood was seeping away. It was a terrifying and shocking experience.

Shortly after this, two other men, William Barber and Liam Bradley joined us. They took up positions beside the young injured man whom we were attending. There was sporadic gunfire at this stage – bursts of automatic gunfire, from time to time, interspersed with single shots. Jackie was rapidly losing blood and there was obviously great need to get him to hospital as soon as possible. At one stage, a woman nervously appeared at the window of one of the lower flats and a member of our group shouted to her 'Have you a phone, have you a phone?' But she shook her head. Few people in the Rossville Flats had phones. The other men in the group then said that if I was prepared to go before them with a handkerchief, they would be prepared to carry this young man somewhere where he could receive the necessary medical attention. There was a discussion as to whether we should carry him back towards the front of Rossville Flats or carry him through the Army lines. Willie Barber was a telephone engineer. He said that there was no point in bringing him back to the flats because the telephone kiosk there was out of order. We reached the conclusion that we had a better chance of calling an ambulance if we carried him to Harvey Street or Waterloo Street. We decided to do that. We desperately needed an ambulance.

Just as we were about to get up and move, a man moved along the gable wall of the last house in Chamberlain Street, about twenty yards from us. The house backed on to waste ground. He suddenly appeared at the corner of this house and moved cautiously along the gable. His movements were rather suspicious and suddenly he produced a gun from his jacket. It was a small gun, a handgun, and he fired two or three shots around the corner at the soldiers. The soldiers in this area facing the flats were stepping out in the open from time to time. I cannot recall the soldiers reacting or firing in his direction. They did not seem to be aware of the gunman. We screamed at the gunman to go away because we were frightened that the soldiers might think the fire was coming from where we were located. He looked at us and then he just drifted away across or into the mouth of Chamberlain Street. I did not see him after that nor, to the best of my knowledge, did I see him before then. I did not recognise him as someone I knew.

At this point we decided to make a dash for it. We got up first of all from our knees and I waved the handkerchief, which, by now, was heavily bloodstained. I went in front and the men behind me carried Jackie Duddy. We made our way into Chamberlain Street, along that street and then turned into Harvey Street. Soldiers challenged us at this point and we saw the BBC News camera crew with cameraman, Cyril Cave and reporter John Bierman. We then proceeded to the corner of Waterloo Street and Harvey Street. At this point Willie Barber took off his coat, spread it on the ground, and we laid Jackie Duddy on it. At that time he appeared to be dead. After being asked by us, a woman called Mrs McCloskey, who, as far as I recall, resided in the street, phoned for an ambulance. Then a patrol of soldiers appeared in Waterloo Street and told us to clear off and I asked the people to calm down and kneel down and offer a prayer. The soldiers moved away. I remember one of the women screaming down the street after them shouting, 'He's only a child and you've killed him.'

We waited until the ambulance arrived. I am not sure how long it took. It wasn't very long. Jackie Duddy's body was brought to the hospital. Mrs McHugh, a resident, kindly offered me a cup of tea. I quickly took a few sips and then I made my way via Fahan Street and Joseph Place to the area of Block Two of the Rossville Flats in front of the shops. I was thunderstruck by the scene that met my eyes. Until then, I had no conception of the scale of the horror. I quickly realised that I had witnessed merely a small part of the overall picture. There were dead and dying and wounded everywhere. I administered the last rites to many of them. I don't know how many. There was no firing at this time. Then an ambulance came and parked on Rossville Street at the corner of the Rossville Flats, near the main entrance. An attempt was made to get bodies out from this area towards the ambulance – and then there was more firing. Father Tony Mulvey went forward, waving a handkerchief, and facing towards the soldiers, in an effort to get them to cease firing. I could not see the soldiers from my position, but this firing was coming from further over Rossville Street.

Then John Bierman of the BBC asked me to do a television interview. We were standing near the telephone kiosk at the southern end of Block One of the Rossville Flats preparing for the interview and suddenly a single shot rang out and we had to dive for cover. I eventually did the television interview beside a doorway on the Joseph Place side of Flat Block Two. In that interview, I described what I had seen as murder. When the interview was completed I stayed around and tried to calm people down. A great number of people were suffering and greatly traumatised by their experiences and all were deeply distressed. People gradually started coming out of their houses and out of the Rossville Flats. Many people had sought shelter in houses in the area. When the wounded and the bodies of those who had died had been taken to the hospital, and the situation had settled somewhat, I eventually headed back towards the parochial house, via the Bogside and Little Diamond where I was stopped and challenged by a patrol of soldiers. I showed them my hands, which were completely covered in blood. I asked what on earth possessed them to do what they did. They did not insist in going through with the search. I arrived at my house. I was angry, frustrated and distraught.

After I got back to the parochial house, the enormity of what I had just witnessed crashed in on me. The kitchen was the place where we all gathered. I wept profusely. Maggie Doherty, our housekeeper, comforted me. She was the mother figure to us all on the many occasions of turmoil or grief. Other people and other priests arrived. Not much was said. Everyone was stunned into silence. Bishop Farren was in and out, asking us what had happened, distressed, bemused, incredulous and confused like all of us. He had been bishop of Derry for more than thirty years, but nothing could have prepared him for this.

I decided to call the Superintendent of the RUC in Derry at that time. Patrick McCullagh had been a contemporary of mine at St Columb's College. I rang him and asked what on earth had happened or why this terrible thing had occurred. He said that he was under the impression that it was only a minor disturbance, that his latest reports were that only two people had been injured and several arrested. I told him that I had seen a number of dead bodies and that many had been seriously injured. He expressed disbelief at this but said that he would check it out. He rang me some time later to tell me that the latest report was that eleven dead bodies had been admitted to Altnagelvin Hospital.

By six o'clock, it was clear that at least thirteen people had died and many were seriously injured and large numbers had been arrested and held in custody. The parochial house was under siege from worried families. Many people had not returned home after the march. Only a few of the dead bodies had been identified. People came desperately asking us had we seen their son or daughter, had he or she been one of those killed or injured. The RUC and Army, to their added discredit, refused to release the names of those who were in custody. A gesture from the RUC or Army, even at this late stage, would have afforded some degree of relief to desperately worried people. To add to the confusion, there were many contradictory reports about identities coming from Altnagelvin Hospital.

There was Mass in the cathedral at 7.30. I cannot remember who celebrated that Mass, but we all sought the Lord's help in our sadness and shock and despair. Mrs McDaid, mother of Michael McDaid, and some members of her family came to the parochial house seeking news of her son who hadn't returned home. Shortly before she arrived, we had received a full list of the names and addresses of the thirteen dead. Michael's name was not among them. We were able to assure her that he must have been arrested or injured. He would be home. She left the house relieved at this news. A few minutes later, word came through that there had been a mistake – one of the dead had been wrongly identified. A body had been incorrectly identified as the body of young man called Gillespie – it was then identified as the body of Michael McDaid! One of my colleagues had to go to Mrs McDaid and her family and break the awful truth to them. After erroneously building up her hopes, I could not face her myself.

Cardinal William Conway telephoned Bishop Farren and asked to talk with Father Tony Mulvey and me. He had seen the television pictures and he sought a first-hand account before he would make any statement to the media. We spoke to him, at length, from Bishop Farren's study describing what we had seen. He repeatedly asked 'Are you sure of this? Are you absolutely certain of this? You are not exaggerating?' Bishop Farren, now almost eighty years old, was perplexed at how radio stations in New York and other parts of the world already knew about the events that had occurred just down the street in Derry. They were calling him for interviews and comments. I then thought of my mother. I called her briefly and assured her that I was all right. She had seen the television news and had been very worried. She had tried to call on the telephone but could not get through. She was relieved that I was safe.

With other priests, I spent much of that night going around the families of the dead and injured. Some of my colleagues went to the hospital. I decided not to go there. I felt that I could not cope with seeing any more dead bodies. Apparently, there were some very tense and angry scenes there between a heavy RUC and Army presence and many anxious and distressed relatives seeking news of their loved ones. Gradually as the evening and night wore on, those who had been arrested were released and arrived home to the relief of their families. Late that night, the families of the dead and injured were all too aware of the fate of their loved ones. The entire community was consumed with shock and grief.

First-hand exposure to the multiple violent deaths of innocent unarmed people on the street leaves a lasting impression. The dreadful events of that Sunday afternoon constituted a defining moment for me and for many others. It was the day when I lost any romantic notions or ambivalence that I may have had about the morality of the use of arms as a means of resolving our political problems. Ever since my experience on that terrible day, I could no longer find any justification for the use of armed aggression by any faction in the North. I have to confess that this was a conclusion reached on emotional as much as moral grounds. Despite the propaganda, there is little that is glorious about armed conflict. Whatever the mythology, it is in reality a nasty, vicious and destructive business. It is my experience that it brutalises both those who participate in it and the society in which the warriors engage in their deadly combat. There may be some circumstances where and when armed conflict is necessary and constitutes the only possible way forward. In such situations, it may be morally justified. It is my conviction that such circumstances did not exist in our situation.

However, these murders, because that is what they were, had a quite different impact and influence on others, particularly younger people. Countless young people were motivated by the events of that day to become actively involved in armed struggle and, as a direct result, joined the Provisional IRA. Many former paramilitary members have gone on record stating that they first became actively involved in the wake of that Sunday. I am not at all sure about how I would have reacted, had I been a teenager and witnessed those same events.

Bloody Sunday cast a long and enduring shadow.

CHAPTER 15

Widgery – The Second Atrocity

Funerals in Creggan – a visit to the United States –
whether to attend Widgery or not - a difficult decision –
evidence to Hearings in Washington – the Widgery findings –
innocent found to be guilty – guilty found to be innocent

Television crews and journalists from many countries arrived in Derry during the Sunday night, and on Monday morning every witness to the events of the previous day was besieged for interviews. I spent the early morning going round the Bogside area, chatting with and comforting people and endeavouring to find out more about what had happened and why it happened. There wasn't so much anger. That came later. Grief and shock were the predominant emotions. The Army and police wisely stayed out of sight. My prevailing memory of that Monday morning in Rossville Street is the silence. After the chaos and uproar of the previous afternoon, now there were just groups of journalists, camera crews, clumps of people quietly chatting and observing the scene. No traffic moved. Few went to work. It was a dead city.

Most of the priests who had witnessed the events of the Sunday afternoon met at midday on Monday. There were seven of us in all. We decided to issue a joint statement. We called a press conference in the City Hotel. We asked Stephen McGonagle, former vice-chairman of the Derry Development Commission, to chair the press conference. He was someone whom we all held in high regard, and had more experience of the media than we had. The priests concerned were Anthony Mulvey, George McLaughlin, Joseph Carolan, Denis Bradley, Michael McIvor, Tom O'Gara and myself.

Father Martin Rooney, a colleague and a father figure greatly respected by all of us, accompanied us at the crowded press conference. Media personnel from all over the world attended. We stated unequivocally that the Army were guilty of wilful murder. We accused the Army of shooting indiscriminately into a fleeing crowd, gloating over casualties and of preventing spiritual and medical attention reaching the wounded and dying. We clearly stated that none of the dead or wounded was armed.

RTÉ, the Irish television service, asked me to go to Dublin that Monday night to participate in special programme to discuss the events of the previous day. It was a current affairs programme called *Seven Days*. A taxi was provided to take me to Dublin. Somewhat reluctantly, despite my emotional and physical exhaustion, I agreed to go. The taxi driver was not very enthusiastic. Like everyone in Derry, he was in a state of bewilderment and depression. We left Derry about 4.30 p.m. He told me several times during the first few minutes of the journey that he had never been in Dublin and didn't know the way. So when we were approaching Strabane, I suggested that a friend of mine who lived in Strabane could drive me to Dublin. The taxi driver eagerly agreed. The friend kindly drove me to Dublin on a dark and bleak evening. The roads were quiet. Even the capital city was quiet. The nation seemed to be in shock, in grief. We arrived at the RTÉ Studios in Donnybrook about 8.30 p.m. John O'Donoghue interviewed me for the live programme. Jack Lynch, the then Taoiseach, was in the studios making a television address to the nation about the events in Derry. He asked to meet me. I had never met him or any Government Minister before. When I met him, he was very kind and comforting. His humanity and sincerity impressed me greatly. We discussed the events of the previous day at length and he expressed concern at the manner in which the British information services were presenting the story in the United States. They were alleging that some or all of the victims were gunmen or bombers. He told me that the BBC news film clip featuring myself and the group carrying Jackie Duddy had been widely shown on US television networks. He asked me if I would be prepared to go to the United States to speak to the media there and set the record straight. He said the Irish Government would be prepared to fund and organise the visit. I had never been in America and I said that I would go there after the funerals if Bishop Farren gave me permission to do so. He said he would phone me in Derry at eleven o'clock the following morning. Afterwards I went for a meal in the Montrose Hotel, just beside the RTÉ studios. The owner of the hotel, Mr P.V. Doyle, happened to be there. He came to our table and introduced himself. He had just watched the television programme, expressed his sympathy, and insisted that he pay for the meal. He also offered to put us up for the night in the hotel as his guests. We declined his generous offer because I wanted to get back North as soon as possible. We travelled back to Strabane through the night and, after a few hours' sleep there, I got back to Derry about nine in the morning. I met with Bishop Farren, told him of the Taoiseach's proposal, and he encouraged me to accept the invitation and go to America. As promised, Jack Lynch himself telephoned me on the dot of eleven o'clock. I told him that I was prepared to go to United States, as he had suggested. He said that his office would see to all the arrangements, and added that an Irish Government car would pick me up in Derry the following day after the funerals.

Tuesday was spent visiting the wakes and families of the victims. During the entire day, huge crowds of people made their way from one home and from one family to another offering sympathy and prayer. That evening the thirteen coffins were carried, one by one, in poignant processions from their homes to St Mary's church in Creggan, where the Requiem Mass was to be celebrated at 12 noon on Wednesday. Large crowds of people walked in each silent procession in the darkness of the chill winter evening. Street lamps illuminated the way to the church. The huge church in Creggan remained open for the entire night and crowds of people gazed in disbelief as they queued to pass the thirteen identical coffins placed inside the altar rails before the altar. I believe that this was the first occasion when many people realised the true enormity of what had taken place on Sunday afternoon. The sight of those thirteen coffins assembled side by side in one place was almost too much to bear.

Wednesday was a wet, dark miserable February day. The weather reflected the profound gloom of the people. Thousands of people came from all over Ireland to join the people of Derry and the bereaved families at the funerals. The people in Creggan prepared for this momentous event with great care and dignity. Tea and other refreshments were offered to all visitors both before and after the Requiem Mass. A large number of public representatives from the Republic, including several members of the Cabinet, attended. President de Valera was represented. There was not a murmur from the Stormont or British Governments – no representatives, little sympathy. The sympathy of the Protestant Churches sadly was somewhat muted. Cardinal Conway presided at the Mass. Bishop Farren was the main celebrant and many other priests concelebrated the Requiem Mass. The ceremony was broadcast live on RTÉ radio. There was wonderful moving music. But the background noise that many will remember was the sobbing, the soft, uncontrollable sobbing of dozens of people, almost in unison. It was haunting and overpowering. The manifest grief and pain of Mrs Kelly, mother of Michael, is still clear in my memory. People do not remember what was said or not said; and little of significance was said; but the atmosphere and super-charged emotion of that Requiem Mass were unforgettable. After Mass, twelve of the victims were buried in the City Cemetery nearby. The thirteenth victim was buried the following day in Iskaheen, just across the border in Donegal.

In mid-afternoon, I met Brian Lenihan, who was Minister for Transport and Power in the Dublin Government. He had been tasked by Jack Lynch to arrange the American visit. He called for me at St Eugene's parochial house. He introduced me to Seán White who was to accompany me to the United States. We travelled together in a State car to Dublin. Ulick O'Connor, the writer, and some other persons were in the car. During the journey, they discussed the events of the previous Sunday with me and told me of the manner in which reports on the murders had been distorted by British influences in the US media. They asked me to tell the truth of what happened simply and in my own words. Seán White was a writer and had lived and worked in the United States for many years. He proved to be a wonderful companion and guide.

I had never been in the United States before. I first had to get a visa. I had an Irish passport. We discussed whether I should seek the visa in the US Embassy in Dublin or elsewhere. It was decided that I should get it in London. Seán and I took the last Aer Lingus flight of the day from Dublin Airport to Heathrow. We stayed overnight in London, went to the US Embassy first thing in the morning, and got the requisite visa without any undue difficulty. We flew to New York from Heathrow at lunchtime on Thursday. During the flight, Seán discussed his plans with me at length. He told me how various Irish Government agencies in the US were setting up the various press conferences and media interviews. In New York, we booked into the Roosevelt Hotel in Manhattan. That interested me because several scenes in one of my favourite movies, *The French Connection*, were filmed there. At Seán's suggestion, I went to bed as soon as we arrived and slept soundly for many hours. I was exhausted and this was my first opportunity to have a full night's sleep since the events of Sunday. In the meantime, Seán was busily engaged in setting up activities for the coming days. Early on Friday morning, I participated in several of the big morning network television programmes. In mid-morning, there was a large press conference presided over by Paul O'Dwyer, the noted Irish American Civil Rights lawyer. I realised very quickly the importance of my visit. Almost all the journalists, to whom we spoke, had an entirely distorted version of Sunday's events. They were under the impression that Sunday's dead and wounded were all either armed or in possession of explosives. The day was filled with interviews and press conferences. It was a whole new and very exciting experience for me. Seán also ensured that I had a lightning visit to some of New York's most famous landmarks. We went to the top of the Empire State Building, to Greenwich Village and other places. We rounded off the evening, after yet another television programme, in a delightful Italian restaurant in Little Italy. It was freezing cold in New York. I only had time to pack an overnight bag, and I was not prepared for such bitterly cold weather so I had to buy some extra clothes.

After further media interviews on Saturday morning, we flew to Los Angeles. Whilst there, we stayed in the famous Beverley Wiltshire Hotel, and held a big press conference there. Again, there was amazing media interest. I trekked from television studio to television studio. I met some celebrities, among them Carroll O'Connor, the actor. He invited us to his home in Hollywood. He was at that time the star of one of the most popular television sitcoms in the States, *All in the Family*. He played the leading role of Archie Bunker. Seán had known him for some years and Carroll made some useful media contacts for us. We also met an executive of the *Los Angeles Times* newspaper, Tom McCartin, who was very kind and invited me to spend a vacation at his home in Las Palomas, outside Los Angeles, which I did during the following summer. The celebrated cartoonist in the *Los Angeles Times*, Paul Conrad, was also very kind and helpful. One of the prized possessions on the wall of my study is a signed copy of a cartoon about Bloody Sunday, drawn and presented to me by Conrad. After a wonderfully exciting few days in Los Angeles, we flew back to New York and more television programmes, including *The Dick Cavett Show*, which was a popular and influential programme at that time. The British had caught up with me at this stage and had sent out a fiery Presbyterian clergyman from Belfast, Reverend Donald Gillies, to confront me on this programme. He had one major disadvantage. He wasn't there when the shooting occurred and I was. It was one of the first questions that Cavett asked him.

When I arrived back in Dublin on the morning of Wednesday, 9 February, the Irish Government had arranged for my mother and the rest of my family to be at Dublin Airport to meet me. It was a pleasant surprise. I hadn't seen my mother since my Christmas break. Seán and I called with Mr Lynch and reported to him on the trip. Mr George Colley, the Minister for Finance and Mr Brian Lenihan, accompanied Mr Lynch. We then had lunch with my mother and the family.

On returning to Derry, I noticed a dramatic change in the atmosphere. The shock and grief in the immediate aftermath of the murders had been replaced by profound and fierce anger. There were dozens of letters waiting for me, many of them with donations for the families of victims. Some of the letters were very moving. They came from individuals and organisations, from groups of workers in factories, from Ireland and abroad. A fund had been established and it was already attracting considerable support from around the world. A committee headed by Derry accountant, PK O'Doherty, managed this fund. It was disbursed to the families of the dead and the injured.

For myself and everyone else who witnessed the murders, there was now a very difficult decision to be made. The British Government had established a Tribunal of Enquiry under the chairmanship of Lord Widgery, the British Lord Chief Justice, the most senior judge in Britain. Each witness had to decide whether to appear before the tribunal or not. Among my letters, there were some urging me to attend the tribunal and others pleading with me not to attend. The people in the local community were hopelessly divided, with most people hostile to the tribunal. They believed that the tribunal would be 'a whitewash'. They did not believe that a British judge could give an objective judgement, where the British Army was concerned. There was a lot of pressure. A decision had to be made quickly. We did not have the luxury of delay. The Tribunal hearings were to begin on 21 February. I received a letter from the tribunal, dated 14 February, seeking a statement. The Derry priests who had been on the scene of the murders came together in St Eugene's parochial house on 17 February. We held a meeting, which lasted for several hours. We first agreed that it would be best if we adopted a common policy or approach to the tribunal. We were not under any pressure from Church authorities to adopt either one position or another. Everyone had an opportunity to speak and put his point of view. I argued strongly that we should attend. I had gone on record in many interviews, describing what had happened as murder, and that the victims I had seen were unarmed. I believed, if I now refused to give that evidence under oath to the tribunal and refused to subject myself to cross-examination, the credibility of what I had said would be seriously undermined. I was particularly conscious of people outside Derry and, especially fair-minded people in England. I was greatly influenced by Lord Scarman, another English judge, who had made a particularly good impression whilst investigating earlier events in Derry. It was also pointed out that, by going to the tribunal, we would be entitled to have QCs* to represent our interests there. As well as

* Queen's Counsel.

representing our interests they would have the opportunity to subject the Army witnesses to probing cross-examination. After a lengthy and very open discussion, it was decided that, if we were called to give evidence at the Tribunal, we would agree to attend.

At a press conference in the City Hotel in Derry, we issued the following statement:

> The Widgery Tribunal, as at present constituted, is not satisfactory because it will not be seen by all to be an impartial enquiry. Its terms of reference are far too restricted in a matter of such gravity. Every available relevant piece of evidence should be admissible. Nevertheless we feel a duty to attend and will do so, subject to clarification of certain matters to our satisfaction.
>
> We ask our people to accept our intentions as sincere. We make our decision in view of our position as priests, and the importance of having the truth about the events of January 30th put before the world. We have also in mind the stand we have already taken on behalf of the dead and injured. We have no interest other than the fullest possible publication of the truth.
>
> We issue this statement in the shadow of a crime that has horrified our people and ourselves. A callous and cold-blooded murder* can do nothing to further any aim. Our sympathy goes to Mrs Callaghan and the relations of the dead man, and we would ask those people responsible for such a terrible act to look at their position before God.
>
> Signed: Denis Bradley, Joseph Carolan, Edward Daly, John Irwin, Michael McIvor, George McLaughlin, Kieran O'Doherty, Anthony Mulvey, Tom O'Gara.**

---

* Thomas Callaghan, a Derry bus driver and part-time member of the Ulster Defence Regiment, was abducted from a bus he was driving in the Creggan area on the previous day. He was found murdered shortly afterwards. At the time of the above statement, nobody had claimed responsibility for his murder.
** Derry Diocesan Archive.

The press conference at which we issued our statement was disrupted by a bomb scare in the City Hotel. Journalists, hotel guests and staff and ourselves had to evacuate the building and wait outside in the street for half an hour until the building was declared safe. Such was Derry at that time.

I submitted a statement to the Widgery Tribunal and was subsequently called to give evidence. The group of priests engaged Mr Liam McCollum QC and Mr Philip Mooney QC as their counsel.

Seven priests subsequently gave evidence to the Widgery Tribunal in the County Hall, Coleraine, Denis Bradley, John Irwin, Michael McIvor, Anthony Mulvey, Tom O'Gara, Terry O'Keeffe and myself. I gave evidence on Thursday 24 February. It was quite a daunting experience. Mr E.B. Gibbens QC, counsel for the Army, subjected me to a probing cross-examination. I was satisfied that my evidence stood up to the test. I had simply told the truth and the events, in every detail, were still fresh in my memory. In the face of such scrutiny, I was glad that I wasn't telling lies!

Jack Chapman was a Welshman, a former Warrant Officer and sergeant major. He joined the Army in the 1930s. Since retirement as a regular serving soldier in the early 1950s, he had worked as a civil servant with the Army. He was still working in this capacity in 1972. He was immensely proud of his long and distinguished Army service. He was married to a Derry woman, and lived in a maisonette in Glenfada Park just across from Rossville Flats. There was a barricade right under his living room window. He had a grandstand view of the events of that Sunday afternoon. Three of those who died were shot dead just outside his home. He was horrified and incredulous that *his* Army could engage in such criminality. I was very friendly with Jack and his wife. He was a man of great decency, honour and integrity. On the morning after Bloody Sunday, at my suggestion, he gave an interview to Peter Taylor, the television journalist, for a Thames Television programme. (It was Peter's first time in Northern Ireland). Jack had spoken to me earlier and gave a powerful and graphic description of the terrible events, using military terminology. I have always believed that, with his Army background, he was one of the crucial witnesses of the events of that afternoon and particularly of the shootings at the

Rossville Street baricade. As he did not have a car, I accompanied Jack to Coleraine when he was called to give evidence to the Widgery Tribunal. The Army Counsel cross-questioned him intensely. I believed that they perceived him as potentially one of the most damaging witnesses against them, and they set out to subject his evidence to the most severe testing. He hated giving evidence against the Army, but he felt, in conscience, obliged to do so. Jack, although a former sergeant major, was, at this time, a timid and nervous man. He was 'in pieces' after the ordeal was over. He died a few years ago.

At the end of February, I found myself back again in the United States giving evidence at other hearings. The Subcommittee on Europe of the Committee on Foreign Affairs of the House of Representatives held hearings on Northern Ireland. I was called to give evidence at these hearings in Washington DC. This was another interesting experience. There was a diverse group of witnesses, ranging from Nell McCafferty, the Derry journalist, to Senator Edward Kennedy and Jimmy Breslin, the colourful New York columnist and writer, Austin Currie, Stormont MP, and Bill Henderson, publisher of the *Belfast Newsletter* newspaper, and a leading member of the Unionist Party and myself. Our evidence was subjected to questioning by members of the Subcommittee. It was an intriguing, and not too challenging, experience. There weren't many opportunities to see Washington. However, there were many opportunities to meet people. I was very impressed by Senator Kennedy and his grasp and understanding of Northern Irish issues. Richard Nixon was President at that time and he had just returned from his triumphant visit to China. The Vietnam War was still raging. When the hearings ended on Wednesday, 1 March, I felt unwell. I was quite exhausted. A doctor, attending the hearings, advised me not to travel back to Derry immediately, as I had planned. He suggested that I stay with him and his wife and family for a few days rest before returning to Ireland. I accepted his advice and travelled with him back to the city of Paterson, New Jersey. The doctor was John Campbell. He was a native of Tyrone, and a consultant gynaecologist. By a remarkable coincidence, unknown to me and to him, the babysitter in his house was originally from Belleek.

Her maiden name was Lily Keown. She had married one of the US soldiers stationed in Belleek during World War II, Rocky Grassano. Rocky was one of the GIs who was enormously kind to us as children in Belleek. I remembered both of them from my childhood. I hadn't met either of them since 1944. So there was reason for celebration. They remembered me as a child working in my father's shop in Belleek. I enjoyed the few days I spent in Paterson and eventually returned to Ireland duly refreshed and rested. Rocky and Lily and I have been in constant touch since then. Dr John Campbell sadly died a few years ago.

The Tribunal of Enquiry into the Bloody Sunday murders was over in double-quick time. Widgery submitted his findings to the Home Secretary and the House of Commons on 18 April. I received summaries by telephone from journalists early that afternoon and could not believe my ears. The doubters had been proved right. It was a whitewash. The guilty were found to be innocent. The innocent were found to be guilty. It was a complete travesty of justice. I was asked to fly to London that evening to appear on the late night BBC current affairs television programme, *Twenty Four Hours*, with some of the other witnesses. We took the opportunity to express our shock and anger and, above all, our sense of betrayal. If the shootings were the first atrocity, the Widgery Report was the second atrocity associated with that fateful day.

I felt profoundly betrayed by Widgery. I felt abused. I shared the anger, if not the cynicism, of the entire Catholic community. I still believe that the other priests and myself made the right decision by attending the Tribunal and giving evidence there. We trusted British justice at the highest level. We found that it was not worthy of our trust. It was a hard and painful lesson. In view of the remarks made by me in the immediate aftermath of the murders, I do not believe that I had any other option. A refusal to attend, in those circumstances, would have been a betrayal of the victims. The fact that we were there highlighted the injustice of Widgery's findings. Our two counsel made a major and important contribution ensuring that the paratroopers' evidence was severely challenged and showing it to be riddled with inconsistencies. I hope that the findings of the Saville Tribunal will be more in harmony with the evidence submitted and tested. This new Tribunal will have the opportunity to hear a great many more witnesses. At the time of writing, it is beginning its inquiry into the events in Derry on that terrible day. I hope that it will investigate the reasons for the deaths as well as the precise circumstances in which they took place and the events and decisions leading up to that fateful day. Most people know what happened. The big question is why did it happen? Who gave the orders? How high up in the chain of command did those orders originate?

The month of February 1972 was one of the most hectic in my life. I didn't have much opportunity to read newspapers or hear or view news bulletins during that month. Many things happened that I was scarcely aware of at the time. The bombing outrage in Aldershot in England on 22 February is one example. The Official IRA in a bomb attack at a Parachute Regiment barracks murdered seven civilians, including a Catholic priest. Five of the dead were civilian women who worked as cooks at the base. It was a dreadful act, a great disservice to the victims of Bloody Sunday.

I have earlier commented on how the events of that day radically changed my life and my attitudes. The death of Annette McGavigan in the previous September had a considerable impact on me, but, at the time, I perceived it as an accident, an unfortunate case of an innocent bystander being caught in crossfire. However, the murders in Rossville Street on that terrible Sunday afternoon were different. Each of the victims was deliberately singled out and shot by professional soldiers. It was callous, clinical and brutal. The IRA and other paramilitaries were also murdering people almost on a daily basis with increasing intensity. I came to have a profound detestation of any group that sought to impose its will on others through force of arms. War and armed struggle are often glamorised. But there was nothing glamourous about the vicious, nasty, often cowardly murders that were a feature of the Troubles in Northern Ireland.

As result of Cyril Cave's BBC news film clip, I suddenly became well known or, in the point of view of some, notorious. Prior to then, I had been an unknown curate ministering in the Bogside, known to a few Derry people and my colleagues in the priesthood. Suddenly and unwittingly, I was thrown into the public spotlight. I lost my anonymity and was recognised wherever I went in Ireland. This experience was very difficult to cope with, as I had always valued my privacy. For years afterwards, I was subjected to many threats and abuse over my role on that fateful afternoon. Threats came by letter and phone, some anonymous, some from organisations, real and fictitious. This still happens occasionally. For better or worse, I am quite sure that I would never have been subsequently appointed Bishop of Derry, had I not been thrust into the limelight because of what happened on that day.

I have no regrets about what I did on that momentous afternoon. I simply did what I perceived to be my duty, as a Catholic priest: to administer the last rites to the injured and the dying. Many other priests did the same as I did on that day and on many other occasions. I reacted in an instinctive manner. Whilst I was very scared at the time, the really intensive apprehension came later. I have to admit that I still feel uneasy and inhibited when I see the pictures of those events reappearing again and again on television and newspapers almost thirty years later.

The memories of that day still haunt me.

CHAPTER 16

Gethsemane

Brief acting career – Ranger Best – Free Derry –
Operation Motorman – two harrowing experiences –
a personal crisis – opportunity for a new position and
new surroundings

When all these other activities were going on, I had only a couple of opportunities to attend rehearsals for the '71 Players production of *The Righteous are Bold.* However, my assistant producer kept the show on the road. On my return from Washington, I managed to attend the final rehearsals before the play was eventually staged. It was good to be back at normal activities. However, there was another twist to the drama. Just before the opening night, one of the male leads in the play was struck down by flu. I was the only person available to stand in for him. Like many people engaged in theatrical production or direction, I am not gifted with acting ability and this handicap was further compounded by the fact that I was playing the part of a grumpy and sour, anti-religious old farmer whose daughter was thought to be possessed by the devil! The play was intended by the author to be a serious melodrama but the audience was convulsed with laughter in response to my opening night performance! So much for my acting skills! Obviously I made the wrong kind of impact. Fortunately, the actor recovered for the second night and the reaction to the performance more closely resembled the author's intentions for the remainder of the run. My acting career was short-lived.

The only positive development, as a result of the Bloody Sunday shootings and their equally bloody aftermath, was the fact that the

214

Stormont Government, which had governed Northern Ireland for fifty years, came to its end. On 24 March, British Prime Minister Edward Heath declared that the Westminster Government was assuming direct responsibility for Northern Ireland. He announced the appointment of William Whitelaw as Secretary of State for Northern Ireland. Direct Rule had begun. The nasty bigoted rule of Stormont that had brought so much misery and suffering had ended.

Early on Sunday morning, 21 May 1972, a woman going to work noticed the dead body of a young man lying just off William Street. A priest was called from the cathedral to give him the last rites. The body was that of William Best, a soldier in the Irish Rangers home on leave from service in Germany. He and his family lived in Creggan. Later in the day, the Official IRA claimed responsibility for his murder. This murder, in the midst of all the others, caused great anger in Derry. I have never been able to assess precisely why this murder triggered such genuine and widespread public outrage. The Best family was popular and respected in Creggan. Perhaps it was because, prior to 1969, there was a long tradition of young Derry Nationalists joining the British Army, Royal Navy or Air Force. The scarcity of work provided few options and a career in the services was attractive. (At one stage of the Troubles, I remember a group of people working out how many of the Derry IRA men then in prison had fathers, uncles or brothers who had served in the British Forces. There were quite a few.) All violent deaths are shocking. William Best was the third young man murdered in Derry in May 1972. However, his death and the nature of his death, and the dumping of his body caused particular revulsion amongst local people and especially local women, who, once again, were the conscience of our society. On the day after the murder, dozens of local women marched to the headquarters of Official Sinn Fein, disdainfully known as 'The Stickies'. They demanded that the Official IRA get out of Derry immediately. The Provisional IRA rather cynically and opportunistically backed their call. The women then called on the Provisionals to end their violence as well. There were several rallies on subsequent days and a group of courageous women emerged as leaders. It took immense moral and physical courage on the part of the women concerned to engage in such activities only a few months after Bloody Sunday. A week later, the Official IRA Command in Dublin announced that they had ordered an immediate cessation of military action 'in accordance with the wishes of the people they represented in Northern Ireland'. Most of the more prominent Stickies disappeared out of Derry, whether out of fear of the people, the Provisionals or British Army was not clear. I suspect that their main fear was the women of Derry. They were formidable opponents. There was, however, a negative response from the Provisional IRA, or 'the Provos', as they were known in Derry. They wanted internment ended and British soldiers off the streets before scaling down their activities. The Provos were getting stronger, growing more confident and attracting more recruits all the time.

One of the most enduring images in Derry during the Troubles was the end gable wall in Lecky Road defiantly proclaiming 'You Are Now Entering Free Derry'. Originally it stood at the corner of Lecky Road and St Columb's Street. The gable now stands in splendid isolation in the Bogside. It was Speakers' Corner, the venue for all the big rallies and the focal point of the area. The proclamation on the wall declared self-government: the Queen's writ does not run in this area – this is a no-go area for British troops. In early 1972, formidable semi-permanent barricades punctuated all the main traffic arteries in the area. Many of these barricades were manned by armed and masked Provos who checked the driving licences and identities of those passing through, right under the noses of the Army patrolling the city walls high above. They were there day and night. At times, they issued passes to drivers from outside the area. But lorries and vans and other vehicles making deliveries were very vulnerable to hijacking. The help of myself and other priests in the area was often sought in trying to recover hijacked vehicles. These ranged from bread vans, to buses, lorries loaded with foodstuffs, to JCBs. The hijackers did not discriminate. Once I recovered a vehicle belonging to 'Meals on Wheels'. Occasionally, we managed to recover the vehicle undamaged and untouched. At other times, we were too late and the missing vehicle was either set alight or looted.

At night, fuel was regularly siphoned from residents' cars and used for petrol bombs or other vehicles. Some cars were hijacked temporarily to 'shift stuff', a synonym to describe moving arms or explosives from place to place within the area. It was a tough time for the majority of the residents of the area who wished to live a quiet law-abiding life and who were concerned lest their teenage sons or daughters be recruited into one or other of the paramilitary groups. Many simply moved out of the area or out of Ireland. On a Sunday in mid-1972, all the priests in St Eugene's spoke out about this criminality at all Masses. However, little changed. Whilst the victims of these activities were usually at Sunday Mass, few of those who were actively engaged in these activities were churchgoers. They seldom darkened our doors, except for funerals.

This kind of situation was politically untenable for the British Government. Action was taken on the last day of July 1972. The action was well telegraphed the previous night, which was Sunday. After the main evening news on television, the Secretary of State, William Whitelaw, warned that action would be taken so that the security forces 'could move freely' throughout all areas of the North. In other words, no-go areas were not going to be tolerated any longer. He advised people to stay off the streets. It was a thinly coded message.

At first light, there was a rolling sound like distant thunder, increasing in volume as it approached. The parochial house shook and vibrated as a couple of massive tanks rumbled their way across Windsor Terrace behind the house. Only once before had I seen real tanks. That was as a child in Fermanagh during manoeuvres for D Day, but nothing of this size. These tanks were massive. From my bedroom window, I watched in fascination as the tanks, each with its huge gun gradually came into view as they crossed the junction of Creggan Road. They were real tracked tanks with a real gun just like those pictured in the movies and they were in the street outside my window! Understandably, there was nobody to be seen on the streets. Whitelaw's admonition was being followed. During the next few days, the Army set about removing all barricades. There was little opposition. After Whitelaw's message, the Provos had obviously and prudently left town. However, two young men were shot dead by the Army in the Creggan area, in questionable circumstances, on the first day of what became known as Operation Motorman.

Claudy is a pleasant village about eight miles from Derry. It is a village in which Protestant and Catholic people have always got on well. It has a good track record of community relations. It is dominated by Desmond's Clothing Factory, which is the major employer in the village and the surrounding rural area. Prior to Monday, 31 July 1972, it was a quiet sleepy peaceful place that the Troubles had passed by. On the same morning as Operation Motorman in Derry and Belfast, the Provisional IRA left lethal car bombs in the small village. As people ran to escape from one explosion, they ran directly into the path of another explosion. Nine people died, six men, two women and one little nine-year-old girl. Protestants and Catholics were among the fatalities. Many others were injured. It was one of the most appalling atrocities of the Troubles and it was inflicted on a small and peaceful, inoffensive community. This atrocity has never received the attention that it deserved partly because of the spectacular events associated with Operation Motorman that were taking place elsewhere on the same morning. The Provisional IRA never admitted responsibility for this atrocity. But it is widely accepted that they were responsible.*

In the wake of Operation Motorman, there was a temporary lull in activities, but after a few weeks, activities resumed and intensified. Despite very tight security, IRA car bombs wreaked havoc in the city. Business after business was wrecked. The spurious reason given for this campaign was that it was an attack on the British economy. It was, of course, nothing of the sort. It was an attack on Derry people, Derry jobs and the community as a whole. The economic life of the city was being destroyed. More and more people lost their jobs and livelihoods. Individuals and families were devastated when they witnessed premises and businesses that they and their families had painstakingly built up for generations destroyed in a second. Among the offices bombed were those of Claud Wilton, the solicitor and 1968 Civil Rights Leader, a friend of

---

* I deal in detail with an aspect of the Claudy bombing in my chapter entitled 'The Troubles' in *History of the Diocese of Derry from Earliest Times* (Four Courts Press, Dublin, 1999), p. 272.

Derry's poor for many years. Nobody was spared – from the big multiple stores to the small local business. It was a most discouraging period. The city was rocked almost daily with huge explosions. After every explosion, a pall of smoke and dust would rise and there would be immediate speculation about which street it was on. People would look and worry and hope that their son or daughter who worked in that street or area was not caught up in it. There was gunfire every day. The Bogside was becoming a very dangerous and frightening place.

There are two experiences that particularly stand out in my mind in the latter months of 1972. In the first incident, in September, to the best of my recollection, I was called out about 6 a.m. one morning to attend an injured man in the Westland Street /Meenan Park area. He was a young man taking a short cut walking to work in a local bakery. Unwittingly, he walked into a gun battle. I was on night duty. A person called at the parochial house and told me precisely where the injured man was lying, and he advised that he would need to be brought to hospital. I made my way to the area in my car, presuming that the gun battle was over. The streetlights were still lit and there was the beginning of daylight. In the dim light, about two or three hundred yards from the place where the victim was reported to be I saw what I thought was a body lying behind a low wall. When I was observing it from about 20 or 30 yards, the 'body' suddenly came to life and opened fire on Army positions on the city walls. 'The body' was an IRA sniper! The Army immediately returned fire and then all hell was let loose. There were snipers in various positions around the area. I took cover for a while and then gradually made my way, briskly moving across entries to lanes and alleyways to the position where I was told the real victim could be found. It wasn't a place to be seen moving around. I was worried that the Army on the city walls would have thought that I was one of the snipers, but reassured by the thought that they must have seen me arrive in the area when I did. I eventually reached the victim. He was shot in the lower leg, had lost a lot of blood and was freezing and shivering with cold. He had dragged himself into an alley behind houses and lain close to a wall. He was terrified to move in case he would be shot again. I managed to awaken and persuade a local resident, whom I knew had a phone, to call for an ambulance that eventually arrived. By now the gun battle had ended, and I accompanied the young man to hospital. We were stopped at Army checkpoints on Abercorn Road and Craigavon Bridge. Soldiers came into the back of the ambulance. I persuaded them that the man was an innocent victim, caught up in a gun battle on his way to work. They let us proceed to the hospital, but soldiers arrived in the hospital soon after us to check the story out. They eventually satisfied themselves that the man was not a participant in the gun battle.

The other experience in late 1972 that stands out in my memory occurred on Tuesday, 28 November. I will relate these events as I understand them. Perhaps there may be another explanation. Three members of the Provisional IRA were engaged in assembling a bomb in a house in Meenan Drive. The bomb exploded prematurely. The house was devastated and the victims were blown to pieces. There was a difficulty. The remains of only two bodies were found in the debris. The Provo command structure knew that there had been three people involved. No survivor had been accounted for. Within a short time, three names were mentioned. Families had to be told. But nobody was sure whether there had been two or three fatalities. If one of the volunteers had survived, his cover would be blown if the three names were published. So the Provos sat tight. In any case, one of the names mentioned as a possible victim was a young man called Jimmy Carr. I knew Jimmy and his parents extremely well. The Carrs were a very good and decent family whom I greatly respected. They lived in Abbey Park in the Bogside. When Jimmy was younger, he did little jobs for me. He went around the sick, elderly and housebound in the area on the evenings before my monthly visit and notified them about the precise time I would be around to attend them the following morning. He used to chat with these people and they were very fond of him. His father, Peter, heard the speculation about his son and came to me some time after lunch to see did I know anything. Peter was perplexed because he hadn't the foggiest idea that Jimmy was involved with the IRA. Jimmy was serving his time as a tradesman with a building contractor and had left for his work that morning as usual. Peter knew that he had a dental appointment that morning. We checked with his place of work in the mid-afternoon. He had been there in early morning, left for the dental appointment but had not returned. I spent a lot of time with Peter and his wife Mary that afternoon, hoping against hope that Jimmy might suddenly come in. Other people were making their own enquiries from his friends and associates, lest he had gone to visit them, instead of going to work. It was then discovered that he didn't have a dental appointment! Peter and I then decided to seek permission from the authorities to view the remains of the victims in the morgue in Altnagelvin Hospital. Permission was eventually granted. It was one of the most horrifying sights that I have ever witnessed, far worse even than Bloody Sunday. The buttocks of one of the victims was intact and wearing a pair of red underpants. Otherwise there were no obvious distinctive features among the remains. The faces were both unrecognisable as human faces. We went back to Abbey Park where the Carr family lived. We told Mary about the underpants. There was a large family in Carrs. Mary said that Jimmy had a pair of red underpants. I shall always remember Mary frantically hunting through presses and drawers and soiled clothes in a desperate search for the red underpants. But they were not there! Our worst fears were realised. Jimmy was one of the victims. He was 19 years old. Shortly afterwards, a message came from the IRA, stating categorically that Jimmy was one of the two fatalities in that morning's explosion. Peter and Mary and the family were distraught. I subsequently heard that the third man had escaped. Apparently, he went outside the house to get something and the bomb exploded in his absence. In the immediate aftermath of the explosion he had gone to ground and didn't make his whereabouts known until later in the day. A member of an Army bomb disposal team, Paul Jackson, was killed on that same day on Strand Road when another IRA bomb exploded. He was 21 years old – three young men dead in one day – another cruel day in Derry in 1972.

But there was still a little glint of sanity in the midst of all this lunacy. When discussing plays for 1972/3 winter season, the '71 Players decided that they should concentrate on comedy or something light. There was enough drama and tragedy on the streets around us. I was asked to direct another production. I chose a play by John B. Keane, the Irish playwright, whose work I have always admired and enjoyed. I was not sure what agency to approach in order to obtain permission to stage the play and to whom I would pay royalties. I wrote to John B. Keane himself at his home in Listowel. He wrote back to me, in typical manner, in a letter dated 14 October 1972:

> Many thanks for yours of today. You have my permission to go ahead with *Many Young Men of Twenty*.
>
> Forget about the royalties. Enjoy yourselves and I pray, please God, that your troubles will soon be over. Give my regards to the '71 Players and tell them they have my permission to eat white as well as black puddings on a Friday.

We staged *Many Young Men of Twenty* very successfully in late 1972. We played to capacity audiences and the performances and music were a source of welcome cheer to ourselves and to the audiences. We were grateful to John B. for his good humour and generosity and for providing us with such enjoyment.

Leon Uris, the American writer, arrived in Derry in the latter part of 1972 or early 1973. He had already written *Exodus* and several other blockbuster novels. He was carrying out research for his new novel, *Trinity*, which was to be set in Ireland and particularly in the North. His wife, Jill, a brilliant photographer, joined him. She was taking photographs and doing research for a book on Ireland. Uris spent a few days walking around the Bogside with me, meeting the people and observing the general scene. It was interesting to watch him at work. *Trinity* was published in 1976. The book of photographs, *Ireland: A Terrible Beauty* was published in late 1975.

1972 ended, as it began, with a multiple murder in Derry. Five men were killed by gunfire in Annie's Bar in the Top of the Hill area in the Waterside on the evening of Wednesday, 20 December. It was, as far as I can remember, the first appearance of Loyalist paramilitaries in the Derry City area. The victims were four Catholics and one Protestant. It was another shocking, dreadful and senseless deed.

There was not much peace or goodwill evident over the Christmas season. There was no Christmas shopping rush. Many of the shops were not there any longer. The Christmas celebrations were very subdued. 1972 was the bloodiest year of the Northern conflict. 467 people lost their lives throughout the North as a result of the violence, at least fifty of them in Derry city. Violent death followed violent death and explosion followed explosion. Hundreds of people were injured. It was very discouraging to preach and try to live Christ's teaching in such an environment. Voices of moderation were being drowned out by the gunfire, explosions and the growing hatred. People were becoming more and more polarised. Preaching moderation was like treating a massive haemorrhage with a bit of Elastoplast.

On the very first day of 1973, there was a double murder of an innocent young couple from Donegal, Oliver Boyce and Breige Porter. Loyalists murdered them just across the border a few miles from Derry. During the early months of 1973, I felt unwell from time to time. I was tired, physically and emotionally, and depressed by the general environment. The Bloody Sunday episode weighed heavily on me. The repeated showing of the film clip with the handkerchief did not make things any easier. The unrelenting violence sickened me more and more. There did not seem to be any future but a continuation of this insane mayhem that was causing so much suffering. I had experienced too much grief and found it very difficult at times to carry on. For the first time in my life, I experienced a crisis of faith and a profound crisis about the priesthood and my continued membership of it. During this time, a number of colleagues and friends were leaving the active ministry. My enthusiasm for personal prayer and my more spiritual activities and duties had waned somewhat. I seriously considered opting out of priesthood. It was a Gethsemane experience, a period of anguish and darkness that persisted for a couple of months.

I remember discussing all these various issues, at length, on several occasions with my spiritual director and an older priest whom I greatly respected. Whilst they did not try to influence me in one direction or the other, they were very reassuring and comforting. I also talked with a few lay friends who did much to bolster my self-esteem, which was very low at that time. A valued and dear friend of mine, Peter Fallon, who was also my doctor, was especially helpful and encouraging. I was particularly inspired by the manner in which the residents of the Bogside carried on cheerfully and brought up their children and endeavoured to make ends meet despite the most appalling obstacles. They helped me to see the environment and myself in a different context. I often sought escape from the harsher realities of this period by becoming more involved in the '71 Players and other activities in St Columb's Hall.

However, I gradually overcame the spiritual problems and, after much reflection, I was eventually rather embarrassed about my weakness and frustration and lack of faith. The Mass gave me great sustenance throughout this period, as always, even in the dreariest times. Thankfully, I had to celebrate public Mass each day, even when I did not feel like it. The cathedral Mass schedules had to be met. It was truly my daily bread. Towards the end of February 1973, I had almost recovered from this crisis. The recovery was gradual. There was no dramatic moment of catharsis when I purged all this negativity. I slowly, but surely, became happier in myself again and found new comfort in my prayer. I became more positive about things and had regained much of my former enthusiasm. I began to experience fulfilment in my priesthood once again. Despite all its difficulties, it is and was the most wonderful and fulfilling way of life.

The Mass of Chrism on Holy Thursday morning is one of the big annual occasions in every cathedral. On that day, the priests of the diocese concelebrate Mass with the Bishop and the Holy Oils are blessed and consecrated. The three Holy Oils used in the administration of the sacraments are the Oil of the Sick, the Oil of Catechumens and Chrism. The Bishop preaches a homily to the priests and afterwards invites them publicly to renew their priestly commitment. It is a beautiful and evocative liturgy, especially for priests.

In 1973, Holy Thursday fell on 19 April. I felt very unwell that morning when I got up. I went over to the cathedral for the ceremony. Some time during the ceremony, I don't know when precisely, I collapsed. I regained consciousness in the parochial house. I remember the ever-faithful Maggie, our housekeeper, being there, but not much else. Dr Peter Fallon was called and diagnosed hepatitis. I was subsequently out of action for many weeks.

Bishop Neil Farren also got a shock later that same day. A group of pupils from St Columb's College were on an educational trip to Rome with some of their teachers. Whilst they were there, on 13 April, they were told by someone in the Irish College in Rome that Bishop Farren had resigned as Bishop of Derry. Somebody suggested to them that they should get copies of the *Osservatore Romano*, which is the official Vatican daily newspaper, to bring home as souvenirs. The official notices on the front page contained the news of Bishop Farren's resignation. The school party arrived home in Derry during Holy Week and one member of the party was deputed to bring a copy of the paper to present it to Bishop Farren. He thought that the Bishop would like to have a copy for his records. Apparently, it was the first that Bishop Farren knew of it! The formal notification from the Holy See had not yet reached the elderly bishop. He had served as Bishop of Derry for almost 34 years. He was 80 years old. Bishop Farren had, in fact, submitted his resignation some years beforehand. Since the Second Vatican Council all bishops are obliged to submit their resignation when they reach seventy-five. The notice in the *Osservatore Romano* simply stated that his resignation had now been accepted. Whilst the failure to notify him formally about the acceptance of his resignation may well have been an administrative error, it was unfortunate that someone who had served the Church for so long and so well during difficult times was treated in this manner. Bishop Farren was now appointed as Apostolic Administrator with responsibility to administer the diocese until his successor was appointed.

There are few things that animate people as much as speculation about succession – whether that succession be political or ecclesiastical. Once the news broke that Bishop Farren was stepping down, the speculation began. The front-runners appeared to be Father James Coulter, President of St. Columb's College – the three previous bishops of Derry in the twentieth century had all been former Presidents of St Columb's College. Besides Father Coulter was generally recognised as being very able and was widely respected.

My colleague and friend for many years in St Eugene's, Father Tony Mulvey, was also widely favoured especially among priests who served along with him in Derry City. Bishop Cahal B. Daly, at that time Bishop of Ardagh and Clonmacnois, was thought to be a possibility if the Holy See opted for an outsider. Bishop Cahal had frequently written and spoken very powerfully and eloquently about the North and he was a Northerner from County Antrim. It was perceived as being a very open race.

Meanwhile, as a result of my hepatitis, I was confined to bed for a week in St Eugene's parochial house. Subsequently I went to Belleek for some weeks of rest and recuperation at my mother's home. I gradually recovered and felt rested and renewed. During my recuperation, an advertisement in the *Irish Times* for a Catholic Religious Adviser to RTÉ caught my eye. The idea of a position in the media appealed to me. I felt that it would give my priesthood a new impetus. I had participated with other Derry priests in a short training course on communications techniques some years earlier in the mid-1960s. I had found this very helpful in my preaching. Bunny Carr and Tom Savage were our tutors. Those of us taking part in that course had never thought that we would need skills in giving radio or television interviews. These were the source of much hilarity during the course. In subsequent years, such interviews had unexpectedly become a regular feature of our everyday lives. That brief training course in communication techniques had proved to be invaluable. I was interested in media generally and television in particular. So I decided to apply for the RTÉ position. I sent for an application form, duly completed and returned it, and then, to my surprise, was called for interview. At that stage, I realised that I hadn't mentioned this to Bishop Farren. So I called with him, told him what I had done and he wished me good luck. He had been consistently kind to me ever since my ordination. I went to Dublin for the interview and subsequently, in a letter of 24 May, was offered the position. I was surprised and delighted. I informed Bishop Farren and asked to be released from my position in St Eugene's in order to take up my new post in Dublin at the beginning of July. He agreed without hesitation. There were lots of tearful farewells with the people of the Bogside. Whilst I was anxious to leave the violence, I was very sorry to leave the parish and the people. When you suffer along with people through a conflict, a great bond of friendship develops.

However, I was only going to Dublin and I promised that I would keep in touch.

CHAPTER 17

To Dublin and Back

Working in RTÉ – 'hang-ups' – Noel Purcell –
a meeting with the Nuncio – Gammarelli the tailor –
a Papal Audience – 'Coraggio' – Archbishop Benelli –
a brush with the Army – episcopal ordination

For as long as I could remember I had loved going to Dublin. I went there for football matches, to attend plays or shows in the theatres, to see new films or just to spend a few days relaxing and browsing around bookshops. I enjoyed it thoroughly. It was my favourite destination for a short break.

I checked in for work at RTÉ Montrose Studios in Donnybrook, Dublin on Monday, 2 July 1973. It was exciting to sit in the canteen and see so many well-known faces and feel part of the whole scene. RTÉ Television, at that time, was just over ten years old and it was a dynamic and vibrant place to be. I was given a salary that was more than four times my average stipend as a curate in Derry. In addition, I was given a company car and, within ten days, I had managed to rent a delightful flat in Woodbine Park, not far from the studios. There was a spare room in the flat, and I planned to bring my mother down as a guest, and provide accommodation for priest friends from Derry. It was the first time in my life that I cooked and washed and did the housekeeping for myself. I thoroughly enjoyed it. I could not believe my good fortune.

However, there was a down-side too. I felt from an early stage that a few of my colleagues in various departments were somewhat suspicious and distrustful of me. I believed that they perceived me as the official Catholic Church person keeping 'an eye' on them –

some kind of 'thought policeman'! In fact, I was not obliged to report back to anyone. I perceived myself as an RTÉ employee hopefully making my contribution on the grounds of my specialised knowledge about religious matters. I also discovered, at an early stage, that Northern Ireland issues were not welcome as a topic of conversation in most gatherings of Dublin people. In 1973, the North was clearly a conversation-stopper in Dublin. However, I experienced a great deal of friendship also, and gradually, as the weeks went by and my new colleagues and I got to know one another better, trust built up.

My formal title was Catholic Religious Adviser. There were religious advisers also from the Church of Ireland and Presbyterian Churches, but they were part-time. I was full-time. The post of religious adviser appears to have been adopted from the BBC. However, whilst the BBC had, as part of its Charter, a Religious Advisory Body to support the Religious Programmes Department and presumably the religious advisers, RTÉ had no such body. Such a resource would have been helpful. Perhaps, because most RTÉ staff members were from a Catholic background, religion, particularly as expressed in Catholicism, was the one subject on which everyone considered himself or herself as an expert. Religious issues were often debated more efficiently on current affairs programmes rather than on specifically religious programmes. The borderline between some religious issues and politico/social issues was blurred. I liaised with programme makers and researchers and I tried to build up contacts with Church authorities around the country. I experienced an inherent distrust of RTÉ and RTÉ people, including myself, among the clergy and particularly among bishops, with a few notable exceptions. I was also taken aback by the number of lay and clerical oddballs who bombarded me with letters and phone calls seeking to get on programmes, whilst many of those who would have something important and valuable to contribute were reluctant to come forward.

Whilst most of my RTÉ colleagues were very friendly and welcoming, I was quite taken aback by the antipathy to Catholicism that occasionally presented itself. In the North, I had only experienced this at second hand and from predictable sources. I had not anticipated it from a self-proclaimed co-religionist, practising or non-practising. All kinds of hang-ups about the Catholic Church emerged to which I had never been exposed before. It was something new for me and became part of my introduction to the wider world. I had come from a part of the country where my Church was in a minority position and relatively powerless. I began to realise that it was, in some ways, easier to be a member of a minority than a member of a majority community. For the first time, I was exposed to people who challenged me on my beliefs, intellectually and morally. In Derry, for example, I seldom became involved in conversations about issues of sexual morality. There were other issues that claimed priority, at that time. In RTÉ, on the other hand, it was about the only aspect of Church teaching that some of my colleagues thought it important to examine and discuss. On the whole though, our discussions and debates were civilised and friendly and I enjoyed the challenges. I was exercised occasionally by the choice of panels for discussion programmes. I felt that they were largely skewed towards the more liberal agenda. However, it was difficult to counter this because of the unwillingness of sensible and moderate spokespersons for the more orthodox camp to come forward, or to make representatives available to participate in such discussions. It was my first experience of working outside a formal Church environment, and, whilst occasionally painful, it afforded me a useful and timely preparation for what lay ahead.

I dwell too much, perhaps, on the negative side of things. There was much that was positive and very enjoyable during my time in RTÉ. I made a lot of very good friends there. I learned a lot. People impressed me with their professionalism. I was fascinated and bemused by the fact that I was invited to join four different trade unions during my first month working in RTÉ. I had the opportunity to visit parts of Ireland that I never saw before. On many weekends, I travelled to the location from which the Sunday Mass would be broadcast on radio. I took the rehearsal on the Saturday evening and was present for the broadcast on Sunday morning. This brought me to many lovely, quaint and remote parishes as well as to major towns and cities. The vagaries of the Irish telephone system at that time tried and tested me. The outside broadcast was sent to

Dublin down a telephone line and this sometimes involved going through a number of local post offices and exchanges. On Sunday morning, it was not the easiest thing in the world to get through to some of these post offices. But the broadcast always got through, although there were some close shaves. There was an engineer, whose name I cannot remember, who looked after the broadcast of Sunday Mass around the country. He was a saint with the patience of Job. I also greatly enjoyed going with camera crews to various places to prepare reports or stories on various issues. I remember one trip to Connemara when it rained for a full three days and we returned to Dublin with virtually nothing to show for our efforts. It was an enjoyable and interesting intermission in my life.

The most enjoyable experience during my time in RTÉ was my association with the actor Noel Purcell. A new weekly 30-minute programme in magazine format was being planned by the Religious Programmes Department. It was to consist of reports on various stories or issues linked together by a presenter in the studio. The producer was Jeremy Johnston, a son of the playwright and writer, Denis Johnston. Jeremy was a larger than life individual and wonderful company. He was pleasantly eccentric. He had, like many in RTÉ at that time, come from the BBC, where he was involved in the production of the Fanny Craddock cookery programme. He was fascinated by religion and had been in and out of several religions. At the time I knew him, he was particularly interested in the Greek Orthodox faith. I suggested to Jeremy that it might be a good idea to get an Irish actor to read Bible stories, something in the style of David Kossoff on BBC Radio. We discussed the idea and it was decided to talk it over with Noel Purcell. I went to see Noel at his home in Sandymount in Dublin. He was very receptive to the idea. We then had to get a scriptwriter. Noel suggested a friend, called Brian Durnin, a retired civil servant. He agreed to write the scripts if I was prepared to help. Our first script was based on the parable of the Prodigal Son. Noel told the story on the programme, in a broad Dublin dialect. The reaction from viewers and people in RTÉ was wonderful. We subsequently wrote many such scripts and the slot was very successful. I was very impressed by the amount of time that Noel spent rehearsing each story. He shaped the script and adapted it and moulded it, working away at the pace, phrasing and intonation until everything was right. He was so professional. Noel was quite elderly at this stage and had a massive white beard and a great shock of silver hair framing a wonderful face. He really looked biblical. I thoroughly enjoyed evenings spent with him and his wife, Eileen and Brian Durnin at his home. After we had finished rehearsing, Noel regaled us with stories about his film and acting career. I especially enjoyed his stories about the filming of *Mutiny on the Bounty* in Tahiti, and his adventures with Marlon Brando. Noel was a lovely, warm, human being.

I celebrated Mass each morning in the School for the Blind on Merrion Road. It was on the route from my flat to the RTÉ studios. This, too, was a pleasant experience and introduced me to a new world with which I was not familiar. The Griffin family, who were my neighbours in Woodbine Park, and who owned the flat I rented, were extremely kind and hospitable. There were regular visits from my mother and members of my family and, of course, there was a constant stream of callers from Derry. I also made new friends among some of the local priests who were kind and hospitable, especially Father Tom Fehilly in Merrion Road.

I became more and more interested in the work. Like everyone else in the department, I was somewhat frustrated by the lack of funding and facilities for religious programmes. I got on well with my colleagues, although there were situations in which we had differing views on things. In such situations, we agreed to differ. However, after a few months, I began to miss the warmth and homeliness of Derry, where I knew nearly everyone and everyone knew me. I got a little lonely. Above all, I greatly missed the pastoral and sacramental ministry that had previously been so central to my life. I felt that I had done the right thing in coming to Dublin, and I was determined to stay for at least a year. I planned to have a chat with the new bishop, when he would be appointed, about a parochial appointment somewhere in the diocese, hopefully a curacy somewhere relatively quiet and away from the Troubles. Somewhere in Inishowen would be very acceptable.

On Christmas Day 1973, after doing a studio voice-over commentary on the Pope's *Urbi et Orbi* blessing from Rome, I travelled to Belleek and joined my mother for Christmas dinner. An elderly parish priest in the Derry diocese, Father Harry McFaul, had died. I decided to attend his funeral on St Stephen's Day in Greencastle, County Tyrone. Since I had gone to Dublin, I had not met many priests from the diocese apart from the close friends who visited me from time to time. Most priests from the diocese were at the funeral and after everything was over, I received considerable teasing and banter from some of them about my being in the running for appointment as Bishop. I had almost forgotten about this and it was the first time that I heard that my name had been mentioned. I was embarrassed, but assumed that it amounted to no more than a little good-natured ribbing. I spent another few days in Belleek and returned to RTÉ two days earlier than planned, only to run into the only serious contretemps that I had in my time there. It had been decided to have a discussion programme about which I had not been consulted; I was very unhappy with the planned format of the programme and the selection of people chosen to appear on it. I felt, rightly or wrongly, that it had been deliberately planned at short notice to take place in my absence. I made my views on the matter known to those concerned. They defended their position. We had a heated discussion, but eventually everything ended amicably. Each knew where the other stood. But a line had been drawn in the sand.

The reason I returned early to Dublin after Christmas was to make the final preparation on the text of a homily I was to preach on the evening of New Year's Day at the Annual Mass for the World Day of Peace in Dublin. It was celebrated in Our Lady of the Assumption Church in Ballyfermot in Dublin. The Archbishop of Dublin, Dermot Ryan, had invited me to preach at this Mass. It is a huge church and it had a full congregation; it was somewhat daunting. The homily, however, was very well received.

January 1974 was a busy month. I had invited the Colmcille Ladies Choir from Derry, which I had helped to found a few years earlier, to sing at Sunday Mass being televised from the studio on the morning of Sunday, 3 February. The Choir had also been invited to appear on *The Late Late Show* with Gay Byrne the previous night. In early January, I paid a flying visit to Derry to discuss with the choir the choice of hymns for Mass and to hear them rehearse.

As always, they were superb. I took the opportunity to visit some other friends. To my relief, the word 'Bishop' wasn't mentioned once!

Cardinal Conway had invited me to lunch in Armagh on Sunday, 27 January. I had met him cursorily on a few previous occasions at the Bloody Sunday funerals and at a few other religious functions since I arrived in RTÉ. He came with his Church of Ireland counterpart, Archbishop Simms, to the RTÉ Studios in Donnybrook just before Christmas to record their joint Christmas Message for television. When he met me on that occasion, he invited me to lunch. Sunday, 27 January, was the first Sunday on which both of us were free. Although, I had never really met him, I always had considered Cardinal Conway as somewhat cold and distant. However, I experienced an utterly different type of person, when I visited him in his own home, Ara Coeli, in Armagh. He was warm and friendly and full of conversation. However, there were no loose words or throwaway phrases. Everything was precisely stated. We had a very pleasant lunch. Over lunch, he discussed my work in RTÉ and general Church/Media relations about which he was very concerned. He felt that the Church was not putting its point of view across as effectively as it could, especially in the South of Ireland. I mentioned to him a problem with Roman documents, which will be outlined later, and he promised that he would do what he could to help in this matter. I also mentioned the difficulties about getting effective spokespersons to represent the Church and the reluctance of many Church people to participate in religious programmes. Finally we discussed the current situation in the North. Once again, the word 'Bishop' in the context of Derry was never mentioned.

From time to time, the Apostolic Nunciature in Dublin had been in contact with me about documents being issued from the Holy See and on one occasion to complain about a television programme, the details of which I cannot remember. I had appealed to the Nuncio personally to give me the Holy See documents under embargo a few days prior to publication, so that they could be presented properly. The RTÉ Newsroom was supportive of me in this issue. In most cases, I only received the documents a few days after they had been issued in Rome; at this stage, their content was yesterday's news and, as such, hardly merited a mention in our news bulletins. The angle or spin given by the accredited correspondents in Rome was the one received universally and reported in all the Irish media, if reported at all. A major document on the New Rite of Penance had been flagged for early spring 1974. I had asked the Nunciature staff to do everything they could to let me have an embargoed copy well in advance, so that it could be presented accurately from an Irish perspective. I knew that there would be considerable interest in this particular document.

On Tuesday, 29 January, there was a Religious Programmes Department meeting at 11.30. It took place most weeks on Tuesday mornings. When I emerged from the meeting in the Administration building about an hour later, there was a message waiting for me at reception. I was asked to ring an unfamiliar telephone number. I strolled back to my office and rang the number. A man answered. It was the Papal Nuncio, Archbishop Alibrandi. He wondered if I could come to see him. I arranged to call at 2 p.m. I had to attend a seminar on Holy Week Liturgy in Clonliffe College at 3 p.m. I said I would call on the way to Clonliffe. I didn't ask him the reason for his request. I presumed that it was about the document on the New Rite of Penance or some similar document. I had a quick lunch in the canteen before setting out for the Nunciature. On the way there, the notion did occur to me that it might be with regard to the appointment of the Bishop of Derry. However, I quickly dismissed the idea as a piece of self-indulgence, a fantasy.

I reached the Nunciature, a beautiful rambling old house set in a secluded corner of Phoenix Park, precisely at 2 p.m. To my surprise, Archbishop Gaetano Alibrandi himself opened the door. There was a twinkle in his eyes. I thought to myself with a little concern, 'This is not going to be about the document on Penance.' Even Papal Nuncios do not get that excited about important documents from the Holy See. He put me out of my agony quickly. I had scarcely sat down when he said, 'The Holy Father wishes you to accept appointment as Bishop of Derry.' I was quite speechless. I didn't know what to say or what to do. 'Would you like a cup of coffee?' I certainly would. I still didn't know what to say or whether to laugh or to cry. The Archbishop was very excited about it. He thought that it was wonderful news. He went on to say that he had sought the views of many people in the diocese, lay and cleric, during the consultation process and that I was the person whom most people nominated. The coffee was served. I gradually regained my composure. I asked, 'What happens next?' He said that he had to send on details about my curriculum vitae to Rome for press releases and so on. He wished me to draw this up and deliver it to him the next day. He asked me about announcing the appointment during the following week. I told him that I had to go to a conference in Geneva during that week. He told me that such announcements were usually made from Rome at 12 noon (Rome time) on a Monday. We agreed that Monday, 11 February, would be the earliest feasible date. He warned me that I was to tell nobody of the appointment and keep it strictly secret until the day it was publicly announced. I expressed my doubts about my ability to take on this daunting responsibility. He told me not to worry that I would do very well. I made my way to the door in a kind of daze, got into the car when suddenly there was a frenzied knocking on the car window. 'Do you accept the Holy Father's appointment?' he asked. He pointed out that he had just remembered that I had not formally accepted the nomination. It had never occurred to me that it could be refused. I said, 'I do.' The Archbishop cheerily nodded and waved me goodbye, and I watched him in my rear mirror standing in the doorway as I drove away.

It was a delightful cold crisp winter's day with a clear blue sky. I stopped the car, lit a cigarette, and went for a short walk in the Phoenix Park in an effort to compose myself. The surroundings were so tranquil and peaceful, yet I was anxious and not a little afraid. I was all too aware that I had been given a great responsibility and a difficult task.

I went to the seminar in Clonliffe College. However, my mind was a million miles away. I left early and went to the lovely college chapel at Clonliffe and sat there for a considerable time in the gathering early darkness of that January evening. I would need the Lord's help and a lot of it. Rather than cook dinner, I went for a meal in a restaurant, on my own, and enjoyed a half bottle of good red wine. After I arrived home, I got out my small Olivetti portable typewriter, and typed out my CV for delivery to the Nunciature in the morning. Later that night, I marked an 'X' in my diary for eleven o'clock (Irish time) on Monday morning, 11 February, the feast of Our Lady of Lourdes.

There was a meeting of the Northern province of the Council of Priests in the Four Seasons Hotel in Monaghan on the next afternoon. I had been active in our diocesan council of Priests and had been elected by the diocesan council on to the Northern provincial council of Priests. This provincial council of Priests had nominated me to be their representative at a meeting of an 'embryo' European council of Priests. This meeting was to take place in Geneva during the following week. I couldn't really absent myself from this meeting. After the meeting in Monaghan and much agonising, I decided to go to on an unplanned visit to Belleek. Since I was a child, I always had a wonderful relationship with my mother. She was my closest confidante and best friend. I decided that she would have to be told the news of my appointment at once despite the Nuncio's warning. I told her that evening. She was delighted and immensely proud but also worried for me. She knew that it was a daunting challenge. She joked with me and asked me would this be the end of the flat in Dublin! She insisted that the remainder of the family would have to be told too. I was worried whether they could all keep it a secret. She assured me that they would. My sisters and brother were invited to join us for tea the following evening and I broke the news to them and warned them about confidentiality.

The Colmcille Ladies Choir and a host of followers arrived in Dublin on that Saturday afternoon. They were determined to have an enjoyable weekend, as was their wont. We had a rehearsal for the Mass and then they performed in *The Late Late Show* to great acclaim. Afterwards, we went to an hotel and a good night was had by all. A few of the women speculated about the 'next bishop' but it wasn't a major topic of conversation. Father John McCullagh, a colleague from St Eugene's, stayed with me in the flat that night and celebrated the televised Mass the following morning. The choir sang superbly. I was proud of them. It was good to meet them all and have some time to spend with them.

I flew, with the three other Irish delegates, one from each ecclesiastical province, to Geneva for the European Priests' Conference. It was my first and only visit to that city. The meeting was interesting and lively. One of the topics discussed was the appointment of bishops! My mind, however, was preoccupied by other things for much of the meeting. As D Day approached, I became more and more worried about what lay ahead. We got back to Ireland on the Friday afternoon.

Archbishop Dermot Ryan invited me for my evening meal to his home on the Stillorgan Road, near my flat, on the Saturday evening. Although I had met him on a couple of prior occasions in the course of my work in RTÉ and the New Year's Day Mass in Ballyfermot, it was the first time that I had met him informally. He told me that he was very pleased by my appointment, and wished me well. We discussed the problems of the North at considerable length. Cardinal Conway had invited me to lunch once again in Armagh on the Sunday at 12.30. It was the day before the announcement. He greeted me warmly and offered me his congratulations and good wishes. He was kind and most affirming and encouraging. I expressed my reservations to him about my relative youth and inexperience and academic inadequacies. I would be the youngest bishop of Derry for several centuries and a few years younger than any of the bishops serving in Ireland at that time. I had celebrated my fortieth birthday just two months previously. He assured me that my relative youthfulness would not be a problem. We spoke about the possible date for my episcopal ordination, and we pencilled in two possible dates that I would check with the Apostolic Nuncio and the folk in Derry. We also discussed the Northern conflict in considerable detail. He was very preoccupied and saddened by this seemingly interminable problem. He also talked about relationships with the media. He said that he hoped that I could do something to improve relations between the media and the Church. He was a good listener too. I was enormously impressed by him at this second meeting. He offered me a considerable amount of valuable advice and I left his residence, Ara Coeli, later that afternoon much less fearful than when I arrived.

The Irish heat of the Eurovision Song Contest took place that evening. I went to the production gallery of the RTÉ Montrose studio in which the contest was being staged for live television. I enjoyed being in the gallery for big live productions. I loved the excitement of such occasions and watching the director and other production personnel in action. Technology has always been a source of fascination to me, especially electronic technology. Afterwards I went to the Montrose Hotel on my own to get a light supper. I didn't want to join the party after the transmission. I wanted to be alone with my thoughts. To my surprise, the first people I met when I arrived at the Hotel were three priests from Derry, who had just arrived to spend a few days in Dublin. We had something to eat. I then invited them to my flat that was nearby. I agonised with myself whether to tell them my big secret or not. I eventually decided that it would be unfair not to tell them. The episcopal appointment had not come up in the conversation until then. At first, they thought that I was joking them! They were surprised and expressed great satisfaction and pleasure and wished me well. I made them promise me that they would not phone anyone in Derry before the announcement at eleven in the morning. We chatted long into the night about Derry and the diocese and the future. We were all optimistic. I invited them to join me for the celebration of Mass in the School for the Blind on the following morning.

On the Monday morning, 11 February, we concelebrated Mass in the School for the Blind and then I made my way to RTÉ, wondering what the impact of the announcement would be there when the news was released at eleven o'clock. The news release of the appointment had been received in the newsroom during the night, under embargo, and a lot of people in the station seemed to be already aware of it. After the formal announcement on the eleven o'clock news bulletins, I was inundated with telephone messages, telegrams and callers. There were radio and television interviews. My RTÉ colleagues, without exception, were most supportive and wished me well. There was not a single discordant note. It was all very encouraging. That evening, the Griffins and some of my neighbours in Woodbine Park held a party for me. The flat and the Griffin home were filled to overflowing with an eclectic group of guests and callers – some relatives who lived in Dublin, a large range of RTÉ personnel and personalities, some clergy including

Archbishop Dermot Ryan, Derry people living in Dublin and many others whom I didn't even know. A few of my priest friends had come down from Derry to join in the celebration. It was a very enjoyable evening.

After clearing up matters needing urgent attention in RTÉ, it was back to Derry on the Tuesday afternoon. It was a very strange feeling driving to Derry that evening. Although I had offers to be driven, I insisted on making the journey on my own. Ever since I had first been made aware of the appointment, I had not had much time to give the matter really serious thought. The realisation gradually seeped in that there would be absolutely no training for this position. I would be thrown into at the deep end. I had spent six years training and preparing for my ordination to priesthood. There was scarcely any preparation for this. The more I thought about it, the more daunting it became. During that journey to Derry, I wondered had I made a dreadful mistake by accepting the appointment. I also realised that it was now too late to change my mind, without causing consternation! Coming through the checkpoint at Aughnacloy, there was a considerable delay. 'What's your name, Guv?' – the clipped tones of the Cockney soldier reminded me, if I needed reminding, that being a Catholic bishop in the North in 1974 had an added dimension of responsibility. In the car, I listened to news bulletins. In the North, I was a news junkie, listening to every bulletin, a habit that I had left behind when working in Dublin. The newscasts were filled with the all-too-familiar reports of everyday life in the North – bombs and shooting and more bombs. I drove through Omagh and Strabane. In contrast to Dublin, the streets were empty and eerie in the early evening darkness. There was relatively little traffic on the road.

My favourite approach to Derry is the road from Strabane. About four or five miles out of Derry, the spires of the two cathedrals can be seen and gradually more and more of the city comes into view. On that dark February night, the lights of Creggan and other higher areas of the city caught my eye from a long distance off, and I began to feel at home again and strangely reassured and more comfortable. I drove up William Street, the site of so much conflict and so many memories, to St Eugene's Cathedral. Here I felt really at home and at ease. There was a wonderful warm welcome from my former colleagues, and from Maggie Doherty and Mary McDaid, the housekeepers. They seemed to be very happy and excited, and had prepared the guest room for me. After a quick meal, I then decided to call on Bishop Farren. I did so with considerable trepidation. He was, however, very welcoming. He told me that he had checked on the Canon Law and explained to me that he was obliged to continue administering the diocese until I had formally presented the Bull of Appointment to himself and the Diocesan College of Consultors. I didn't know anything about Bulls of Appointment! He told me that he was moving to Buncrana in a few weeks. We discussed possible dates for the Episcopal Ordination. He assured me that he would be available to assist me if I wished such assistance. I took the opportunity to thank him for his many acts of kindness to me over the years, ever since he accepted me as a seminarian for the diocese. Towards the end of our meeting, he went to a drawer in his desk and produced a beautiful ancient bishop's ring and pectoral cross. He told me that these were worn by some of his predecessors and he would like me to have them. I accepted them gladly.

There followed a few intense days. After meetings with the Diocesan Council of Priests and others, the date of the Episcopal Ordination was agreed for Sunday, 31 March, in St Eugene's Cathedral. An organising committee was set up. I had given some thought, over the previous week, to the appointment of a Vicar General. I decided to ask Father Bernard Kielt to accept this appointment. I appointed Father James Clerkin, a fellow curate in St Eugene's, to be my Diocesan Secretary. I was sorry to hear that Father Tony Mulvey was in hospital with a chest complaint. He was now administrator in St Patrick's Parish in Pennyburn in Derry. As noted earlier, I greatly admired and respected Tony. He taught me a great deal about ministry and particularly the social responsibilities of ministry. I had also believed that either he or Father James Coulter would have been appointed as Bishop Farren's successor rather than myself. I felt that, on a personal level, Tony Mulvey would have been disappointed by my appointment. On my second morning back in Derry, I went to visit Tony in hospital. I brought him a large box of chocolates as a peace offering, because he loved chocolates. He feigned shock and anger at not being appointed. I do not think that he was serious, however. We had a good and happy meeting. There was lots of gentle banter and teasing about my qualifications or lack of them! I told him that I planned to go to Rome in a couple of week's time to prepare for the episcopal ordination and invited him to accompany me there. He thanked me for the invitation and said he would consider it, if he were well enough. I went to spend the weekend with my mother in Belleek. On the Sunday, I celebrated Mass in the local church. The people there greeted me with great warmth.

During the following weeks, there were many meetings with the excellent organising committee. The Episcopal Ordination ceremony had to be planned in detail. Music and choirs had to be decided upon. Invitations had to be sent out. I insisted that there should be lay representatives from every parish, chosen by ballot, present at the ceremony. I was required to choose a motto and a coat of arms. I chose '*Pasce Oves Meas*' (Feed my Sheep) as my motto, and on the advice of my friend, Father Tom Fehilly in Dublin, commissioned Archbishop Heim, the Apostolic Delegate to Great Britain to design a coat of arms for me. The Archbishop, who is a world authority on Church heraldry, spent a considerable time discussing the design with me. I was very pleased with the design he eventually produced. It incorporated a cluster of oak leaves and a dove, both symbols of St Columba and of peace. Columba was one of those who first preached the Christian faith to our part of Ireland and is still the object of much devotion, especially in Derry City.

From the day my appointment was announced, I was inundated with letters, telegrams and messages of congratulations, good wishes and promises of prayers. It was all very encouraging. I had to wind up my work in RTÉ. My colleagues there were warmly supportive and encouraging. Just a few days before my call to the Nunciature, I had submitted my application for membership of a trade union in RTÉ. After the announcement of my appointment, I was advised that consideration of the application had been deferred until a later date!

For some strange reason, I was advised that I was expected to make courtesy calls on the President of Ireland, Erskine Childers, and the Taoiseach, Liam Cosgrave, before I left Dublin. I cannot recall who suggested this or why it was suggested. However both President and Taoiseach greeted me with great kindness and courtesy. The last two weeks of February were spent commuting between Dublin and Derry.

The only really sad and distressing experience in these weeks took place on one of my first days back in Derry after the announcement. A diocesan priest telephoned me and asked for an appointment to talk to me. He told me that he wished to resign from the priesthood. He said that he had wanted to do this for some time, but did not wish to upset the ageing Bishop Farren by approaching him with this news. He had decided to wait until the new bishop was appointed. I was taken completely by surprise and was stunned and deeply upset. It was one of the many things that I had not anticipated. This was the first formal meeting between a diocesan priest and myself as Bishop Elect. It was an early reminder that episcopal responsibility would be accompanied by a lot of pain and heartbreak and disappointment. There was a counterbalance, however. Around the same time, a priest, who was a native of the diocese and had served abroad for a number of years, applied to be accepted into the diocese of Derry. He was subsequently accepted, and has made and continues to make a significant contribution to the priestly ministry in the diocese.

On Sunday, 3 March, I flew to Rome. Father James Clerkin, my Diocesan Secretary, and Father Tony Mulvey who had, by now, recovered from his chest complaint, accompanied me. In Rome I planned to make a retreat, have a short holiday and get fitted with my episcopal robes. We stayed in the Irish College where I received a wonderful welcome. On the Monday morning, the first stop was at Gammarelli's to be measured and fitted out for my episcopal robes. My two cohorts accompanied me to, perhaps, the most famous ecclesiastical tailors in the world. We were fascinated by the place. None of us had ever been there before. This family business has been going for several centuries. It is set in one of the oldest areas of Rome, near the Pantheon and Piazza Minerva. Across the road is the wonderful 13th-century church of Santa Maria Sopra

Minerva, which contains a magnificent marble statue sculpted by Michelangelo. Gammarelli's provides a wonderfully efficient, if rather expensive, service, and the quality and cut of their work is superb. Going there is quite an experience. One of the first telegrams that I received after my appointment was from the afore-said Gammarelli! They have provided robes for everyone from Popes to humble seminarians for several centuries.

After being measured and placing orders for the various items, I travelled to a retreat house in Nemi, up in the Alban Hills about 30 kilometres from Rome, to begin my retreat. I spent five or six blissful days there in silence and had a chance to think and reflect and pray. I had a wonderful retreat director who helped me to focus on my spiritual life and reflect on what lay ahead. It was the first time since my appointment that I had time and space to consider my new situation in any kind of detached manner. Up until then I had been buoyed along on a mixture of excitement, euphoria and appre-hension. There had been little time to think or pray since the announcement. In the quiet and peace of Nemi, I was able to address my situation, rationally and sensibly, for the first time. I gave a lot of thought to the conflict at home and how I would deal with it. I was never more aware of my inadequacies, especially in theology, but I ended my retreat with a great peace and tranquillity in my heart, and with a new confidence that the Lord and the Holy Spirit would guide me in my future ministry.

I had often seen Pope Pius XII at ceremonies in St Peter's Basilica when I was a student in Rome. I also saw Pope John XXIII on one occasion in St Peter's during a visit to Rome when he preached a wonderful sermon about an upcoming Corpus Christi procession through the Roman streets and in which he would be participating. He was, for all the world, like an old Irish parish priest urging his people to take part in this great event. When I came back to the Irish College in Rome after my retreat, I was told that Pope Paul VI had granted me a private audience. I had to bor-row a rather ill-fitting soutane for the audience, because I had not brought one with me. I had the private audience with the Holy Father, just after the public audience on a Wednesday morning. I attended the public audience and then met the Holy Father in an anteroom off the audience hall. I was nervous and quite overawed initially, but the Holy Father quickly and gently put me at my ease. There was nobody else present but one of his secretaries. I was surprised that he was so small in stature. From his pictures and from television, I thought that he was much taller. I was considerably taller than him. We sat down and conversed for about fifteen or twenty minutes in Italian and English. His English was better than my rusty Italian. I was astounded at how much Pope Paul VI knew about the problems in Northern Ireland. He was extraordinarily well briefed. He asked a lot of questions about various issues. He was wonderfully kind, friendly and affirming. After a few minutes I felt quite relaxed. I told him of my apprehensions and nervousness about episcopal responsibility and he gave me great encouragement. He was fatherly. Towards the end of the audience he asked me to visit Archbishop Benelli, who was then acting as Secretary of State. When the audience was over and I was preparing to leave, he gave me his blessing and a personal gift of a bishop's ring. His parting word to me was 'Coraggio.' 'Courage'. Since then, I came to have a special affection and respect for Pope Paul VI. Prior to meeting the Holy Father, I had the impression of a person who was some kind of superhuman with whom it would be difficult to relate on a personal level. To my surprise, I met a pleasant, warm human being, a fellow priest, with whom I felt very comfortable and who was very reassuring and down to earth.

When I got back to the Irish College, the Secretariat of State had already been in touch! Archbishop Benelli wished to see me that afternoon at 4.30. The Vatican certainly does not hang around. I had a two-hour meeting with the Archbishop and one of his staff, whose brief it was to monitor the situation in Ireland. I quickly learned why the Holy Father was so well briefed. I was astonished at the breadth of knowledge that Benelli had of the situation in the North – policies, ideas, events, names of people and names of places poured out, as if he were a native of Belfast or Derry! His grasp of the situation was quite extraordinary. He knew as much or more about the political life of the North than I did! He had served for a time, many years previously, in the Apostolic Nunciature in Dublin. There was evidence of comprehensive briefing from a number of sources. I was very reassured by the fact that most of the briefing seemed to be from Irish sources, rather than from British sources. This had been a problem in the Vatican in the past. The staffer asked me if he could telephone me, from time to time, in the future, to obtain my point of view on particular political developments and issues, and to get an update. He did this on a regular basis for several years afterwards, until he was reassigned. Archbishop Benelli was a very impressive individual. I left the Vatican that evening convinced that I had met the next Pope!

Iceland was never mentioned. I draw attention to this, because another official of the Secretariat, a Dutch priest, had contacted me on the previous Monday. We spent a considerable time together, during which he asked me if the Derry diocese would consider taking Iceland under its pastoral care. He explained that the Catholic population of Iceland was tiny and that their pastoral care, for many years, had been provided by Dutch priests and religious sisters, members of the De Montfort Order. The main Catholic presence was a large hospital in the capital, Reykjavik, owned and administered by Dutch religious sisters. These Dutch priests and sisters planned to pull out in a few years time, because of a shortage of personnel. He wondered if Derry would be prepared to take on this added responsibility. I told him that I would bring the matter to the attention of our Diocesan Council of Priests, and the Sisters of Mercy and that I would give the matter due consideration. Subsequently, Sisters of Mercy from Derry served in Iceland for a number of years.

I had twice returned to Gammarelli's for fittings. Eventually everything was ready and I was fitted out with robes for every occasion and eventuality. Gammarelli's provided a car to bring Father Mulvey, Father Clerkin and myself back to the Irish College with all the garments. Having looked over my shoulder when I was paying the bill, James Clerkin wondered did we get the car to keep as well! I began to learn that being 'bishoped' was a very expensive business!

On my last night in Rome, the Irish Ambassador to the Holy See hosted a dinner in my honour. Two Cardinals attended, including Cardinal Wright from the USA, as well as some representatives of the Irish community in Rome. It was a very pleasant occasion graced by interesting and stimulating conversation and good food.

We got back to Derry on Saturday, 16 March. At that time, St Patrick's Day was not an occasion for significant celebration in Derry. It was celebrated with much more enthusiasm and energy in the United States and by the Irish abroad than it was in the North. It was a religious holiday marked by the Catholics, and largely ignored by Protestants. The Provisional IRA, too, treated it as an ordinary working day. On St Patrick's Day 1974, a young British soldier was murdered in the Brandywell area of Derry. Ironically, his name was Michael Ryan. Both his parents were Irish. They originally came from County Tipperary and had emigrated to Leeds. His brother was studying for the priesthood in the English College in Rome. Exactly one year later, on 17 March 1975, his mother wrote a deeply moving and memorable letter to me. It was a powerful testament to Christian faith and forgiveness from a heartbroken mother.

On the Tuesday after I returned from Rome, there were lengthy meetings with the organising committee and the Diocesan Council of Priests. The preparations for the 'big day' were going very well and the general atmosphere was very upbeat and optimistic. The priests were circulated my schedule for Parish Confirmations due to take place in the Derry City and County in April and May. We discussed many things about the future and the administration of the diocese. I listened carefully to all their various suggestions.

I went to Dublin for a few days to pack up my belongings in the flat and bid farewell to my colleagues in RTÉ and other people whom I had come to know during the time I was there. I engaged a friend in the furniture business in Strabane to look after the transportation of my belongings in a furniture removal van from Dublin to Derry. All the required documents had been prepared and completed. In the early afternoon of Saturday, 23 March, I received a telephone call in Derry from the two men who were transporting my things from Dublin to Derry. They were calling from Aughnacloy. They were greatly agitated. They advised me that the Army, at the cross-border checkpoint in Aughnacloy, had held them up for a considerable period of time. My belongings had been thoroughly checked and the Army had seized the box files containing all

my letters and correspondence and told them to proceed! I immediately phoned the Army authorities in Derry to complain about
this and demanded the immediate return of the seized materials. I
was directed by them to call the Army in Armagh. I demanded that
none of the documents be photocopied. I also phoned the Northern
Ireland Office. Included in the documents seized were a large numbers of letters that I had received after the events of Bloody Sunday.
Some of these were quite sensitive. Among them was a letter from
Harold Wilson. In January 1972, he was leader of the Opposition in
the House of Commons. But in March 1974, Harold Wilson was
Prime Minister. I advised the Northern Ireland Office that, unless I
had a phone call from the Army promising the return of the documents within thirty minutes, I would call 10 Downing Street. I had
a phone call from the Army within twenty minutes! There were
profuse apologies and an assurance that arrangements were being
made to have the materials flown immediately by helicopter to
Derry and delivered to me. There was also an assurance that none
of the documents had been photocopied or noted in any way. The
documents arrived in Derry, delivered at St Eugene's by Army Land
Rover, only a short time after the furniture van arrived with the rest
of the consignment. I also received letters, dated 23 and 24 March
1974, from Major R.G. Buckton of the Royal Fusiliers in Armagh,
apologising for the incident and assuring me that none of the material had been copied, and that there was no question whatever of any
information in the documents being used in evidence in any legal
proceedings. This was followed by a letter dated 24 March from
Brigadier J.D.F. Mostyn, Commander of the Eighth Infantry
Brigade, based in Derry, who wrote:*

> May I reassure you personally of the following:
> (*a*) The checkpoint which searched the furniture van was a
> 'snap' check point which by pure and utter coincidence
> stopped the van which was carrying your belongings.
> (*b*) The solider in charge felt that the material was 'subversive'
> and therefore took possession of it. He passed it directly to
> his Battalion HQ who realised the moment they saw it that

* Derry Diocesan Archive.

it was of entirely personal nature and hence they returned it
by helicopter to us for forwarding on to you immediately;
which we did.

(c) I can assure you, on the word of my colleague commanding
3 Brigade that the papers were not photographed and will
certainly 'not be used in evidence', whatever Fr O'Neill
might meant by that.*

I am most sorry that this situation should ever have arisen,
particularly at this moment of your return and my departure.

The *Derry Journal* was anxious to have a photograph of me in
my episcopal robes that would be circulated in the edition covering
the episcopal ordination. The newspaper arranged for me to have
the photograph taken in a photographer's studio in Queen Street.
Paddy Hegarty was the photographer. A few days before the episcopal ordination, Father Clerkin and I went to the studio as
arranged. I changed into the episcopal robes and Paddy was arranging the lighting when suddenly we heard footsteps and excited voices on the stairs. 'Everybody out. There is a bomb outside!' The IRA
had hijacked a fully laden fuel tanker at the City Gas yard attached
high explosives under it and parked it outside police headquarters,
a few hundred yards from the studio in which we were sitting. It was
due to explode in ten minutes. There was no time to change and, in
my full regalia, I had to join the fleeing crowds from shops, factories and offices in Queen Street and obtain shelter in a house in
Great James Street. Albeit undignified, it was my first public
appearance in episcopal robes in Derry! The huge bomb, thankfully, failed to detonate and the photograph was successfully taken later
that night.

The Bull of Appointment eventually arrived from Rome and
was duly presented by me to Bishop Farren and the Diocesan
College of Consultors, convened specially for the occasion.

The last few days before the Episcopal Ordination were spent in
silence and quiet in a place of retreat, offering me time for some
more prayer and reflection on the way ahead. I was still very appre-

* Father Bennie O'Neill, Adm., St Eugene's, had phoned Brigadier Mostyn
to protest about the seizure of the documents.

hensive. It was a responsibility about which I had little knowledge and no experience whatever. However, I was boosted by the good wishes and encouragement of the Holy Father, Cardinal Conway, my brother priests and especially the laity who had written to me in their hundreds assuring me of their unequivocal support and prayers.

I took great comfort from the words of the prophet Jeremiah in the passage I had chosen for the First Reading at the Episcopal Ordination ceremony:

> The word of the Lord came to me saying, 'Before I formed you in the womb I knew you and, before you were born I consecrated you; I appointed you a prophet to the nations. Then I said, 'Ah Lord God! Behold I do not know how to speak, for I am only a youth'. But the Lord said to me, 'Do not say, "I am only a youth"; for all to whom I send you, you shall go, and whatever I command you, you shall speak. Be not afraid of them, for I am with you to deliver you, says the Lord'. Then the Lord put forth his hand and touched my mouth; and the Lord said to me, 'Behold I have put my words in your mouth'. (Jeremiah 1: 4-9)

I had never been present at an episcopal ordination, the ordination of a bishop. However, during those final days of quiet and prayer as my own episcopal ordination day approached, I felt a great and growing sense of peace and serenity.

On the afternoon of Sunday, 31 March 1974, one chapter of my life ended and another began.

PRIESTHOOD

My dear friends accept us as we are;
The priest is not an angel sent from heaven.
He is a man, chosen from among men,
a member of the Church, a Christian.
Remaining man and Christian, he begins to
speak to you the Word of God. The Word
is not his own: he speaks it because God
has told him to proclaim his Word. Perhaps
he has not entirely understood it himself,
perhaps he adulterates it, but he believes,
and despite his fears, he knows that he must
communicate God's word to you. For must not
some one of us say something about God, about
eternal life, about the majesty of grace in
our sanctified being: must not some one of us
speak of sin and of the judgment and mercy
of God? So, my dear friends, pray for us,
carry us, so that we might be able to sustain
others by bringing them to the mystery of God's
love revealed in Christ Jesus our Lord.

Karl Rahner SJ
(1904-84)

Index

252

254 / Index